AN AMERICAN'S IRELAND

AN AMERICAN'S IRELAND

Don Fullington

RANAFAST PRESS
NEW YORK

GRATEFUL ACKNOWLEDGMENTS

* Excerpt from *A Portrait of the Artist as a Young Man* by James Joyce: copyright 1916 by B. W. Huebsch Inc., 1944 by Nora Joyce, 1964 by The Estate of James Joyce. Reprinted by permission of Viking Press.

* Excerpts from *A Celtic Miscellany* translated by Kenneth Hurlstone Jackson, Routledge & Kegan Paul, Ltd. London, England and Boston, Mass.: copyright 1951. Reprinted by permission of Routledge & Kegan Paul, Ltd.

* Excerpt from *In Kerry* from *The Complete Works of John M. Synge,* Modern Library/Random House: copyright 1935. Reprinted by permission of Random House.

* Excerpt from *The Brook Kerith* by George Moore, Macmillan Publishing Co., Inc., New York: copyright 1926. Reprinted by permission of Macmillan Publishing Co., Inc.

* Excerpt from *Lake Isle of Innisfree* from *Collected Poems* by William Butler Yeats, Macmillan Publishing Co., Inc., New York: copyright 1906. Reprinted by permission of Macmillan Publishing Co., Inc. Also *The Stolen Child,* copyright 1899.

Library of Congress Catalog Card Number: 83–62185
ISBN: 0–914089–00–5

Printed in The United States of America

FIRST EDITION

To my assistants
STEPHEN AND KEVIN FULLINGTON

INCLUDING

Entertainments
Family Roots by Area
History and Heritage
Hotels and Other Lodgings
Legends
Literature
Pubs
Restaurants
Shopping
Special Places
Sports

With Personalized Itineraries for Each Area

CONTENTS

Ireland: Introduction   3

**Book One: Dublin Through the Southeast to Cork,
Killarney, and Shannon**   17

I Dublin   19
  Vital Dublin Notes   20
  Your Personalized Dublin Itinerary   22
  Dublin's History   28
  Dublin's Special Places   29
  Lodgings   36
  Restaurants   39
  Pub Luncheons   50
  Luncheon Theater   51
  Breakfast in Dublin   51
  Cabaret   52
  Night Clubs   53
  Theater   53
  The Wonderful World of Dublin's Grand Old Pubs   54
  A Dublin Shopping Spree   57
  Sports   59
  Dublin's Stalwart Literary Heritage   60
  An Optional Tour: The Boyne Valley   63

II The Haunting Journey from Dublin to Wexford   71
  Your Personalized Dublin-to-Wexford Itinerary   72
  Details on the Special Places Along the Way   73

III Wexford   79
  Your Personalized Wexford Itinerary   80
  Wexford's History   84
  Wexford Lodgings   85
  Wexford Activities   86
  An Optional Journey Through the Nore Valley to Kilkenny   90

IV **Kilkenny**   91
    Your Personalized Kilkenny Itinerary   92
    Kilkenny's History   93
    Kilkenny Lodgings   95
    Kilkenny Activities   95

 V **A Long Day's Journey to Waterford and Cork**   99
    Your Personalized Itinerary to Waterford and Cork   100
    Waterford's History   105
    Waterford Lodgings   105
    Waterford Activities   106

VI **Cork**   109
    Your Personalized Cork Itinerary   110
    Cork's History   116
    Cork Lodgings   117
    Cork Activities   119

VII **Kinsale and Environs**   125
    Your Personalized Kinsale to Kenmare Itinerary   126
    Kinsale's History   128
    Kinsale Lodgings   129
    Kinsale Activities   129

VIII **Kenmare and the Ring of Kerry**   131
    Your Personalized Kenmare Itinerary   132
    Kenmare Lodgings   132
    Kenmare Activities   133
    Your Personalized Ring Itinerary   135
    Activities Around the Ring   140

IX **Killarney**   141
    Your Personalized Killarney Itinerary   143
    Kerry's Optional Travels   147
    Killarney's History   148
    Killarney Lodgings   148
    Killarney Activities   149
    An Optional Trip to the Dingle Peninsula   153

 X **Shannon**   167
    Your Personalized Shannonside Itinerary   168
    Shannon Area Lodgings   171
    Shannon Area Activities   172

**Book Two   The Optional Tours from Limerick City to the
High Reaches of Donegal**   175

XI   Limerick City   177
Your Personalized Limerick Itinerary   178
Limerick's History   179
Limerick Lodgings   179
Limerick Activities   180

XII   Galway, the Aran Islands, and Connemara   183
Your Personalized Galway Itinerary   184
Galway's History   187
Galway Lodgings   188
Galway Activities   188
Your Personalized Aran Islands Itinerary   194
Aran Lodgings   196
Aran Activities   197
Your Personalized Connemara Itinerary   201
Connemara Lodgings and Restaurants   204
Clifden Activities   208

XIII   Mayo   211
Your Personalized County Mayo Itinerary   213
Ashford Castle   213
Other County Mayo Sites   217
County Mayo Lodgings   219
County Mayo Restaurants   219

XIV   Sligo   221
Your Personalized County Sligo Itinerary   222
Sligo's History   224
County Sligo Lodgings   224
County Sligo Activities   224

XV   Donegal   227
A Major Note About County Donegal   228
Your Personalized Donegal Itinerary   229
Donegal Lodgings   239
Donegal Activities   241

Index   249

Come away—To the waters and the wild
—William Butler Yeats
The Stolen Child

Ireland . . .

. . . whether rising from purple shifts of morning mist, or gleaming in its dark verdant splendor on the strands of a shimmering golden sea, you have the sense that this is a land confected in a dream, one that might well disappear before you awaken and the plane has a chance to land.

Ireland is truly a very special place—unlike any other in the world. Its peace and splendor, beauty and quiet grace, will long live in your memory.

Most Americans think of Ireland as a tiny country that can easily be seen in its entirety in two days. Well, part of this, at least, is true: Ireland is a small country (about the size of West Virginia), but in no way can it be covered in two days' or even two weeks' time. Since the roads are myriad, and the majority of Americans traveling there are self-drivers, a simplified approach to touring is desirable.

An American's Ireland is designed to guide you to the country's most historic and most exciting places. It is *not* designed to cover every nook and cranny—there are plenty of books like this on the market already. Instead, this guide takes the work out of travel by honing in on the key routes, places, and sites and exploring them in detail.

The basic area covered runs from a Dublin starting point down the southeastern coast through Wicklow, Wexford, Kilkenny, and Waterford; around the coastal base of the country through Cork (with a lap-off to Mallow); and up the southwestern coast through Kerry to Limerick and Shannon.

Extended stays move you up through Galway to Connemara and the Aran Islands, then onward to Mayo, Sligo, and sections of Donegal. Of course, this agenda can be done in reverse, starting from Shannon, then later cutting back from Dublin to cover the northwestern regions.

This book offers you a personalized itinerary especially planned for Americans. It allows for variations to meet your own specific needs. There's a one-week version with two- and three-week extensions, plus variations in between. Besides the sites, there are suggested lodgings, restaurants, entertainments, pubs, shops, and sports.

For those interested in tracing family ancestry, the key surnames relating to each area are listed under the heading *Roots*. Buildings, monuments, and other landmarks associated with these names are described or mentioned. If Irish literature is your interest, there's information on the writers relevant to each area under the heading *Literature*. Fascinating *Legends* of the various regions are included as well.

This book offers much more extensive sections on dining facilities than the average guidebook, because many Americans indicate that dining is a major interest in their travels. Most of the restaurants, pubs, and lodgings listed here are referred to favorably. If places were found to be below standard, they were eliminated to avoid waste of space and time. This does *not* mean that every place not listed here is undesirable. No guidebook could cover every establishment in the country, and new ones are opening constantly. If you discover a place that interests you, but which is not listed here, check with the nearest Irish Tourist Board (Bord Failte) office to get an accurate rundown before committing yourself.

One final note before going to specifics. When traveling Ireland, keep uppermost in mind the beauty, inner peace, and splendid moments you can have in viewing this wondrous country. Do take the time to absorb it. If you find yourself rushed, pare down your itinerary, on the principle that it's better to see less and take in more than to see all and recall nothing but a blur. Besides, you can always come back—and most likely you'll be eager to do so.

One more reminder: Be sure to take this guide with you, as it is designed for use as you travel.

A WORD ABOUT PRICES

As a state of economic chaos has become the international norm, there is no enduring financial certainty. Prices may rise or decrease after this book goes to press: chances are they will rise. Although Ireland is insular, there is no escape from this reality, which may at least be alleviated by some mesmerizing Irish landscapes.

JOURNEYING TO IRELAND

There are three airlines offering the majority of flights to the Irish Republic from the U.S.A.

★ Aer Lingus offers the most flights—and the best hours. It also carries 70 percent of all American travelers to Ireland, which must say something about the quality of its service.

In the old days people always said that when you travel to a foreign land, take the airline of that country. In Ireland's case, this is certainly valid. Aer Lingus does carry the country's flavor wherever it goes. Its staff is still all Irish—and they're good. The headphones offer a wonderful cross-section of the country's entertainment. The menus proffer things like smoked salmon, or, even better, smoked trout (if this is listed, be sure to try it). If chicken is one of the main-course selections, go for that too, because it's very good.

Prices on the special Apex (must reserve three weeks in advance) seven- to eighteen-day trip from New York to Shannon are between the $500 and $600 mark round trip. Regular fare would be in the upper-$800 range. There is an executive-class fare that runs considerably over $1000 round trip, while the first-class one way is in the $1500 range. All these are slightly more to Dublin versus Shannon. Boston fares are slightly lower; Chicago slightly higher; Los Angeles and San Francisco fares are several hundred dollars higher (depending on internal domestic fares). Check with the airline via the American phones and addresses below.

* Northwest Orient, a fine American line, is on the scene with very slightly lower prices in these categories than Aer Lingus at this writing. They do some interesting and even lower-budget trips in key and off-season. It's worth investigating if you're pinching pennies. Northwest Orient operates out of New York, Boston, and Chicago to and from Shannon only.

* Transamerica, the discount American carrier, offers a $500 round-trip fare from New York to Shannon, $800 from Los Angeles or San Francisco—cheaper in off-season. Transamerica operates to and from Shannon only. The food is good.

Aer Lingus:	Toll-free all states except New York	800–223–6537
	Toll-free New York State	800–631–7917
Northwest Orient:	Toll-free all states except	
	New York	800–223–5100
	New York State	212–563–7200
Transamerica:	Toll-free all states except California	800–227–2888
	State of California, except San	
	Francisco	800–772–2694
	San Francisco	415–577–6300

Note: If you are beginning your Irish visit in Dublin (you can, as previously noted, reverse it and begin at Shannon), you will want to take an Aer Lingus flight, since it's the only airline from America which lands in Dublin. And you are strongly advised to take the earliest flight leaving America. This is designed to arrive Dublin in the early morning so that you don't waste much of the day. The early arrival time also links up best with the personalized itinerary offered in the next section.

CAR RENTALS

There are several ways to rent cars in Ireland. First there's the straight rental from an Irish car-hire firm, as listed below with their 800-line American-branch phone numbers.

There are also a number of very attractive fly/drive packages with the Irish airline, Aer Lingus, whereby your fare includes both the plane trip and an unlimited-mileage car which you pick up upon arrival at the airport.

Taking this a step further, you may arrange for an even more economical package that includes the plane fare, the car, and vouchers to cover stays at a range of the country's hotels. You choose the hotels and book them from the listing offered by the airline or tour operator. Naturally, the more you pay, the more expensive the accommodations. Some packages even include free breakfasts and other meals, along with other discounts. An important point is that the first night is usually planned for a specific hotel, so you won't have the problem of making a reservation the minute you step off the plane. Aer Lingus's "Irish Heritage Vacations" is a prime example of a high-quality Irish package.

Another possibility is to take advantage of the package deals offered by some of the car-hire firms. These include an unlimited-mileage car; accommodations at well-rated hotels, guest houses, or farmhouses including breakfasts; and vouchers for tourist attractions.

Any of these can be arranged personally or through your travel agent. For airline phones, see the preceding section. Car-hire phone numbers in America are:

Avis Rent-A-Car:	800–331–1212
Budget Rent-A-Car/Brendan Self Drive:	800–421–8446
for California:	800–252–0351
Flynn Brothers Self Drive/Auto Ireland:	800–343–0395
for Massachusetts:	800–852–1000
Hertz Rent-A-Car:	800–654–3001
Johnson & Perrott:	800–223–6764
Kenning Car Hire/American International Rent-A-Car:	800–527–0202
Murray's Europcar/National Car Rentals:	800–328–4300
Dan Ryan Rent-A-Car:	800–654–3090
TM Nationwide/Tom Maloney Tours:	800–621–3405

All of these, of course, have offices at the major Irish airports. Note: Other Irish car-hire firms which don't have U.S. branches or representatives can be located through The Irish Tourist Board (see below).

Vital Points About Car Rentals

* In Ireland, as in England, you must drive on the left side of the road. This may take a little getting used to. It might be wise to minimize your city driving at first by heading directly to your lodgings, parking your car, and using city transportation or walking. Some people beginning their journey in Dublin don't even pick up their cars until they're ready to head for the hills, as it were. It is also possible to take delivery on a car at your hotel, and the delivery driver, or shunter as he's called, can give expert advice on the best way to leave the city.

* As in the United States, you must produce a complete and valid driving license from the country of your residence. You must have held the license for at least two years. And you must have one of the major credit cards or else be prepared to leave a sizable security deposit before you're allowed the rental. Arrangements for the latter may be made at the time you reserve the car. Many car-hire firms will not allow rentals to drivers under 24 and over 70, even if they're properly licensed and carry credit cards. Be sure to check this point at the time of reservation, if applicable.

* Reserve your car well in advance—especially if you're planning on a July, August, or early September vacation.

* Do not, repeat *do not*, expect that the car you reserve will be an automatic unless you so specify. Ireland is not like the United States in this respect. Unless you state very specifically that you must have an automatic, you'll end up with a standard transmission. While there are many more automatics available than there were a few years ago, it could prove virtually impossible for you to switch from a standard shift to an automatic once you arrive in Ireland, especially in the peak summer season. Don't let this ruin your vacation.

* Rates for car rentals vary greatly according to the deal you opt for and, of course, the type of car. Those packages involving plane fare are discussed under the previous airline section. If you rent an average car (nonautomatic) for a week of unlimited mileage, the cost moves to approximately $225 in off season, $250 in peak, with taxes included. A chauffeur-driven car would cost you over $100 per day, tips not included.

* Car rates are inclusive of third-party and passenger liability coverage. But if you are responsible for an accident, you must pay the cost of the repair work. Of course, full collision damage is available, as in the U.S., but in the rush to dispatch cars to incoming airline passengers this vital aspect may be forgotten.

* Gas (called petrol in Ireland and England) is expensive—around the £2.50-per-imperial-gallon mark at this writing.

* It's always a good idea to fill your gas tank the night before a

long journey. Otherwise you may have to search around for an open station early in the morning. And don't count on running into one a little farther down the road. You may be lucky, but then again, you may not—as in the case of the Wicklow Mountains or parts of Donegal (to name just a few places), where you seem to drive for hours without seeing houses or people, let alone "petrols."

★ Another important word about gas stations: almost none of them has public toilets. Your best bet is a pub or a hotel. Public toilets are labeled in Gaelic, which can be confusing: *Fir* is for men and *Mna* for women.

★ Road sign terminology:

  Black spot indicates an upcoming dangerous twist or curve in the road
  Cul-de-sac is a dead end
  Dual carriageway is a divided highway
  No overtaking means no passing of other vehicles
  Roundabout is a traffic circle

★ Important car terms

  Bonnet is the hood
  Boot is the trunk
  Dynamo is the generator

★ A special note about the type of car-hire package you choose. Rather than rushing into it, you may want to do some investigating first. While the fly/drive packages with hotel vouchers are undoubtedly excellent value, are they for you? The potential problem is that you are limited to a set list of hotels or other accommodations from which you can choose. While these lodgings are all highly rated, rarely do they include, for instance, any of the fine Irish countryhouses. And suppose you've had your heart set on staying at one? The best course is to ask the airline or travel agent for such a listing and then check with this guide for descriptions of the places to see if they'll suit you. If not, just take the fly/drive package without the lodgings vouchers.

IRISH TOURIST BOARD OFFICES IN AMERICA

The Irish Tourist Board is considered by nearly all other tourist organizations to be the finest such organization in the world. It is held in such high esteem by other countries that they come to it for advice in dealing with their own tourism matters. What it can do for you is provide you with information on all areas of the Irish Republic and all aspects of Irish life—and it does so with great pride and pleasure. So don't hesitate to call, write, or stop in if you have any questions. There are also Tourist Board offices (called Bord Failte in Ireland) all over the Irish Republic which will do the same. They will even make reservations for you after you arrive in Ireland. These addresses and phone numbers will be provided later.

* New York City: 590 Fifth Ave. Zip 10036. Phone 212–869–5500
* Chicago: 230 North Michigan Ave. Zip 60601. Phone 312–726–9356
* San Francisco: 681 Market St. Zip 94105. Phone 415–781–5688
* Toronto: 69 Yonge St. Zip M5E IK3. Phone 416–364–1301

LODGINGS

Don't expect every place you stay to supply you with a private bathroom complete with toilet, sink, tub, and shower. Don't even expect a private phone, much less a radio and a color TV. Having said this, it is only fair to say that you will be surprised at many places. A large number of lodgings throughout the country are modern or have modernized to offer not only full baths and direct-dial phones, but color TVs linked to cable systems that offer the latest movies. At these you may well find heated pools, saunas, and exercise rooms. But the point is you can't assume anything. (This guide defines the individual lodgings and their facilities). For instance, some of the finest accommodations in ancient castles and elegant country houses offer bedrooms filled with antiques and antiquated baths, because that's part of their appeal to those who want things the way they were in olden times. Some of them have modernized the baths with showers, others haven't. Some have added color TVs. Others don't have so much as a radio in the sitting room, because they feel it spoils old-time ambiance. And many Americans agree, making this a strong feature in the selection of their lodgings. Whatever your preference, it is wise to check first so you won't be disappointed.

A WORD ABOUT CHILDREN

Little is said of children in this book—because the majority of Americans traveling to Ireland do not travel with them. This is truly a shame, because the Irish love children. Large discounts for children's meals and lodgings abound. Many accommodations cater to families with children and offer special baby sitting and sporting facilities, such as pony rides. This is not to say that if you would rather avoid children on your vacation you can't do it in Ireland. Many of the stately country homesteads cater to romantic couples rather than families, as do the fine big-city hotels.

CURRENCY

The Irish pound is divided into 100 new pence. Notes are issued in Irish pounds running in denominations from 1 to 5, 10, 20, 50 and 100 sequences. Coins range from ½ pence to 1p, 2p, 5p, 10p, 50p.

Note: Ireland is now a member of the European Monetary System. This means that English currency is no longer acceptable in the Irish Republic—nor is Irish currency received in Great Britain. You would want to check with your bank or your newspaper for the value of the pound compared with the dollar, as the value changes daily. But the dollar is strongly rising against the Irish and English currency.

RESTAURANTS

If you're from a large American city where you can pretty much call your own dining hours—breakfast at noon, lunch at three, or dinner at ten—you'll want to change your habits. Dining in Ireland is very much like dining in small-town America where hours are concerned. Breakfast is rarely served after ten o'clock. You can get coffee or tea and some rolls between then and noon, but that's about it. Lunch usually runs from noon or 12:30 to 2:30 or 2:45. Dinner is usually served from 6:30 or 7 to around 9, sometimes to 10. Now, you will find coffee shops in some of the larger modern hotels that are open from 7:30 A.M. to midnight, offering a complete range from snacks to full meals. Jury's, Dublin, is open even longer hours. But most of these places are limited to the cities and are few and far between. It's easy to be critical of what many would consider pinchy dining hours, but if the restaurateurs kept on the staff needed to cater to the few who drift in at odd hours, they'd be out of business. If you do find yourself stranded on the dining scene, many pubs and hotel bars can supply you with a sandwich and tea or coffee.

PUBS

Pubs are open daily from 10:30 A.M. to 11:30 P.M. during the summer. Wintertime hours are only to 11 P.M. Sunday hours are from 12:30 P.M. to 2 P.M. and from 4 to 10 P.M. throughout the year. But wine may be served in restaurants up to midnight. Remember, though, in Dublin, Cork, Limerick, and Waterford pubs close from 2:30 to 3:30 P.M. each day in what is called an observance of the holy hour. Why here, and not in the rest of the country? Legend may say the holy hour, but in fact most Irish in the know contend that if the bars weren't closed in these key business luncheon communities, many would never go back to work again.

Remember that as a visitor, you enjoy special status. If you're a resident of a lodging with a bar, you can be served alcoholic beverages long after the stipulated hours. Legally.

Advice: If you're going on a pub crawl, leave your car at your lodging. Irish laws are strict, and the combination of drinking and driving in the unfamiliar left-hand pattern could be doubly hazardous.

COSTS

For Lodgings:
* Inexpensive starts at under $15 per person sharing per night up to as much as $20.
* Moderate moves from the lower $20 range per person sharing to $40.
* Expensive is anything from $40 upward

For Dining Places:
* Inexpensive is anything up to $10 per person
* Inexpensive to moderate includes those places offering meals in both ranges
* Moderate is in the $10 to $15 range
* Moderate to expensive, $15 to $20
* Expensive, $20 and up.

CREDIT CARDS

Most hotels take the major credit cards: American Express, Visa, MasterCard, and Diners Club (hereafter abbreviated to AE, Visa, Master, and Diners). Some take Carte Blanche (CB) and Bank Americard (BA), but many don't. Castles (Ashford and Dromoland) and *some* of the elegant countryhouses do take them. If they don't, this will be stated in the individual descriptions. Most guest houses, farm houses, and inexpensive lodgings do *not* accept the cards. Since this is almost invariable, it will *not* be stated in the individual descriptions. Restaurants and other dining places that accept the cards will be so noted.

It is very important that you check with the lodging or restaurant if there is any doubt about credit-card acceptance before you commit yourself. No one will be offended, and it will make for a much pleasanter stay if you're not living with anxiety about this point. Rarely— and for obvious reasons—are personal checks accepted. Of course, travelers checks are welcome everywhere, provided you don't sign them in advance.

Almost all major stores and many small stores (including craft shops) throughout the country accept some major credit cards.

TIPPING

Be sure to check your dining bills to see if there is a 10- or 15-percent service charge. If so, no additional sum is required, unless you feel the service rendered and the quality of the meal were so extraordinary that you'd like to leave a little more. Never tip for drinks served at a bar. However, you may wish to tip a waiter or waitress for drinks served at a table in the bar.

Taxi drivers are usually tipped 10 percent of the total meter amount, while porters are given 50p to a pound, depending on the number and/or weight of the bags.

LICENSING

All hotels have full license to serve all alcoholic beverages, and that goes for the restaurants as well as the bars within these premises. Therefore no reference to licensing has been made in the descriptions of hotel restaurants. In the case of free-standing restaurants, some have full license, others only a wine license, and some no license at all. A reference is included with the individual descriptions of those which have full or wine license. It's important to note that a wine license allows for the sale of wine only (sherry, other aperitif wines, port included), and does not allow for the sale of beer, stout, lager, or brandy. All pubs have full licenses, but this does not mean that all pubs stock wine. Many do, and the list is growing every year as wine drinking becomes increasingly popular. However, don't expect a wide array of superlative wines in the pubs. It is better to ask what kind of white or red wine they have before committing yourself, because some of it (especially in the more rural areas) can be pretty desperate. On the other hand, many of the country's restaurants have become very sophisticated in the wine area. An ever-growing number have a finer selection than many of the top American restaurants.

TAXIS

As in the U.S., taxis are expensive. They do seem to be more so in Ireland—but then gasoline is far more expensive and the drivers have to live. A ride from Dublin Airport into the city (six miles) can run from $7 to $10, maybe more. In many other areas of the country, there are gypsy cab drivers with no meters. If you look prosperous, you may be charged Park Avenue prices: it's best to establish the fee before you enter the vehicle.

CLIMATE/CLOTHING

Ireland lies within the Gulf Stream and therefore has a springlike climate most of the year. This does not mean that it's eternally balmy. It can be cold and rainy or warm and rainy. It can be cold or warm and cloudy. It can also be dazzling under halcyon skies. You can be prepared for all these conditions by packing medium-weight clothing along with a little rainwear. Forget all the heavy-weight tweeds and bulky sweaters. It's the rare occasion when you'll need them. What you really have to be concerned about—especially during the peak season—is the heat. Everyone, and every travel guide, insists that the average temperature during the peak season ranges from 60 to 66 degrees Farenheit. Well, this may be true at times, but in recent days in Dublin that figure has risen well into the 80s. There are very few restaurants or hotels capable of dealing with this, since they don't have air-conditioning (Jury's, Dublin, *Kish* restaurant is one of the few exceptions). So you can see that if you drift in wearing heavy tweeds, you're going to wilt immediately. Stick to medium weights, but be sure to slip in some light-weight wool sweaters (you may want to purchase some beautiful ones in Ireland) to layer in if it really gets cold.

Regardless of the weather, be prepared with an easy system of dressing up for one of the fine city or country evening-out experiences. Many think of Ireland as completely rural and jeans-oriented. Not so—at least, not anymore. Men should pack a tie, dress shirt, and blazer, while women should pull together a dressy evening outfit—unless you will keep entirely to the farm or guest houses.

Don't forget swimwear, running shorts and shoes, golfing and tennis apparel, fishing equipment (which you can rent in numerous places in Ireland), if you're so inclined. As many Irish lodgings don't provide washcloths (or facecloths, as they're called), you may want to pack a few of these.

TIME ZONE

Ireland is five hours ahead of American time—except during March and April when there is a six-hour difference in favor of Ireland due to a variance in time changes.

PASSPORTS

All Ireland requires from Americans is an up-to-date passport: no visas. But don't fail to have such a passport when you land in Ireland.

Very close checks are made at American airports before you're allowed to board, but occasionally there is a slip-up. Don't arrive with an out-of-date passport.

ELECTRICAL APPLIANCES

The standard Irish current is 220V, the standard in the U.S. is 110V. So be prepared. Even if there is a conversion button on the appliance, you will have to have plug adaptors if you want to use your favorite hairdryer. Such adaptors are available in many U.S. drug and hardware stores, designed to fit the vast array of Irish outlets. Most major hotels will be able to supply you with an adaptor. As for electric razors, most hotels and even guest and farm houses have wall units that convert to 110V and accept the standard American electric razor plug.

SHOPPING

When you see something you're dying to purchase—don't wait. Buy it. The likelihood of your finding it at a cheaper price somewhere else is remote, since Ireland is not discount-oriented like America. You are much likelier not to see the same item again at another locale.

Note allowances in your return to America. You must declare all goods you're bringing home. You may bring in articles valuing $400, Irish prices. Included in this limit are 100 cigars and 200 cigarettes. The same duty-free allowances would apply to only one liter (35 ounces) of alcoholic beverages.

Gifts not exceeding $25 retail in the Irish Republic may be sent to friends and all relatives in the U.S. duty free—if the same person does not receive more than $25 dollars in gift value in one day. But you *must* write the words *unsolicited gift* on the package and label it 'under $25.' Then you must indicate the contents in large letters. *Do not* include alcoholic beverages, tobacco, or drugs in any such shipments—or you'll never be allowed to make them again.

SPORTS

The wonderful thing about Ireland is that just about anywhere you go—especially if you follow the personalized itineraries herein—you will have access to a wide variety of sports and spectator sports. Some of the possibilities are: golfing, tennis, swimming, surfing, water skiing, canoeing, boating, sailing, riding, bicycling, hunting, shooting, fishing (sea, river, lake), mountain and cliff climbing. In Dublin, you'll even find polo. And running is becoming popular just about everywhere. There's even a 10K race on Inishmore in the Aran Islands in July. One of the world's leading runners, Eamonn Coghlan, developed his record-breaking skills in Ireland. And with such beautiful scenery, what a place to run. As a matter of fact if you need to be inspired to move into any sport, you will be here.

As for spectator sports, you can literally have a field day. There's horse racing, polo, Gaelic football, handball, hurling, regattas, fishing contests, tennis. The Dublin Horse Show is a world-famous spectator event. The country is a sportsman's paradise.

An important note: While few references to fishing or hunting licenses are made within the text (they vary from year to year), you must check with the local authorities or you may find yourself in legal difficulties. Some areas require no license for fishing—others definitely do. Most are stringent about hunting. So remember not to go casually firing or casting away. The Irish Tourist Board can advise you best.

IRISH TOURIST BOARD (BORD FAILTE) OFFICES IN IRELAND

	Telephone
Cork: The Tourist House, Grand Parade	(021) 23251
Dublin City: 14 Upper O'Connell Street	(01) 747733
Dublin Airport	(01) 376387/8
	or 375533
Dun Laoghaire: 1 Clarinda Park North	(01) 808571
and St. Michael's Wharf	(01) 806984/5/6
Ennis: Bank Place	(065) 21366
Galway: Aras Failte, Eyre Square	(091) 63081
Kilkenny: Shee Alms House, Rose Inn Street	(056) 21755
Killarney: Town Hall	(064) 31633
Letterkenny: Derry Road	(074) 21160
Limerick City: 62 O'Connell Street	(061) 47522
Shannon Airport	(061) 61664
Skibbereen: 14/15 Main Street	(028) 21766
Sligo: Temple Street	(071) 61201
Tralee: 32 The Mall	(066) 21288
Waterford: The Quay	(051) 75788
Westport: The Mall	Westport 269
Wexford: Crescent Quay	(053) 23111

OTHER IMPORTANT ADDRESSES/NUMBERS

The American Embassy, 42 Elgin Road,
   Ballsbridge, Dublin   (01) 764061
American Express Co., 116 Grafton Street,
   Dublin   (01) 772874
EMERGENCY: (fire, police, emergency
   medical, ambulance, throughout the
   country)   999

Book One

DUBLIN THROUGH THE SOUTHEAST TO CORK, KILLARNEY, AND SHANNON

Wicklow Hills

I. DUBLIN

St. Stephen's Green

*The trees in Stephen's Green were fragrant of rain
and the rainsodden earth gave forth its mortal odour,
a faint incense rising upward through the mould of
many hearts.*

—James Joyce
A Portrait of the Artist as a Young Man

VITAL DUBLIN NOTES

Dublin is an exciting old European city with an abundance of memorable places to see and things to do—far too abundant for a short stay. Perhaps that's part of the city's appeal: it leaves you longing for more, thinking *I'll have to come back here again.* And that puts Dublin on the elite list of the world's most captivating cities.

Dublin is like Boston in many ways. It's very old, and it's fascinating to wander its twisting streets and lanes, getting lost, finding treasures—that is, unless you're driving. Then if you become lost, excitement may turn to anger and exasperation, as you waste the precious time you've allotted yourself. (1) Be sure you get a detailed map, like one of the Geographia Dublin Streetplanners maps available at newsagents and bookshops (others may omit many of the smaller thoroughfares) and study it before you start out. A good navigator is worth gold.

(2) A number of Americans take one of the city's half-day (three- or four-hour) bus tours to get the feel of the city before they attempt driving. If they rent a car at the airport, they park it at their accommodations in favor of an initial (and inexpensive) tour. C.I.E. (The Irish Transport Company) runs excellent, well-documented, half-day tours daily at 10 A.M. and 3 P.M. They feature clean and comfortable coaches with personable drivers—'real Dublin.' Phone 300777 at 35 Lower Abbey Street. The buses leave from Busaras, Amiens Street. Another city-tour operator is Dublin City Tours at 3 Wilton Place, near Baggot Street Bridge (786682/766887).

(3) Think left. Not only will this save you time and traffic hassles, it may save your life until you get accustomed to the unfamiliar driving pattern. You may want to stand and watch the traffic flow for a time. It's also worth noting that many choose not to rent a car while in Dublin and use one only for their travels through the rest of the country. Taxis and buses are usually readily available, walking is enjoyable—and you'll avoid Dublin's sizable parking problems.

(4) When making your Dublin plans, bear in mind that the city has two major annual events that have been known to fill its lodgings to capacity. You will want to reserve early so you won't be disappointed.

The Dublin Horse Show, usually held the second week in August, attracts the horsey set from America and the Continent in droves, making it Ireland's best-attended special event.

The Dublin Theater Festival, usually scheduled for the first two weeks in October, is not quite as well known as Scotland's Edinburgh Festival, but it's still immensely popular and attended by a cross-section of theater people from around the world.

For exact dates of these events, contact The Irish Tourist Board.

(5) The nationwide emergency number, 999, will also provide the name of the nearest hospital. Doctors for tourists through Doctor on Call (976108); Contractors Bureau (300244); Medical Ltd. (972541).

(6) Don't forget to leave. Dublin is so attractive that you may neglect the rest of the country, but you'll be wronging yourself if you do.

YOUR PERSONALIZED DUBLIN ITINERARY

City Centre

Three Days, Three Nights of the Best

Day One

* Arrive Dublin Airport. Pick up car (see Car Rentals), taxi (easy to get but moderately expensive), or bus (pleasant, clean, huge sightseeing windows, and inexpensive, but only to one destination—Busaras, the central bus station on the city's north side at Amiens and Store Streets).

* Head for your lodgings, preferably on Dublin's south side since it's closer to most of the places you'll want to see. If you prefer a modern grade-A* hotel (as rated by The Irish Tourist Board) try *Jury's Hotel*, Ballsbridge. All the A* hotels mentioned here are dependably good. If you want an old European-style grade A* Hotel, *The Shel-*

bourne on St. Stephen's Green is a sound choice. But truly pleasant (and cheaper) are the Georgian and Victorian townhouses which have been converted into small hotels or guest houses. Try the *Ariel House* on Lansdowne Road, the *Mount Herbert* on Herbert Road, or *Kilronan House* on Adelaide Road.

* Check in. Make reservations for the next two evenings (see Day Two). Have a shower and head for lunch in one of the Old World's most beguiling cities. Review the Restaurant section, but the suggestion here is *Bewley's* on Grafton Street for a real slice of turn-of-the-century Dublin, as it was in James Joyce's time. And at inexpensive prices. Finish by 2 P.M.

* Take a taxi or city bus to *Busaras,* the central bus station, for a 3 P.M. half-day bus tour to acquaint you with the city and save you time later when you travel Dublin on your own. Try to plan it so you have a few minutes before your bus tour to walk across Beresford Street and look at the old *Custom House.*

* The tour is usually finished between 5:30 and 6 P.M. Return to your lodgings and prepare to dine at one of Dublin's truly fine restaurants. Heading the list—and strongly suggested—is *Le Coq Hardi,* 35 Pembroke Road. If reservations aren't available, or if you'd rather select another place, you can choose from the Restaurant section, which lists and describes all of Dublin's finest.

* After dinner you'll probably want to call it a day, since you'll already be missing a night's sleep. But if you're not tired, you may wish to taxi to one of the old pubs mentioned in the Pubs section.

Day Two

* Breakfast at your lodgings. Make sure it's before ten o'clock, when most places stop serving breakfast. Grade A*-hotel residents, try the coffee shops in your abodes—they're quick, cheap, and most important, good. If you're exhausted, then breakfast in bed—costly, but maybe you should treat yourself this once.

If you're staying in one of the Old World townhouse/guesthouses, drop into the dining room for a hearty Irish breakfast: juice, porridge, bacon/sausage/egg, toast, and tea—often accompanied by home-made jam, marmalade, freshly baked scones, and a dish of rhubarb or strawberries (in season).

The morning is then open for sight-seeing. The Irish Tourist Board publishes a booklet called *The Tourist Trail* which is a walking guide to all the spots of historic interest on the signposted Trail through Dublin. And this will cover just about everything. But here's a suggestion.

* Start with a stroll around Merrion Square, so you get a true picture of Georgian Dublin from the magnificent townhouses.

* Move from the northwest corner of the square across to *The National Gallery,* which you should visit. Behind the Gallery is *Leinster House,* a Georgian mansion dating from 1745 which now houses both seats of the Irish Parliament—the Dail and the Seanad.

* From here, it's a short walk down Nassau Street to College Green and the entrance to *Trinity College* (you'll be walking past its gardens as you move down Nassau). You'll want to spend some time at the College, and at its library with the famous *Book of Kells.*

* Across the way from Trinity is an enormous curved building which was once the old parliament house and is now *The Bank of Ireland.*

* From the Bank, walk along Dame Street past South Great Georges Street. There's a fascinating old pub, *The Long Hall,* just a short distance up this street on the right, if you want to make a swift detour. If not, keep going on Dame Street up a slight incline known as Cork Hill, and there on the left you can visit *Dublin Castle* and just past it, on Lord Edward Street, *The City Hall.*

* At this point, you can drop by the second floor of a fine old pub, *The Lord Edward,* at Christchurch Place for a pub lunch. Or if you're not hungry as yet (remember that most places, especially pubs, stop serving lunch at 2:30), visit nearby *Christ Church Cathedral* (Church of Ireland) in what is said to be the oldest part of the city.

* Here curve around onto Nicholas Street and follow it along until it bleeds into Patrick Street, where you may visit *St. Patrick's Cathedral* (Church of Ireland).

* Then walk down Upper Kevin Street, cross Bride Street bearing to the right onto Lower Kevin Street, and follow it to its end; cross over and you'll be on Cuffe Street, which will lead you to *St. Stephen's Green.* If you haven't eaten, try the *Paddock Bar* of the Shelbourne Hotel, located on the north side of the Green, for a pub lunch.

* After lunch spend a little time strolling in the Green before heading off for an afternoon shopping tour, which you might wish to combine with some pubbing.

* The shopping is all within easy reach of the Green. At its northwest corner is Grafton Street—a brief street with a multitude of shops. Off Grafton to the right, as you head down it from the Green, are Anne, Duke, and Nassau Streets for more shops, boutiques, and old pubs. Off Grafton to the left is a little lane called Johnston Court, which will soon lead you to Clarendon Street and the magnificent new *Powerscourt* shopping complex. More time has been allotted for shopping and pubs if you decide to spend the optional third day in Dublin. For more details, see Shopping and Pubs.

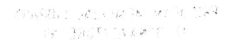

* Nighttime plans call for an evening of theater, cabaret, or ballad singing: your option. Remember to make reservations early so you won't be disappointed. If you choose the theater, you'll probably want to attend Ireland's most famous, *The Abbey,* on Lower Abbey Street. The curtain is at 8, so you'll be a little more pressured for time with this choice where dinner is concerned. Most of the best Dublin restaurants don't start serving until 7 or 7:30, and their last orders are around 10, so they're out. Your best bet is to finish your shopping so as to arrive back at your hotel about 5:30. Then head for the nearest hotel coffee shop, which will be open. There are those at Jury's, Ballsbridge; The Shelbourne, Stephen's Green; Bloom's Hotel, Anglesea Street; and The Berkeley Court, Lansdowne Road. Another thought is Casper & Guimbini's pub on Wicklow Street—open all day, full licenses, and fast.

Those who have chosen an evening of cabaret have a much more leisurely course. *Jury's Cabaret,* for example, at Jury's hotel, is an excellent selection. The doors open at 7:30, but the show doesn't begin until 8:15, and you're served your dinner. So you could linger a little longer shopping if you like, or drop by one of the pubs mentioned in the Pubs section. Arrive back at your hotel around 6:30 to prepare for the evening. Incidentally, while you're at Jury's check out the excellent-value shop here called *Shop At Jury's* (open till midnight). See Shopping notes.

For those interested in an evening of ballad singing (dinner included), the place is the *Abbey Tavern* in Howth, nine miles from Dublin's city center. If you don't have a car at this point, remember that taxis are expensive. The No. 31 bus that you get where O'Connell Street crosses Lower Abbey Street will take you there in about forty minutes, but 11:30 P.M. is the *last* return bus. So plan to arrive at The Abbey about 8:30 (it's open from 7:00 to 11:00).

* Head back to your lodgings for the night. If you are ending your Dublin stay at this point, you will want to plan on an early start for your journey to Wexford beginning the following morning. It's a good idea to top up your gas tank the night before, if you've already used a lot of gas.

An Optional Day in Dublin
(for those on longer stays)

* Breakfast at your lodgings.

* Head for O'Connell Bridge, cross it, then walk down O'Connell Street on the left side past Abbey Street to view the *General Post Office* (GPO).

* Just past it is Henry Street (closed to traffic). Turn down Henry

a very short distance and on the right is Moore Street, Dublin's old market street. Stroll along it for local color.

* Then return to O'Connell Bridge, but don't cross it. Instead, turn right up Bachelor's Walk which leads into Ormond Quay. Continue on along the Liffey until you come to *The Four Courts*, which you'll want to stop and study.

* Now you can either catch a bus for the *Phoenix Park* (a 10-minute ride) or walk straight on along the Liffey until you come to Parkgate Street and you're there (half an hour).

* Take time for a brief stroll in this very large city park (one of Europe's biggest and most beautiful). Sample either the gardens or the zoo, or just sit on a hillside bench enjoying one of the vast expanses of verdancy.

* Upon leaving, take time to pop into *Ryan's* on Parkgate Street, one of Dublin's finest old pubs.

* This should bring you up to lunch: here are several possibilities. If you didn't select theater the previous night, you might want to sample one of Dublin's lunchtime theaters. A listing is provided in a later *Luncheon Theater* section. Second, since the afternoon has been left free for shopping (or your own pursuits), you may want to taxi back to the *Powerscourt* Shopping Centre. Here, do dine at the inexpensive *Periwinkle*. Third, you may wish to pursue the wonderful world of pub luncheons, on which there is a detailed section later. Or fourth, you may want to stay where you are and either grab a sandwich (maybe at Ryan's) or pull together—from one of the local grocers—a few items for a picnic in the park, so you can visit the nearby *Guinness Brewery* and *Kilmainham Jail* in the afternoon.

* As you see, you're free to go in many varied directions in the afternoon. This is an important part of a visit to any city. Do the established things first, then take the time to do your own exploring: this reaps you a harvest of special, personal memories. The city's there—and it's all yours.

* Return to your lodgings around 5:30, relax and prepare to have dinner there before embarking on a leisurely and fascinating trip through the pubs of Dublin. It you're staying at one of the A* hotels, most of them have a selection of restaurants ranging from the relatively inexpensive coffee shops, to the moderate roast and grill rooms, to the elegant, very expensive rooms emphasizing the finest in continental and Irish dining. If you've followed this itinerary foodwise, you've already had at least one expensive meal in Dublin. So why not opt for the inexpensive or at most the moderate? You're at an advantage if you're staying at one of the Georgian or Victorian guest house/hotels. Most of the owners are so proud of their occupation—

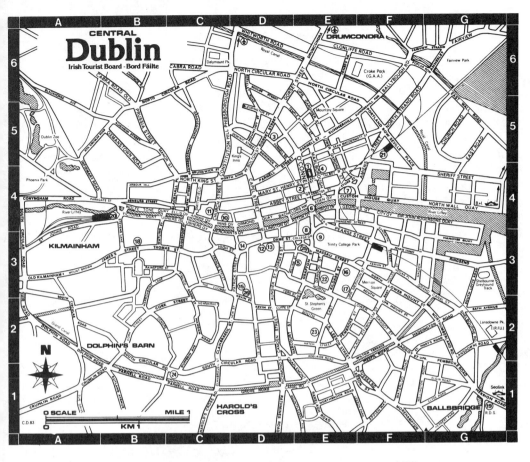

CENTRAL
Dublin
Irish Tourist Board · Bord Fáilte

The routes to Dublin Airport, 6 miles north of city centre, are signposted thus:

INDEX TO MAP OF DUBLIN

1. Tourist Information Office
   O'Connell Street (E4)

2. General Post Office,
   O'Connell Street (E4)

3. Municipal Art Gallery,
   Parnell Square (D5)

4. Catholic Pro-Cathedral,
   Marlborough Street (E4)

5. Civic Museum,
   South William Street (D3)

6. O'Connell Bridge

7. Custom House, Bus Station
   and Airport Terminus,
   Store Street (E4)

8. Bank of Ireland,
   College Green (E4)

9. Trinity College,
   College Green East (E3)

10. The Four Courts,
    Inns Quay (C4)

11. St. Michan's Church,
    Church Street (C4)

12. Dublin Castle,
    Dame Street (D3)

13. City Hall,
    Dame Street (D3)

14. Christ Church Cathedral,
    Lord Edward Street (D3)

15. St. Patrick's Cathedral,
    Patrick Street (D3)

16. National Library, Leinster
    House and National Museum,
    Kildare Street,
    National Art Gallery,
    Merrion Street (E3)

17. Government Buildings,
    Upper Merrion Street (E3)

18. Guinness's Brewery,
    James's Street (B3)

19. R.D.S. Showgrounds,
    Merrion Road, Ballsbridge (G1)

20. Heuston Station
    (Kingsbridge) (B4)

21. Connolly Station, (Amiens
    Street) (F5)

22. Mansion House,
    Dawson Street (E3)

23. National Concert Hall,
    Earlsfort Terrace (E2)

24. National Stadium,
    South Circular Road (C1)

25. Automobile Association,
    Suffolk Street (E3)

26. Marsh's Library,
    Patrick Street (D3)

The 'Ireland' map, printed in colour, contains maps of the major cities and indicates 'through-routes' from airport and ferry terminals. The map is on sale at all tourist information offices, and most bookshops in Ireland.

entertaining you—that the food (while basic) is to the highest standard. But the prices are not; in fact, they're extremely modest considering the quality.

⋆ After dinner take in some of Dublin's finest old pubs. Start off by trying some in the Grafton Street area: *Doheny & Nesbitt,* 5 Lower Baggot Street; *The Bailey* and *Davy Byrnes,* Duke Street; *Neary's,* Chatham Street. If at this point you still have the energy to stray, take a taxi to *The Brazen Head* (Dublin's oldest pub) at 20 Lower Bridge Street. Move from here by taxi again to *Mulligan's* on Poolbeg Street. Then top the evening off by heading back to the Grafton Street area (make sure its before 11:30, or 11 in the wintertime—Irish pub closing hour) and stopping off at *O'Donoghue's,* 15 Merrion Row (traditional music—musicians and singers). If your lodgings are somewhere in this area, as they probably are, and the weather's fair, stroll back under the Dublin sky. It's an especially relaxing and rewarding experience. (But first, make sure you're certain of the directions.)

⋆ Plan an early start on your journey to Wexford the following day.

DUBLIN'S HISTORY

Dublin is truly an Old World European city and one of Europe's finest capitals. Some of its medieval and many of its Georgian buildings still stand, lending a splendid sense of history to the city that so gracefully arches Dublin Bay. The northern arm extends to the fishing port and the rocky hill of Howth, while the southern arm rises to the sweeping sea-vista headland of Dalkey. The heart of the city is divided by the River Liffey, and this is how Dublin got its Irish name. *Baile Atha Cliath* means literally The Town of the Hurdle Ford. Later, Norsemen called the city *Dubhlinn,* which is Irish for dark pool, because such a pool formed one of the boundaries of its settlement.

Folklore has it that St. Patrick visited the area around A.D. 400 to convert the hedonistic inhabitants to Christianity, and for the next few centuries the settlement developed around the river. During the ninth century the Norsemen arrived and established a fort in the area where Dublin Castle and Christ Church Cathedral are now located. From there, they sent out warring factions in an attempt to conquer the country and plunder the churches. But as destructive as they were, they did establish centers of trade which fostered Irish commerce.

Warfare between the Irish and the Norsemen continued until 1014 when, at the Battle of Clontarf, the Irish were victorious under the leadership of the famed chief Brian Boru. After this the Danes converted to Christianity and helped build Dublin's first church on the site where Christ Church Cathedral now stands.

The Anglo-Normans, having seized control of Waterford and much of Leinster, stormed and conquered Dublin in 1171 under the leadership of the Earl of Pembroke (Strongbow). Soon after, Henry II came to the city to establish himself as ruler and secure the loyalty of the Irish chieftains. During this visit he granted Dublin its first charter. In the years that followed, Dublin was attacked frequently by two native Irish clans, the O'Tooles and the

O'Byrnes. Finally, in desperation, King John ordered the construction of a castle and a wall to encircle the city.

During the 17th and 18th centuries, Dublin grew and prospered. This is the period when the great public buildings, such as the Parliament House in College Green, and the mansions of noblemen were erected. It was also the era of the creation of Phoenix Park by the Duke of Ormonde to display the government's majesty. (A visitor's must, this is the most beautiful, peaceful, and spacious of European city parks.) Trade with England flourished and brought Dublin to major commercial importance.

In 1783 England gave the Irish Parliament autonomy, but not for long. Repressive English policies began to reassert themselves. This led to an unsuccessful Irish uprising in 1798, followed by the Act of Union, giving Great Britain strict control. In 1803 the famous Irish patriot Robert Emmet led another insurrection, which also failed and which brought him to the gallows.

More than a century later, during the spring of 1916, the Irish patriots staged the bloody Easter Rising that led to the Irish civil war. It ended after much bloodshed and great destruction of property in 1922, with the establishment of the Irish Free State.

DUBLIN'S SPECIAL PLACES

Georgian Dublin

Trinity College

* Merrion Square has been said by many Irish historians and writers to exemplify the finest Georgian architecture in Europe. There are some magnificently constructed buildings here, with haunting reminders of the past. Note: If you're truly interested in Georgian, you can move from here a few blocks to the southeast and linger over the smaller, but very beautiful, Fitzwilliam Square.

* Leinster House, which is now in back of the National Gallery on Kildare Street, is the magnificent Georgian mansion dating from 1745 where both houses of the Irish Parliament (*Dail* and *Seanad*) sit. The Duke of Leinster built it, and later Lord Edward Fitzgerald lived here. In 1815 it passed to the Royal Dublin Society. On its spacious lawn is a memorial to Irish heroes Michael Collins, Kevin O'Higgins, and Arthur Griffith.

* Trinity College was founded in 1591 by Elizabeth I to further the Protestant Reformation in Ireland. Located on the east side of College Green, the only remnant of the original building is a rendering of the Royal Coat of Arms near Trinity's library. What we see as Trinity today is the magnificent 300-foot facade designed by Henry Keene and John Sanderson, both of Britain, and erected in 1759. David Sheehan did the superb carvings.

You enter Trinity through an enormous gateway facing into a large square, known originally as Parliament Square because the English Parliament provided the funds for its construction in 1752. To the right of the square is the Examination Hall and Public Theater designed by William Chambers and constructed in 1787. Inside are the gilt oak chandelier that once belonged to the British House of Commons and some fine examples of stucco-work.

To the left of the square is the Chapel, which was designed by Graham Myers, with more good stucco-work.

In one corner of the square is a printing house that was built around 1727 to resemble a Doric temple. Across the way is the museum building constructed in 1857 and housing a famous Irish stone carving of the O'Shea Brothers.

Without question, Trinity's most famous building is the library. Constructed from the designs of Thomas Burgh, it was completed in 1732. Originally there was a grand open-ground arcade, with a strong central wall to support the weight of the upper stories. This ground floor was enclosed in 1892; it is 270 feet long and is divided into 27 bay areas. There are over 2000 ancient manuscripts, including Egyptian papyri and Latin and Greek texts. But the library's most famous document is the Book of Kells. This masterpiece of Celtic art, which is believed to date from the eighth century, depicts the gospels magnificently in text and graphics. It is worth a visit to the library to see this treasure alone.

In 1967 a new library building of contrasting modern design was added to the grounds. Within the two buildings there are well over half a million books. It is interesting to note that an act passed in 1801 allows Trinity the right to a free copy of every book printed in Ireland or Great Britain if a request is made to the publishers within a year of publication.

* The Bank of Ireland at College Green—across the road from Trinity—was originally Parliament House, which included The House of Lords, The House of Commons, and The House of Requests. After the creation of the Irish Free State in 1922, parliament disbanded and the building was purchased by the Bank of Ireland.

The building was constructed in 1729 from the designs of Sir Edward Lovett Pearce and James Gandon. Originally it had a sweeping open colonnade with grand entrance arches complete with tympanums (carved with the Royal Arms) and a portico with Ionic columns. In 1782 another sweeping portico was added, extending the building in an eastward curve to connect with the original colonnade. Corinthian columns were used, lending the complex an even greater pageantry.

After its sale to the bank, plans were developed for the building's alteration. The House of Lords, with its fine Diocletian windows, still stands, but the House of Commons is gone and the House of Requests has become a central cash area. Original carvings and stucco-work are still intact, and there's a rococo ceiling of Venus Wounded by Love by an unknown artist in the bank directors' dining room.

* The Custom House on the banks of the River Liffey near Butt Bridge is esteemed by many as the finest example of Dublin's historic architecture. In 1791 the architect, James Gandon, fought severe criticism and untold financial problems to erect this building. Facing the river, it is 375 feet long and 204 feet deep. The central portico, with its grand Doric columns, is crowned by a magnificent dome. The statue of Commerce, sculpted by Edward Symthe, stands atop the dome, and its tympanum bears the arms of Ireland. Stretching out from either side of the main portico is a series of arcades with a pavilion at each end. In 1921, during the War of Independence, the building was gutted by fire, but after the war, it was beautifully restored.

* The Four Courts are on the north bank of the Liffey at Inns Quay near Butt Bridge. Originally these courts of law were housed in Dublin Castle, and later in Christ Church Cathedral. The united Four Courts building was

The Four Courts

completed in 1796. This stately edifice consists of a central block with a portico featuring Corinthian columns and housing a statue of Moses with figures representing Justice and Mercy. There is a circular central hall in this block, covered by an enormous dome. Flanking the main building are squares connected by rusticated arcades.

The Four Courts, whose frontage is 450 feet, was built at a cost of 25 million pounds from designs by Thomas Cooley and James Gandon. In 1922, with the Civil War raging, the building was bombed and burned, but the solid-granite exterior walls remained intact, and later the interiors were reconstructed. Today ten courts, including the Irish Supreme Court, are housed here.

* The City Hall on Lord Edward Street, designed by Thomas Cooley and built between 1769 and 1779, was originally planned as the Royal Exchange. It is a square Corinthian building with an interior central ring of columns that support a domed roof. The central ring sets off the ambulatory, which is now filled with statues created by noted Irish artists.

* Dublin Castle at Cork Hill on Dame Street was built between the years 1208 and 1220. What is known today as the Upper Castle Yard is the area where the original castle walls stood, fortified by four formidable towers and surrounded by a moat. All that remains today are two greatly reduced towers and a segment of the wall. The main entrance is the site of the original gate. On the south side are the state apartments, which during the reign of Elizabeth I became the residence of the British Lord Deputies or Viceroys. They remained as such until the creation of the Irish Free State. One of the most impressive buildings here is St. Patrick's Hall, over 80 feet long

and 40 feet deep. Its dramatic paneled ceiling is decorated with paintings of
St. Patrick, Henry II, and George III. In the nearby Throne Room is an enormous 200-year-old chair of state, complete with canopy. At the southwestern
area of the complex is what remains of the Bermingham Tower (the sloping
base). It was built in the 1400s and rebuilt in 1776. For years it was used
as a prison. One of its prisoners was the legendary Red Hugh O'Donnell,
who made two escapes to fight against the English occupation of Ireland.

* The walls of the Record Tower in the Lower Castle Yard are 16 feet
thick and a fine example of the sturdiness and longevity of Norman construction. Today the building houses the State Paper Office, a repository for historical documents. Also in this yard is the Church of The Most Holy Trinity,
built between 1807 and 1814; it was originally the Chapel Royal. The exterior
features nearly 100 carved heads of royalty, ecclesiastics, and other historical
figures. Inside the church are oak carvings displaying the arms of all the
English viceroys. Of particular note are the ancient stained-glass windows,
one of which is divided into four sections—the arrest of Christ, Christ before
Caiphas, Christ before Herod, and Christ before Pilate. The church has been
Roman Catholic since 1943.

* Christ Church Cathedral stands dramatically on a high slope on Lord
Edward Street at Christ Church Place. Without question, it is one of the
city's grandest historical buildings. The original cathedral, founded by the
Anglo-Normans in 1172, took 50 years to complete. It was almost completely
restored in the late 19th century from the plans of George Edmund Street.
Some insight into the original buildings can be gleaned on the south side of
the transept, where you'll find the remains of a chapter house and the cloister
and garth.

The striking appearance of the current cathedral owes much to its rugged
but simplistically classical design. The awesome stonework interior, on the
other hand, has beautifully proportioned pointed arches and finely carved
columns. The western bay of the choir and part of the nave wall date from
medieval times. Under the church is the vaulted crypt, which was built in
the 12th century. It contains statues of Charles II and James II and the taber-
nacle and candlesticks used when the latter attended Mass here. Some of
the crypt's vaults were used as taverns and wine cellars during the 16th
century.

A multitude of historical events associated with the Cathedral have taken
place here. In 1394 Richard II knighted four Irish chieftains as he received
their homage. In 1487 pretender to the throne Lambert Simnel was crowned
Edward VI of England during the reign of Henry VII. The first Protestant
to occupy the See of Dublin, Archibishop Browne, became Henry's instrument
for establishing his religious policies, which resulted in the Book of Common
Prayer of 1551. It was the first time the English liturgy was read in Ireland.
Here, in 1689, James II briefly reestablished the rites of the old faith and
heard Mass on his way to the Battle of the Boyne in 1690. There he suffered
defeat at the hands of the original Orangeman, William III, who then came
to the Cathedral to give a Protestant thanks for his victory.

* St. Patrick's Cathedral is a brief walk south of Christ Church Cathedral
on Patrick Street. It is the national cathedral of the Church of Ireland (Protestant) and was founded in 1190 on the site of what was once an island in a
river called the Poddle, which now flows underground. This is the body of
water where St. Patrick is said to have baptized his converts and followers.

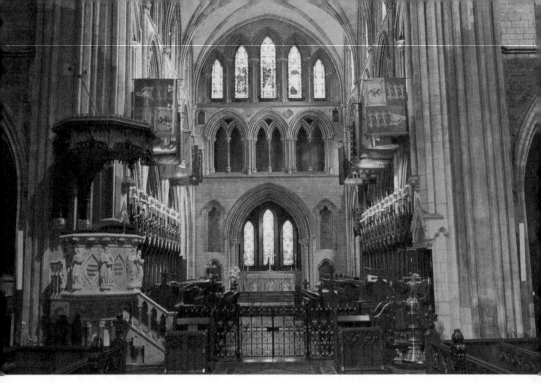

St. Patrick's Cathedral

The saint's well of holy water, which was said to be near the western tower
of the present Cathedral, was marked by a large inscribed stone preserved
in the nave's southwestern corner.

The Pope founded a university in 1320 and made St. Patrick's its home
until Henry VIII abolished it. Late in the 14th century the original cathedral
was almost entirely rebuilt after a disasterous fire. During the fateful wars
of the 17th century, Cromwell's troops turned the church aisles into stables
for their horses. The building fell into such a state of disrepair that during
the late 19th century it had to be completely restored. What we have today
is an early-English style cathedral of cruciform shape, but its stately square
tower is 14th century, while its grand spire was added in the 18th century.

Within the cathedral, which is 300 feet long, are many monuments, including the Boyle monument erected in 1631 by the first Earl of Cork and statues
of Turlough O'Carolan, the last of the Irish bards; Samuel Lover, the novelist
and poet; John Philpot Curran, the famous orator; and the Duke of Schomberg,
who was the Williamite commander at the Battle of the Boyne.

Over the stalls of the choir, you can see the helmets and swords of the
Knights of St. Patrick, the famous order instituted by George III in 1783.
Around the walls are the flags of Irish regiments who gave honor to their
country on the battlefields of Europe.

St. Patrick's is probably best known for its historical connection with Jonathan Swift, who was the Dean of the cathedral from 1713 to 1745. The pulpit
he preached from is still there, as is his tomb with the epitaph: *He lies where
furious indignation can no longer rend his heart.*

Dublin has many museums and libraries, all of which have their points of interest, but there are far more than one could see in a single visit to the city. The following are at the top of the list.

* The National Gallery on Leinster Lawn in Merrion Square seems straight from the pages of Joyce. Opened in 1864, the building today houses works of the Renaissance masters, along with those of Rubens, Van Dyck, Goya, El Greco, and Murillo. In the Irish section are paintings by John Butler Yeats (W. B. Yeats's father), Osborne, and Lavery. 10 to 6 weekdays and Saturday (open till 9 on Thursday). 2 to 5 on Sunday.

* The Municipal Gallery of Modern Art is ensconced in a magnificent Georgian mansion on Parnell Square and owns several excellent paintings by the French Impressionist Corot. Among its sculptures are those of Rodin and the famous Irish sculptor Andrew O'Connor. 10 to 6 Tuesday–Saturday, 11 to 2 Sunday.

* The State Library on Kildare Street is the country's largest, with well over half a million books and many Irish literary and historical manuscripts and prints. Fine arts, zoology, and botany are covered in depth, and there's an enormous collection of Irish newspapers. 10 to 6 daily.

* The Chester Beatty Library is at 20 Shrewsbury Road in the Ballsbridge section. New Testament manuscripts, picture scrolls, Manichaean papyri, and Far Eastern jades are among the attractions here. 10 to 1 and 2:30 to 5:30 Tuesday–Friday. 2:30 to 5:30 Saturday.

* Trinity College Library, with its legendary Book of Kells, is a must (covered as a special entry under Trinity College). 10 to 5 weekdays, 10 to 1 Saturday. Closed Sundays.

* The National Museum on Kildare Street houses all the major ancient Irish art finds, including prehistoric gold workings, the Cross of Cong, the Tara Brooch, the Ardagh Chalice, the Viking artifacts from the oldest section of Dublin City, and the Irish silver, glass, and Belleek china collections. 10 to 5 Tuesday–Saturday and 2 to 5 Sunday.

A Special Place Near Dublin

Howth, the small fishing village about nine miles northeast of Dublin's city center, is famous in literature for its hilltop overlooking the vast expanse of dazzling sea where Leopold and Molly Bloom made love among the rush of rhododendron in the closing pages of *Ulysses*. It was memorialized by an unknown 14th-century author in ancient Celtic words that translate: "Delightful to be on the Hill of Howth, very sweet to be above the white sea; the perfect fertile hill, home of ships, the vine-grown pleasant warlike peak."

Howth is the peninsula forming the northern arm of the horseshoe that cradles Dublin Bay. The rich green hills of Wicklow are visible from this point. When you descend the hill from the north side, you can see straight out the tiny island called Ireland's Eye. Boats are available for trips to the Eye, where many go to picnic. Howth Harbor is a noted yachting center and the fishing boats dock here. The harbor was the scene of the landing of arms for the Irish Volunteers in 1914. In the village itself are the ruins of an abbey that adjoins the demesne of Howth Castle and a massive dolmen marking an ancient tomb. There are two good restaurants in Howth: King Sitric and The Abbey Tavern, which features ballad singing (for details, see Restaurants). The Howth area also offers swimming and fishing. Five miles away is the resort town of Portmarnock, with its velvety sand beach and championship golf course.

DUBLIN'S UNIQUE STOPS

⋆ *The Guinness Brewery,* St. James Gate. No trip to Dublin is complete without it, brew enthusiasts insist. And why wouldn't they? This place has been operating since 1759 and is said to be the largest in the world, producing untold pints per day. Some say the brews (Guinness stout and Harp lager) surpass the finest French vintages and the best of German beers. Whether they do or not, the brewery is worth a visit, if only to sample the newly culled brews. Unfortunately for the visitor, if not for progress, the brewery is being renovated and it will be some time before the process can be observed again except on film. But you'll still get to taste. 10 A.M. to 3 P.M. Monday–Friday only. No children under 12.

⋆ *St. Stephen's Green.* Placid, well-kept, with gazebos, duck ponds, a children's playground, and quiet gardens furnished with convenient benches, this park (donated to the city by Sir Arthur Guinness in 1880) was once the center of Georgian Dublin. The statues of Irish freedom fighters here and there are a continuing reminder of an earlier day, and of the fact that the real Irish cause is—and always has been—peace. A good thought not only for Ireland, but for the world. A good reason for going there.

⋆ *The Phoenix Park.* The 2000 acres of beautiful terrain encompass a zoo, a floral garden, a race course, a polo ground, and even a cricket pitch. In some areas cattle still graze, and late in the evening you're quite likely to see roaming deer. The Irish president's residence is here, along with that of the American ambassador.

⋆ *Kilmainham Jail,* Kilmainham. This is one of Dublin's most disturbing reminders of the past. Political prisoners were held behind its bars from 1796 to 1924—many to receive the death sentence. The greatest of Irish freedom fighters spent time here at the hands of the English. The prison was phased out in the late 1920s, but in the 1960s voluntary Irish workers pulled the place from disrepair, and the late Irish President deValera insisted on reopening it as a museum in 1966 on the anniversary of the Irish Revolution. Open Wednesday & Sunday 3 to 5 P.M. only. Inexpensive conducted tours.

⋆ *Moore Street,* off Henry Street. This is just off Dublin's main thoroughfare, O'Connell Street. An engaging route, which remains today only in part. Like the old Les Halles of Paris, this was once Dublin's great market area. Now that a shopping center has taken over, what is left are some of the die-hard women who still sing out in legendary fishmonger style the prices of the 'collies—the finest in Ireland' (cauliflowers, that is), lettuce, potatoes, all kinds of produce. They compete fiercely in traditional 'price wars,' but they form a strong fellowship and are the truest of friends in times of hardship. This is a real slice of Dublin life. Out of the way, but if you're interested in local color—go.

LODGINGS

Expensive

Dublin has six hotels that have been granted the Irish Tourist Board A⋆ rating. In order to receive this, a hotel must meet and maintain extremely high standards in all phases of hotel and restaurant management and presentation. Two in this category are old hotels; the other four are relatively new. Sadly, a wonderful old A⋆ hotel—one of the world's few 'elegant' coaching inns, The Royal Hibernian—has closed its doors to the ring of the property developer's cash register.

   * *The Shelbourne,* Stephen's Green (766471), is still the *grande dame* of Dublin's hotels. Built in 1842 as an elegant townhouse, then revamped in the 1860s, it remains much the same, although it has acquired some of the neighboring Georgian houses over the years and added a modern wing in recent times. A fine example of a 19th-century European hotel, The Shelbourne has excellent dining rooms and bar and a charming Old-World sitting room where you can have tea and scones. If you're into the past, be sure to request a room that hasn't been modernized or renovated. There are 166 in total (including some suites), all with private bath. Expensive.

   * *The Gresham,* Upper O'Connell Street (746881). This is one of Ireland's most historic hotels. Built in 1817, it found itself in the heart of the Irish Revolution less than a century later. During the Easter Rising of 1916, the lobby and halls of the Gresham were transformed into emergency wards, turning the place into a kind of railroad-yard scene from *Gone With The Wind.* An interesting anecdote that affected the course of Irish history: Cathal Brugha, an Irish patriot and the leader of the united Irish movement, held out at the Gresham against his own blood, the Free State Army, which was willing to accept a partitioned Ireland. Brugha was assassinated, shelled to death as he fled the burning Gresham. You can't help but wonder what would have happened had he not been killed.

   After the revolution, the place was elegantly restored. It remains today a fine example of Regency architecture, and one that you shouldn't miss even if you don't stay here. It's just across the street from the General Post Office—the major setting of the 1916 rising against the British. At the Gresham, you'll still see the old Waterford chandeliers and remnants of the Regency furniture, which hint at the grandeur of old Dublin. Unfortunately, what you won't see or feel is the same sense of the Grand Hotel the Gresham once was (even in the late 1960s). In those days you wouldn't stand a chance of booking a room at the Gresham in peak season and often into off season unless you reserved months in advance—or knew someone. Not so today. Managements have changed and changed again. The north-side location has gone out of style, and its south-side neighbors are the chic places now. The Gresham neighborhood has been infiltrated by the rise of young Dublin rowdies. This isn't to say the hotel isn't well kept: it is. But interest has dwindled to the point that its fine Old-World restaurant has had to close. A very good coffee shop still remains—but it isn't quite the same. If you stay there, it's wise to take taxis in and out late at night. But do see it. Moderate to expensive.

   * *The Berkeley Court,* Lansdowne Road (601711), is one of the country's newest hotels. Opened in 1978, its theme is Old-World elegance. Its plush antique-laden lobby is palatial, as though designed solely to entertain royalty. The rooms are comfortable, traditionally furnished, but not as enormous as the lobby would suggest. Two hundred rooms (including suites), all with baths. Health center, indoor pool, sauna. Fine dining places (see Restaurants). Fifteen-minute walk, short bus ride to St. Stephen's Green, Grafton Street. Expensive.

   * *Bloom's,* Anglesea St. (715622), is another of Dublin's new hotels, this one designed to achieve a feeling of turn-of-the century Dublin, as its Joycean name would imply. There are 86 rooms with bath, and they're cozy, comfortable, and richly green. Excellent places to eat (see Restaurants). Very centrally

located near Trinity College, Grafton Street, St. Stephen's Green. Moderate to Expensive.

★ *The Burlington,* Upper Leeson St. (605222). If you want a large hotel, this is the one by Irish standards. It's the country's largest, with 500 light, airy rooms with bath, television (including closed-circuit movies) and direct-dial phones. If you're into circular tubs, the mirrored bath of the Presidential Suite has one. Good restaurants, cabaret, night club-disco (see under separate headings). Shops, indoor pool, sauna. Parking for 600 cars. Ten-minute walk, short bus ride to St. Stephen's Green, Grafton Street. Expensive.

★ *Jury's,* Ballsbridge (767511), is a fine, smoothly run large hotel with an almost American atmosphere. There's a newly added wing and a total of 310 rooms, suites with bath, television including closed-circuit movies, direct-dial phones. A great shop called *Shop At Jury's* (see note under Shopping). An indoor-outdoor pool. Fine restaurants, cabaret (see under separate listings). Fifteen-minute walk, short bus ride to St. Stephen's Green, Grafton Street. Expensive.

Smaller Hotels and Guesthouses

Many Americans find these places, especially the guesthouses, extremely appealing. The Old-World atmosphere, along with more personalized service, seem to be the attractions. Many of them are less expensive as well.

★ *Sachs,* Morehampton Road (680995), is a relatively new grade-A small hotel made up of three early 19th-century mansions—the central of which was the old Morehampton Hotel. The Regency flavor has been maintained here even in the renovation. The bar, though, is more Victorian, with its masculine emphasis on mahogany and brown leather. Here you're likely to run into members of the Dublin literati, along with visiting film stars and stage personalities. There's a drawing room for afternoon tea, a marble fireplace, an old Waterford chandelier, and antiques extending to the 20 bedrooms and baths. Fine restaurant and food (see Restaurants). There's even a nightclub (Raffles) in the basement. Expensive.

★ *Buswell's,* Molesworth Street (764013), is rated B* by the Irish Tourist Board. Small, simply decorated, centrally located (near Grafton Street, St. Stephen's Green)—yet away from it all. A tidy hotel with a cheery staff. The restaurant food is hearty Irish. Cocktail bar frequented by Irish politicians. There are 53 rooms with bath, television, phone. Moderately priced for central Dublin.

★ *Ariel House,* 52 Lansdowne Road (685512). This red-brick Victorian town-house built in 1850 for a monied marquis is special—so special that its present owner, Michael O'Brien, had to add an entire wing. People (especially Americans) love this place. Even though it's a charming house loaded with antiques, the real reason the Ariel is so popular is probably O'Brien himself. He loves his business and his guests. Having spent several years working at prestigious American West Coast hotels, this Irishman knows what people want better than they do themselves. If he senses that a couple at breakfast are tense about being in a strange new city without a clue as to where to go first, he'll immediately go to their table and not only alleviate their fears, but plan a whole itinerary for them. As he does, he'll bring out fascinating little gems of Dublin history. Yet with all this camaraderie, the place is remarkably well run: tidy and spotless. His restful garden restaurant serves excellent— and very reasonable—dinners with wines. Actually, the restaurant has become so popular that O'Brien is opening it to non-residents (by reservation only). (See under Restaurants). There are 16 rooms with bath. Warning: You must reserve early; this place has caught on. Also specify if you want one of the Victorian rooms. All rooms are equipped with color television and phone. Be sure you have a look at the Victorian sitting room, which is one of the loveliest. St. Stephen's Green/Grafton Street are a five- to ten-minute bus ride, 15-minute walk. There's a taxi rank just down the road between the Berkeley Court and Jury's. Inexpensive.

* *Egan's House,* 7–9 Iona Park, Glasnevin (303611), is a cozy old off-the-beaten-path guesthouse. Close to Dublin Airport, a good 20-minute bus ride to city center, there are 23 rooms with bath, a television lounge, restaurant with wine license. Inexpensive.

* *Iona House,* Iona Park (306217), is a small red-brick Victorian guesthouse. A kind of home-away-from-home coziness. Only 14 rooms with private shower, television, phone. There's a restaurant/coffee shop with wine license. Inexpensive.

* *Kilronan House,* 70 Adelaide Road (755266), was built in the late 1800s but emulated earlier Georgian architecture. Its old crystal chandlier, antiques, and marble lend it the elegance of another day. This place is clean, tidy, and very comfortable. Its restaurant serves fine basic home-cooking-type meals. The owner, Mrs. Josephine Murray, is another gracious host(ess) who loves to help visitors with their Dublin itinerary. Centrally located near St. Stephen's Green, Grafton Street. Eleven rooms, six with bath. Very popular; reserve well in advance. Inexpensive.

* *Mount Herbert,* 7 Herbert Road (684321), is a grand three-story townhouse—actually it's four 19th-century townhouses joined together—that's more of a hotel than a guesthouse (which is how the Tourist Board classifies it). It has 88 rooms, 77 with bath, and simple, homey decor. A large, bright dining room faces the gardens. Wine license. There's also a solarium, a sun bathing area, a sauna, a badminton court, and a miniature golf course. A short five-minute bus ride, or a 15-minute walk to the St. Stephen's Green/Grafton Street area. Inexpensive.

* *Elgin,* 23 Elgin Road (684497), is a red-brick townhouse run by an amiable Irishwoman named Mrs. Kelly. Antiques, including a beautiful patchwork marble-top table and a brass chandelier, abound in the parlor. There's a pleasant garden behind the house. Breakfast only (but the area is riddled with excellent dining places—see Restaurants). Across the street from the American Embassy. A five- to ten-minute bus ride, 20-minute walk to the Grafton Street/St. Stephen's Green area. Inexpensive.

* *Embassy,* 35 Pembroke Road (684130). The exciting advantage of staying in this attractive Georgian townhouse is that downstairs is one of the country's finest restaurants, Le Coq Hardi (see under Restaurants). So if you want, you can spend your entire Dublin stay here and be spoiled for life. Cozy, comfortable rooms, 10 of them, two with bath. Near Ballsbridge and only a short ride or 10-minute walk to the St. Stephen's Green area. Inexpensive (except for the restaurant—but it's worth it).

RESTAURANTS

Fxpensive (Note that there are a few restaurants listed here that are more moderately priced for lunch. Others are not open for lunch. These points will be mentioned.)

The Lord Edward Restaurant

* *The Bailey,* **Duke Street** (770600/773055). If you're a James Joyce addict, this place is mentioned in *Ulysses* (it was called Burton's in those days). Here since the 1880s, this restaurant with a lounge bar downstairs houses the famous door from 7 Eccles Street, the fictional home of Joyce's Leopold and Molly Bloom. (The Eccles Street house is now being demolished.) The Bailey still does excellent seafoods, game birds, beef Stroganoff, and a fine Chateaubriand in an old-Dublin atmosphere. Full liquor license. L—12:30 to 2:30. D—6:30 to 11:30. Closed Sunday. AE, Diners, Visa, Master.

* *The Berkeley Room* of the Berkeley Court Hotel (601711). Truly elegant, Old-World dining rooms aren't uppermost in the minds of those building most new hotels around the world today. But P. V. Doyle, one of the country's leading hoteliers, insisted on having one in his sweepingly graceful new hotel. Ornamented by pastoral oil paintings, it achieves its serene elegance without a loss of the sense of intimate dining. Fine foods are abundant here. The avocado stuffed with Dublin Bay prawns is a favored starter. The wine-poached sole or the cider-baked plaice with mushroom purée are popular seafood entrees. The filets of beef, either plain or with mushrooms and a rich red wine sauce, are very good choices. L—12:30 to 2:30. D—6:30 to 10:30. AE, Visa, Diners, CB.

* *The Anna Livia Room* of Bloom's Hotel, Anglesea Street (715622). The atmosphere of this room in one of Dublin's newest hotels is disappointing. In trying to achieve the aura of Joycean Dublin, this downstairs dining area comes across a little more gloomy than Old World. But if the architects and decorators seem to have gone astray—not so the chefs. Foodwise this place

is streets ahead of many fine Dublin dining places, and the lively, young, yet extremely knowledgable staff make up for any decorative grievances. While such dishes as escalope de veau, Gaelic steak, and filet of sole poached in white wine with mussels in a lobster-and-cream sauce are fine, two other house specialties are superlative. As an appetizer, the crab claw salad served with a cloudlike lemon mayonnaise, and as an entree, the lobster poached in brandy and butter, make for truly memorable dining. They go down very well with a reasonably priced white Hermitage (either '78 or '79 vintage). Maitre d' Johnny Bacon, a very conversant down-to-earth young Dubliner, suggests you don't overwhelm these with loads of vegetables (as many Irish restaurants do), but instead sample a light green salad. He's right. For dessert, try the wonderful wild strawberries (in season). Raspberries or apples (dashed with port) are fine. Great cheese cake. Or try a cut of Stilton served with vintage port. L—12:30 to 2:30. D—6 to 10:45. Note: While expensive, the lobster prices are still among the lowest in town. AE, Diners, Masters.

* *Celtic Mews,* 109A Lower Baggot Street (760796/682327). Irish stew and spectacular seafoods in this cozy out-of-the-way mews restaurant. Special and romantic. D—6:30 to midnight. Closed Sundays, bank holidays, July 18–31. AE, Visa, Diners.

* *The Kish* in Jury's Hotel, Ballsbridge (767511). Very modern, terraced, air-conditioned dining room overlooking Jury's Pavilion Bar, gardens, and a pool. Named after a lighthouse in Dublin Bay, and the seafood is unusually good—especially the salmon, sea trout Bearnaise, and lobster Newburg. Expensive at night, but at lunchtime there's a special seafood buffet that lets you sample everything at a much more moderate price. A truly good value for lunch—after which you won't need dinner. L—12:30 to 2:30. D—6:30 to 11. Closed Sunday. All credit cards.

* *Le Coq Hardi,* 35 Pembroke Road (689070). An outstanding restaurant; not only one of Ireland's finest, it must be among the world's best. Chef-patron John Howard and his charming wife Catherine are garnering citations from all quarters (Michelin, Egon Ronay, Good Food, Woodford Bourne Wine Awards). The Howards have recently moved into this marvelous Georgian townhouse and decorated it regally, in the manner it deserves. When you arrive you're escorted to the basement sitting-room bar with its masculine deep brown tones, white marble fireplace, richly appointed love seats, and even a magnificent black-leather chaise, plus stately oil lamps. Vases of long-stemmed mums grace the tables. Fine aperitifs are served while you nibble on nonfilling (rightly so) crisp celery and freshly picked cherries on the stem as you ponder the menu. And what a menu. Scallop, lobster, prawn, mussel, turbot, sole, and angler dishes were the seafood selections one evening. Meat and fowl included rack of lamb, Gaelic steak, sweetbreads, calves' liver, ribs of beef, filets, and chicken. Roast goose is a specialty. Everything is done in the grand French manner and served in the elegant first-floor dining room of rosewood and mirrors. A lobster salad appetizer was enormous. Served in the shell, the lobster was icy fresh and wonderfully tasty. The rack of young lamb entree was superbly done and served in its own rich juice laced with fine wine. The young Argenteuil asparagus was equally tender and flavorful. John Howard whisks up the hollandaise for the latter after you've ordered, as he does all sauces (you can hear the whisk from a table near the kitchen). The wine list is enormous: excellent wines, moderate to very expensive. The restaurant's suggestion of a 1976 Chanson Bourgogne proved smooth and light

but extremely rich—perfect with the lamb. The wine price was moderate, actually inexpensive, considering the quality.

Writing a restaurant review is always risky: you might have had gambler's luck and chosen the best in the house. But this reviewer arrived unannounced to overhear the subdued sighs and murmurs of other diners as they received various courses from a chef who seemed to work wonders. Desserts are excellent, but the cheeses are even better . . . so good that the place has won dairy awards, and that's rare in Ireland. Do try the Mileens— a tangy smooth cow cheese that tastes like one of the great French goat cheeses. It's prepared by a young Irish couple living on an island near Cork's Beara Peninsula.

Note: If you have one life to live in Ireland—or one night in which to go money-mad—and you like superlative food in elegant, yet intimate, surroundings, go to Le Coq Hardi. Not only won't you regret it, you'll never forget it. L—12:30 to 2:30. D—7 to 11. Closed Sundays, bank holidays, and three weeks in January. Wine license. All credit cards.

  * *Le Provence,* 120 Pembroke Road near Jury's Hotel (600629/603438). If you're in love and want romance with your dining, this is the place. The lights are low, the room long and alcoved. And do these people believe in candlepower—even at lunchtime. Fine French cuisine, especially veal, quail, beef filet, monkfish, and poached salmon. And watch for their hot goose liver with olives. Fine wines. A charming place altogether. L—12:30 to 2:30. D—7 to 11:30. Closed Sundays, bank holidays. Lunch is moderate to expensive. Wine license. AE, Master, Visa, Diners.

  * *Lobster Pot,* 9 Ballsbridge Terrace (680025). Fine seafoods, fowl, roasts, flambées. Moderate and intimate. L—12:30 to 2:30. D—6:30 to 10:30. Closed Sundays, bank holidays. Wine license. AE, Master, Visa, Diners.

  * *The Lord Edward,* 23 Christchurch Place (752557). Charmingly woody Victoriana. This is a superb place for seafood served in the grand French manner. (Don't be put off by the first-floor bar, where the best of the Dublin grassroots *bowsies* reside. This is a rather unusual place that includes an expensive and fashionable upper level, a businesspeople's elite middle-level lounge, and a real down-to-earth Dubliner bar on the lower level. Try them all.) L—12:30 to 2:30. D—6 to 10:45. Closed Sundays, bank holidays. Full license. AE, Master, Visa, Diners.

  * *Restaurant Patrick Guilbaud,* 46 James Place, Lower Baggot Street (764192). Designed by one of Ireland's bold new architects, Arthur Gibney, this intimate new restaurant would be a knockout anywhere for its romantic French elegance, including cool pink-striped upholstery, interior garden, and skylight. You'd go far in Dublin to find a place even close to this Mediterranean lightness. The cuisine is strictly French, with some dishes tastier than others. Try the John Dory if it's on the menu: a hearty white-fish served with a delicious red wine sauce. Rack of lamb and veal dishes are good. Lunch, 12:30 to 2, is moderate to expensive. Dinner, 7:30 to 10, is expensive. Closed Sundays, bank holidays. Wine license. All credit cards.

  * *Sach's Restaurant* in Sach's Hotel, 21 Morehampton Road (680995). This place achieves an Old-World restaurant atmosphere in a hotel formed from a group of Regency townhouses. The dining room is cool and green. The poached turbot or the veal Cordon Bleu are excellent choices from an extensive menu. L—12:30–2:30. D—7 to 10:30. Lunch moderately priced. Closed Sunday, Saturday lunch, bank holidays. Full license. AE, Master, Visa.

* *Shelbourne Restaurant* in the Shelbourne Hotel, St. Stephen's Green (766471), is still one of Dublin's grandest hotel dining rooms, although service flags a bit these days. The food is superbly prepared. Especially good—crab dishes, baked scallops, veal, Tournedos Shelbourne. L—12:30 to 2:30. D—6:30 to 10:30. Closed Sundays. All credit cards.

* *Small Home,* 41/43 Shelbourne Road (608087). Everything but the thatched roof—open fires, candlelight, romantic and cozy. The food is good. Meat and fish done in rural style. L—12:30 to 2:30. D—7 to 10:30. Closed Sundays, bank holidays. Wine license. All credit cards.

* *Snaffles,* 47 Lower Leeson Street (760790/762227). Touted for years as one of Ireland's finest restaurants, this rather small (seats 40) Georgian basement with all its 19th-century horsey trappings still serves superb food. For starters, the Andalusian soup (an Irish version of gazpacho) was light but alive with succulent flavor. The famous Snaffles mousse of cream cheese and garlic was beautifully zesty, perhaps a little too much so for lunch. The entrees of quail stuffed with grapes (perfectly rendered) and tender steak filet with Béarnaise sauce (theirs is one of the finest) will remain memorable months after the occasion. There are veal, lamb, and fish dishes as well. Wine license only, but excellent selections: reasonable to expensive, as you would expect in a restaurant of this caliber. L—12:30 to 2:30. D—7 to 11. Closed Sundays, Saturday lunch, Monday dinner, bank holidays. AE, Visa, Master, Diners.

* *Tandoori Rooms,* 27 Lower Leeson Street (762286/688618). Well-established candlelit basement restaurant specializing in Tandoori-style Indian food. Spicy and unusual. Especially good lamb dishes. Moderate wine list. D (only)—7 to 12. Wine license. AE, Visa, Master, Diners.

* *Wednesdays,* 15/17 Ballsbridge Terrace (681049). Small, cozy, tucked-away restaurant specializing in good seafoods. Leisurely ambiance. L—12 to 3. D—7 to 11. Wine license. Closed Sundays, bank holidays, week after Christmas. AE, Master, Diners.

* *The Sussex Room* in the Burlington Hotel, Upper Leeson Street (605222). This sizable hotel dining room (somewhat American in ambiance) offers both Irish and Continental dishes, of which the best are the beef. L—12:30 to 2:30. D—6:30 to 10:30. All credit cards.

Moderate to Expensive

* *The Rooftop Restaurant* of the Burlington Hotel, Upper Leeson Street (605222). Excellent dining value at this glimmering candlelit restaurant where you can wine, dine, and dance until one o'clock in the morning. Obviously more subdued, but still busy, at lunchtime. Here you pay on entrance, then it's all yours: appetizer and soup to start, then all the freshly carved meats and fowls you can eat—just keep asking for more. Roast ribs of beef, ham, turkey, chicken, pork . . . eat forever. Well, at least till closing time. If you have lunch here, you can skip dinner. Save room for something from the fine dessert table. House wines and Beaujolais are very reasonable. L—12:30 to 2:30. D—8 to 1. Closed Sundays, Saturday lunch. All credit cards.

* *The Grey Door,* 23 Pembroke Street (763286/766011), is Dublin's answer to New York's Russian Tea Room minus the sprightly Faith Stewart Gordon. But wonderfully rich Russian and Finnish dishes. L—12:30 to 2:30, moderate. D—7 to 11:30, moderate to expensive. Closed Sundays, Saturday lunch. Wine license. AE, Master.

* *The Embassy Room* of Jury's Hotel, Ballsbridge (767511). Popular for

business lunches and dinners, but fine for any occasion. This place has long been known for its wandering roast-beef trolley. Your favorite cut is carved right at your table, and it's delicious. If you prefer, there are steak, lamb, and many other well-prepared dishes. Wines are reasonable. L—12:15 to 2:30, moderate. D—6 to 9:45, moderate to expensive. All credit cards.

* *The National Gallery Restaurant* in The National Gallery, Merrion Square (765268/763240). The dramatic backdrop of Ireland's most famous museum is the setting for tasty meals of meat and fish (especially good are the crab pâté and the roast beef). Varied menu. Monday–Saturday 10 to 5:30. Thursday 10 to 9. Sunday 2 to 5. Morning and afternoon tea also served. Wine license. AE, Diners, Master.

* *The Saddle Room* of the Shelbourne Hotel, St. Stephen's Green (766471). If your interest is prime beef, this place is for you; also good grills and seafood. More leisurely, less formal than the hotel's Shelbourne Restaurant, but service is slow. L—12:30 to 2:45. D—6 to 10:45. Sunday dinner 6 to 9:30. All credit cards.

Moderate

* *The Coffee House* in the Berkeley Court Hotel, Lansdowne Road, Ballsbridge (601711). A fine grill room where you can get full meals or lighter fare at a fraction of the price in the hotel's stately Berkeley Room. Omelettes, salads, steak, mixed grills: good value. Open 7:30 A.M. to 11 P.M. (10 P.M. Sunday). AE, Visa, Diners, CB.

* *Blazes Boylan Coffee Shop* in Bloom's Hotel, Anglesea Street (715622). Among its varied offerings, this coffee shop/restaurant has Biddy Mulligan's Irish stew and fine mixed grills. Open 7:30 A.M. to 11:30 P.M. (Sunday to 9 P.M.). AE, Master, Diners.

* *The Burlington Grill* in the Burlington Hotel, Upper Leeson Street (605222). This coffee house-type restaurant offers grills and steaks, snacks and light meals. Open 12:30 P.M. to 11:30 P.M. Closed Sundays from 4 to 5 P.M. All credit cards.

* *Casper & Guimbini's,* Wicklow Street (775122). The restaurant part of this new pub-restaurant offers extremely good meat and fish dishes at moderate verging on inexpensive cost. (For further details, see listing under Pub Luncheons.) Open noon to midnight daily (opens 11 A.M. on Saturday). Closed Sundays, bank holidays. Full license. Visa, Master, Diners.

* *Dobbins Wine Bistro,* Stephen's Lane (764670/764679). A variety of fish and meat dishes, mainly good, but the steak can be a bit tough. Open noon to 11:30 P.M. Closed Sundays, bank holidays. Wine license. AE, Visa, Master, Diners.

* *The Coffee House* of the Gresham Hotel, O'Connell Street (746881), serves a wide variety of moderate verging on inexpensive meals. Steaks, omelettes, grilled fish, chicken, and the house specialty, crusty meat pies. Open 7:30 A.M. to 11:30 P.M. Full license. AE, Master, Diners.

* *Kilmartin's Wine Bistro,* 19 Upper Baggot Street (686674). Once a bookie joint, now a small (very small—seats 35) intimate rendezvous. The menu is brief but quite good. The brandied chicken liver pâté and the oversized steak and kidney pie make this place worth a visit. It's one of Dublin's in little restaurants, where the food and the prices are right. Reasonable wines. Open 12:30 P.M. to 11 P.M. Sundays 1 to 10. Closed bank holidays. Wine license. AE, Visa, Diners.

* *Mitchell's Cellars Restaurant,* 21 Kildare Street (680367). This little place located in the cellar of Mitchell's Wine Shop is enormously popular. Open only for lunch; the sirloin salad is excellent, but so are the quiches. Wines are good and reasonable. But get there early, you can't reserve. L—12:15 to 2:30. Wine license. Visa, Master.

* *O'Casey's Bistro,* 17A Lower Baggot Street (604498). This neat, charming little candlelit restaurant is one of Dublin's latest entries on the romantic dining scene. With its intimate tan-clothed tables and rustic straw-seated chairs, it's completely disarming. It looks expensive but borders on moderate/inexpensive. A steak and kidney pie was succulent, a tender minute steak perfectly medium rare—as ordered. A number of other meat and fish dishes and good salads. L—12:30 to 2:30. D—6 to 11. Closed Sundays, bank holidays. Wine license. AE, Visa, Master, Diners.

* *Shrimps Wine Bar,* 1 Anne's Lane (713143), is a little like a Greenwich Village bistro with a lovely fire and either classical or jazz background music. Tiny and popular, so reserve in advance. The food list changes daily and ranges from pizza to fish pies, crabs to curries. The rhubarb desserts are unforgettable. Cheeses and wines are excellent. A special place. Open noon to 10 P.M. Closed Sundays, bank holidays. Wine license. Visa.

Inexpensive

* *Ariel House,* 52 Lansdowne Road (685512). The restaurant in this Georgian-townhouse guesthouse is so popular that its manager, Michael O'Brien, is opening it to non-residents as well (by reservation only). Overlooking the peaceful gardens and lawn, this place offers homemade pâtés and soups, mushrooms in beer batter for starters. Entrees vary, but typical are tender steaks, zesty chicken scaloppini, salmon, plaice served with fresh vegetables, and crisp salads. The hazelnut torte and ice cream (both homemade) are fine dessert selections. Reasonable wines. Very good value. 6 to 8 P.M. Wine license.

* *Bewley's Cafes Ltd.,* 78/79 Grafton Street; 11/12 Westmoreland Street; 13 South Great Georges Street (776761). The Grafton Street location is the largest and most interesting, although all are fine. Established in 1840 as classic tearoom/coffeehouses, little has changed at Bewley's. Mahogany paneling, stained glass motifs, enormous dining rooms with tables shared by various parties, displays of tea chests and baked goods—above all, the wonderful aroma of coffee—make these places memorable. A cross-section of Dublin life sits and sips its coffee here each day, and the roving waitresses are all authentic Dublin characters. It's easy to sit back with a tea or coffee (the best in Dublin) and a rich pastry or buttered sugary currant bun (delicious) and see what it was like when James Joyce used to frequent these cafes.

Note: Sandwiches and hearty full meals are available, including breakfast. The fried plaice and chips are delicious. Considering the very reasonable prices, you might want to eat your main meal of the day here and skip the heavy cost of an evening restaurant. Open Monday–Friday 8:30 A.M. to 5:30 P.M. Saturday 8:30 A.M. to 1 P.M. (except Westmoreland Street, which is open to 5:30.) Closed Sundays, bank holidays.

* *Burger King,* 39 Grafton Street/*McDonald's,* 9/10 Grafton Street. Probably the fastest and the cheapest you'll find. Here good Irish hamburger is used, tenderer and tastier than that used in most American counterparts of the chains, although the catsup is a touch sweeter than some Americans

would like. Open every day 10 A.M. to 11 P.M. PS: There's another branch of McDonald's at 62 Upper O'Connell Street.

* *Department Store Dining: Brown Thomas Club 76* and *Sandwich Shop,* Grafton Street; *Arnott & Co. Salad Bar,* Grafton Street. If you're shopping at either of these distinguished stores and want to grab a bite, try one of these. Brown Thomas also has a slightly more expensive *Brown's Restaurant* with waitress service. All have wine licenses and are open 9 A.M. to 5:30 P.M. Closed Sundays, bank holidays.

* *The Connacht Restaurant,* 13/14 Dame Street between Dublin Castle and Trinity College (770831). This family-run restaurant in one of the oldest sections of the city prides itself on good food at good prices. If you're on a budget, you can stuff yourself with a fine meal here without unstuffing your wallet. Roast beef, roast leg of lamb, shoulder of spring lamb, turkey, ham, quiche, chicken, minute steaks, scampi . . . the menu is unending, the food wonderfully cooked. But be forewarned that it's a bit hard to find and has an almost hospital-cafeteria decor. Very busy, especially at lunch hours. Open 11:30 A.M. to 8:30 P.M. Closed Sundays, bank holidays. Wine license.

* *The 18th Precinct,* 18 Suffolk Street, is Dublin's oddest place. Patterned after Manhattan's 18th Precinct, this fast-food restaurant (hamburgers, etc.) features waitresses in New York City police uniforms who storm your table brandishing pistols and demanding 'Your order or your life!' Menu items like 'the electric-chair sizzler'—a well-done hamburger steak with fries— abound. Despite all this zaniness (which customers don't seem to respond to), the food is quite good, more than adequate for a place of this type. It's very busy and open late. It just seems that with this theme (and the American accents which some of the staff struggle to perfect) the whole operation would be more appropriate in one of those recycled California ghost towns. Maybe they should dress up like Vikings and flourish bronze swords instead. Well, it *is* different. Open Sunday–Thursday 11:30 A.M. to midnight. Friday–Saturday 11:30 P.M. to 1 A.M. Wine license.

* *The Granary Buffet Restaurant,* 34/37 East Essex Street (713187). Excellent food, self-service. Salads, sandwiches, homemade soups, full meals, including meats and seafoods. Home baking. Extremely popular despite the cafeteria atmosphere—and rightly so. Open 10:30 A.M. to 11:30 P.M. Closed Sundays, bank holidays. Full license.

* *Jury's Hotel Coffee Dock,* Ballsbridge (767511). Certainly, this is one of the best coffee shops in the city: *and it's open 23 hours a day.* The after-hours hamburgers are excellent, but there are full meals as well: steaks to traditional Irish dishes. Very reasonable and popular. Closed 5 to 6 A.M. Sunday open 6 A.M. to 10:30 P.M. only. Full license. All credit cards.

* *The Kilkenny Shop,* Nassau Street (777066). This pleasant little self-service restaurant in the Kilkenny Shop overlooks the gardens of Trinity College. Salads, scones, cakes, tea, coffee. Open 9 A.M. to 5 P.M. Closed Sundays. Wine license.

* *Murphs,* 99 Lower Baggot Street (681205/760784). Great value in this Tiffany lamp-shaded wine bistro with its bentwood chairs. Historically, it's interesting to note that this was once the wine cellar of an old Georgian mansion; how many of those have you been in? If all you want is a hamburger, you can get it. The Irish stew is zesty. There's sole Connemara and fresh salmon salad (in season). Boiled bacon, shepherd's (or cottage) pie, Scotch egg with ham salad are house specialties. Farther out of the way at 21 Bache-

lor's Walk (a leap from O'Connell Street) is another branch housed in a 300-year-old warehouse on the River Liffey banks. Note: Murphs has received the coveted Irish Tourist Board award for excellence in inexpensive dining. Same prices all day. Open 12:30 P.M. to 11 P.M. Closed Sundays, bank holidays. Wine license.

* *Murphy Doodle's,* 18 Suffolk Street (711038). You'll get a strange mix of cuisines here, from pizza and canneloni to steak and kidney/shepherd's pies. Food okay—and open late. Rather bland basement decor. Closed Sundays, bank holidays. Wine license.

* *The Periwinkle* in the Powerscourt Townhouse Shopping Centre, South William Street (711979). One of Dublin's best new mini-restaurants, with nautical decor against a gleaming white background. Fast food—seafood only—and delicious. Salads, sandwiches, periwinkles, shrimp rolls. The crabmeat sandwiches are enormous, jampacked with crab; coupled with a glass of zesty white wine, the tab is less than most U.S. restaurants would charge for a tuna sandwich and a Coke. Open daily 11 A.M. to 6 P.M. If you like seafood, don't miss this bargain. Wine license.

* *The Pink Bicycle,* The Powerscourt Shopping Centre, South William Street. Good self-service place where you can eat on balcony terraces overlooking the entire Powerscourt Centre while an ever-changing parade of musicians entertains far below. Homemade soups, salads, tacos, hot chicken dishes, desserts. Open daily 11 A.M. to 6 P.M. Wine license.

* *Regency Fare Delicatessen,* 28 South Anne Street (777340). The kind of deli food that all cities should have but don't, especially not at these prices. Fresh prawns and prawn salads, smoked trout/salmon/mackerel, hearty country-style pâtés, quiche, steak and kidney pie, oversized sandwiches, freshly carved cold roasts, pastries. Breakfast. Open 8:30 A.M. to 6:30 P.M. Closed Sundays, bank holidays. Wine license.

* *Coffee Shop of the Shelbourne Hotel,* St. Stephen's Green (766471). A wide variety of foods from snacks to full meals at very reasonable prices in one of Dublin's finest old hotels. Hamburgers, steak, chicken, a special dish every day. Also a variety of fish and omlettes. Good service. Open 10:30 A.M. to 11:30 P.M. Closed Sundays. All credit cards.

* *Solomon Grundy's,* 21 Suffolk Street (774804). A mix of Irish and Italian foods here. Spaghetti, pizza, and the steak and kidney pie which is a specialty (this varies according to the day; one was succulent, another a little too fatty). But it's reasonable and open very late. Monday–Thursday noon to 11:30; Friday–Saturday noon to 1 A.M. Sunday to midnight. Wine license.

* *Timmerman's Wine Cellar,* The Powerscourt Shopping Centre, South William Street. Salads, buffet style, with wines, served in the original vaulted kitchen of Viscount Powerscourt's Dublin home. Church pew seating. Inexpensive. Open daily 11 A.M. to 6 P.M. Wine license.

Suburban Dining

There are some fine places on the outskirts of Dublin, most of which are covered briefly, because unless you've planned an extended Dublin stay it's doubtful you'd have time to visit them.
North of the city:

* *The Abbey Tavern,* Howth (322006). Dublin's little fishing village on the north arm of Dublin Bay, about nine miles from city center, houses this large, bustling tavern that offers a superb Irish ballad sing every night except Sun-

Abbey Tavern

day. This combined with a wonderful new seafood restaurant (Old-World decor), warming turf fires, stone walls and flagstone floors, and gas lights make for a wonderful evening. Plus there's a special traditional song pub. Stroll down toward the shore afterward and watch the twinkling lights of boats at sea. It's memorable, especially on a starry night. The Abbey is open 7 P.M. to 11 P.M. Closed Sunday. Full license. AE, Diners, Visa, Master. Expensive.

 * *King Sitric*, East Pier, Howth (325235). A charmingly sleepy candlelit restaurant in the old Harbour Master's house. Have a pre-dinner drink in a lounge (wines only) as you watch the lonely lights of ships at sea, then enter the dining rooms to feast on superb seafood dishes. This place used to be praised far and wide as Dublin's finest. It's doubtful if it can still claim that illustrious position, but then look at all the new competition. It's still a wonderful standby. Open 7:30 P.M. to 11 P.M. Closed Sundays. Wine license. AE, Diners. Expensive.

South of the city:

 * *Digby's Restaurant and Wine Bar*, 5 Windsor Terrace, Dun Laoghaire (804600). Seafront seafood in batik-roofed dining area. Open Monday–Saturday 7:15 to 11:30 P.M. Lunch from 12:30 to 3 P.M. Closed Sundays. Wine license. AE, Diners, Visa, Master. Expensive.

 * *Restaurant Mirabeau*, Marine Parade, Sandycove (809873). A Georgian house serving French cuisine. But beware: not of the food, which ranges from good seafood dishes to game, but of the Waterford glass and other expensive accoutrements of the whole serving experience. There are no prices on the

menu, and you do get a staggering check when it's all over. Worth it? Some say yes, others disagree. Regardless, most Dubliners consider it their most expensive dining experience. Open from 7:30 on (at these prices, why not?). Wine list, staggering! Closed Sundays. Wine license only. All credit cards. Enormously expensive.

* *Resturant Na Mara*, Dun Laoghaire (806767). More seafood, but with a selection of fine Irish meat dishes, as you overlook Dun Laoghaire harbor. L—12:30 to 2:30. D—7 to 10:30. Closed Sunday and Monday. Full license. AE, Visa, Master, Diners. Expensive.

* *Chez La Hiff*, 21 Railway Road, Dalkey (859559). Fondues, barbeques, and other unusual dishes in this snug restaurant furnished with antiques. 7 P.M. to 12:30 A.M. Closed one week in October. Wine license. AE, Visa, Master. Expensive.

* *The Guinea Pig*, 17 Railway Road, Dalkey (859055). Relaxed, homey seafood restaurant, mentioned in Michelin and Egon Ronay guides. D—7 to 11. Closed Sundays, bank holidays, two weeks in January and July, also Holy Week. Wine license. All credit cards. Expensive.

* *Nieves Restaurant*, Dalkey (856156). Cozy place that offers both meat and seafood: good fare. L—12:30 to 2:30. D—7 to 11. Closed bank holidays. Wine license. AE, Diners, Visa, Master. Lunch moderate to expensive; dinner expensive.

* *Restaurant Baroque*, Main Street, Dalkey (859455). This place over Arches Lounge, with its snug open fireplaces, does everything well from seafood and game in season to suckling pig. Open 7 to 11 P.M. Closed Sunday and Monday. Full license. AE, Diners, Visa, Master. Expensive.

* *The Sand Castle*, Castle Street, Dalkey (850552). Refreshing new game and seafood restaurant with fresh vegetables cooked to order. Intimate ambiance. L—12:30 to 2:30. D—7 to 11. Closed Sundays. Wine license. AE, Master, Diners. Expensive.

* *The Island Restaurant* in The Court Hotel, Killiney (851622). A pleasant restaurant with extensive menu in this stately Victorian hotel (with modern wing) overlooking Killiney Bay. Good seafood, traditional Irish dishes, international cuisine. Expensive. But the hotel also has its Library Coffee Shop, with meals at much lower prices served among displays of old books, so you can browse while you eat. L—12:30 to 2. D—7 to 10. Coffee Shop open 12:30 P.M. to 11:30 P.M. Full license. AE, Visa, Master.

* *Fitzpatrick Castle Hotel*, Killiney (851533). If you dream of Victoriana and silver trolleys—go here. Excellent carvery roast beef, lobster, steak, rack of lamb, served by candlelight. Expensive, but the hotel does have a considerably less expensive grill located in a former dungeon and connecting with a 'dungeon bar' (piano music and an open turf fire). L—12:30 to 2:30. D—7 to 11:30. Grill open 12:30 P.M. to midnight. Full license. AE, Diners, Visa, Master.

Note: Both the Court Hotel and Fitzpatrick's have rooms if you should want to stay in this beautiful seaside area.

* *Eamon's Restaurant*, Seafront, Bray (829072). A little farther out (just into County Wicklow) is this very pleasant, surprisingly inexpensive little Victorian seafront basement restaurant. It's a family-run operation, with kids in and out and a host who prides himself on creating good dishes. Excellent pâté, prawns, chicken curry, plaice, raspberry/chocolate cake, cheese mousse. The spinach is beautifully spiced with ginger. Open 7 P.M. to midnight. Closed

Sunday and Monday, bank holidays. Wine license. AE, Diners, Visa, Master. Moderate to inexpensive.

PUB LUNCHEONS

Excellent dining value

This phenomenon, a long time on the British scene, is relatively new to Ireland and is spreading rapidly throughout the country. While lunch has been a custom at some pubs for years, it is only recently that most have moved beyond the stale-sandwich stage into fine, hearty luncheons. At most places you can stuff yourself for around $5.00. It's great value by any standards, so you may want to consider these for your main meal of the day and forego the expensive evening restaurants.

Dublin's Best Pub Dining Places

* *Bloom's Bar* in Bloom's Hotel, Anglesea Street (715622). New hotel and bar done with turn-of-the-century styling. Fine foods. Hot and cold buffet, salads. Open daily 12:30 P.M. to 2:30, with a Sunday brunch combining Irish-style breakfast with buffet lunch. AE, Master, Diners.

* *Casper & Guimbini's*, Wicklow Street (775122). On the site of the old Wicklow Hotel, this spacious new pub-restaurant somehow manages to be bright and glittery even with its dim Tiffany-shaded lighting. The bar where you're served the pub food is massive, the chair-stools comfortable. And there's air-conditioning (a rarity in Ireland). Chicken and fish platters, smoked salmon, submarine sandwiches, salads, shepherd's pie, bangers & mash. Good and very reasonable. Brunch on Saturday. Open daily noon to 11:30 P.M. Closed Sundays, bank holidays. Visa, Master, Diners.

* *The Castle Inn Bars* in The Castle Inn, Lord Edward Street (780663). Posh and comfortable. The food is hearty—hot meat and fish dishes. Or you can have a lighter but tasty salad. L—12:30 to 2:30 P.M. Closed Sundays. All credit cards.

* *The Granary Bar* 34/37 East Essex Street (713187). Marvelous Victorian pub with excellent food: cold buffet, soups, meats, seafoods. L—noon to 2:30. Closed Saturday, Sunday, bank holidays.

* *The Dubliner Bar* in Jury's Hotel, Ballsbridge. (767511) A real bargain in this room at Jury's with its winged chairs, dark rich woods, and fireplace— all recalling Edwardian days. Carvery luncheons from joints of the day are thick, tender, bountiful. A dozen different salads to choose from, and a vegetarian meal as well. You wouldn't get this for double the price in most Dublin restaurants in the evening. L—12:30 to 2. Closed Saturday, Sunday, bank holidays. All credit cards.

* *The Lord Edward*, 23 Christchurch Place (752557). Woody, cushiony Victorian pub-lounge on the second floor of the three-story Lord Edward complex, serving salads and delicious hot meat and seafood dishes. Popular businessmen's haunt. L—12:30 to 2:30. Closed Saturday, Sunday, bank holidays. AE, Visa, Master, Diners.

* *Neary's*, Chatham Street, has beautiful sandwiches of smoked salmon on home-made brown bread and (in season) oysters with stout.

* *The Paddock Bar* of the Shelbourne Hotel, St. Stephen's Green (766471), is adjacent to the Shelbourne but with its own separate entrance on the Green. Cushiony, comfortable, bright old-townhouse atmosphere. Fine hearty food, including steak and kidney pie, curries, sliced melt-in-your-mouth cold sirloin,

tasty cold chicken, solid sandwiches, and a platter of oversized sausages and potatoes that turns some diners wild with delight. This place is very pleasant all around, and one of the most popular. Go early. Open 11 A.M. to 2:30 P.M. *Note:* This is one of the few pubs that serves food into the evening, from 4:30 P.M. on. Closed Sundays. All credit cards.

★ *Sachs Bar* in Sachs Hotel, Morehampton Road (746881). Pâtés, fish salads, crepes, roasts, wonderful desserts. All good to excellent in this fine Victorian bar of a renovated Regency hotel, where the Dublin literati meet. L—12:30 to 2:30. Closed Saturday lunch, bank holidays.

★ *The Stag's Head,* 1 Dame Court. Hardy hot lunches, especially good sandwiches. Meeting spot of the legal profession.

LUNCHEON THEATER

This is a rapidly growing form of divertissement for Dublin, and it's good to see such a phenomenon flower, given this country's uniquely rich heritage of drama. But luncheon theater doesn't confine itself to plays; there are prose and poetry readings (often based on the Irish heritage), traditional music hours, and concerts. Still so relatively new that you must check schedules frequently, but the programs are good and the cost is minimal, even with the snack food (which is optional). If you don't have time to go to a full evening of theater, this is an excellent way to fit some into your itinerary.

While times vary, most luncheon theater begins between 12:30 and 1:00, ends between 1:30 and 2:00 P.M. Some of the best:

★ *The Peacock Theater,* Lower Abbey Street (744505). Under the Abbey Theater, this experimental house has programs that vary from jazz trios to Beckett one-acts.

★ *Tailors Hall,* Back Lane off High Street (780797). One-man shows, brief plays in this 18th-century hall.

★ *Trinity College,* College Green. (772941). Reviews, traditional music, drama within the Trinity complex.

★ *Focus Theater,* just off Pembroke Street (682993). A variety of entertainments in this experimental theater.

★ *The National Concert Hall,* Earlsfort Terrace (711888). Lunchtime concerts on an occasional basis in this new concert hall.

★ *The Royal Dublin Society,* Ballsbridge (680645). Occasional concerts, often featuring international pianists and cellists, at this the venue of the Dublin Horse Show.

★ *The Shelbourne Rooms* of the Shelbourne Hotel, St. Stephen's Green (766471). Mainly concerts and recitals at this stately old hotel.

BREAKFAST IN DUBLIN

Expensive

★ The Coffee House in The Berkeley Court Hotel. Opens 7:30.
★ The Coffee House in The Gresham Hotel. Opens 7:30.
★ The Embassy Room in Jury's Hotel. Opens 7:00.
★ The Saddle Room in The Shelbourne Hotel. Opens 7:15.

Moderate

★ The Blazes Boylan Coffee Shop in Bloom's Hotel. Opens 7:30.
★ The Coffee Dock in Jury's Hotel. Opens 6:00.

Hearty Irish Breakfast

Inexpensive

* ★ Arnott & Co. Opens 9:00.
* ★ Bewley's. Opens 8:30.
* ★ Brown's and Club 76 in Brown Thomas Department Store. Opens 9:00.
* ★ The Kilkenny Shop. Opens 9:00.
* ★ Regency Fare Delicatessen. Opens 8:30.

Most of the above serve either full Irish or Continental (lighter) breakfasts. The food is good, because the Irish really believe in breakfast. As a rule of thumb, the faster service is usually in the coffee shops. Note that nearly all restaurants in Dublin, and in the rest of the country as well, stop serving breakfast at 10:00. After that, you may be able to get coffee or tea and scones, possibly (if you're lucky) toast.

CABARET

There are four major cabarets in Dublin, and when you consider that they offer between 90 minutes and two and a half hours of traditional entertainment, along with a full dinner, the price falls into the moderate to inexpensive category.

★ *The Braemor Rooms,* Churchtown (982308/988664). A traditional Irish musical tour de force (1½-hour) dinner show with dancing to the Braemor Trio. The Rooms also offer you a choice of six starters, entrees, and desserts. 8 P.M. (show 9:30). Open all year. Closed Sundays. Full license. All credit cards.

* *The Burlington Irish Cabaret* at the Burlington Hotel, Upper Leeson Street (605222). Harps, fiddles, ballads, shanties and the Rory O'Connor Irish Dancers entertain you for well over two hours. The set traditional dinner consists of potato soup, salmon, steak filet, colcannon (cabbage, kale, and boiled potatoes mashed together and well buttered), and an Irish Mist souffle. 7:00 (show 8:15). Closed Sundays and November through March. There's a special low price for those who just want to see the show. All credit cards.

* *Clontarf Castle Show,* Castle Avenue (332271/331898). Singers, dancers, harpists, and other musicians bring you a two-and-a-half-hour program of the Irish traditional. Dinner features a variety of meat and fish dishes and is optional, so you can pay a low entrance fee for the show alone. Eight-thirty, with dinner served at the table during show. Dancing afterward until 12:30 A.M. Open all year, but closed on Sundays. Full license. AE, Visa, Master, Diners.

* *Jury's Irish Cabaret* at Jury's Hotel, Ballsbridge (767511). This is Ireland's longest-running and probably most popular cabaret. Marvelously skillful performers and show. Traditional music, comedy, Irish dancers, plus the attractive Anne Byrne singing *Love's Old Sweet Song* so beautifully that all Joyce lovers can close their eyes and imagine it's the twilight of 16 June 1904 once more. The food: a five-course dinner with five entree selections, including Irish traditional dishes. You might want to try the corned beef and cabbage or the baked cod in oatmeal. Good hearty fare. 7:30 P.M. (2½-hour show begins at 8:15). Dinner optional. Special low price for show and two drinks. Closed Mondays and from mid-October through April. Full license. All credit cards.

NIGHT CLUBS

It's safe to assume that most Americans vacationing in Ireland don't go there with night clubs/discos uppermost in their minds. Otherwise they'd probably make for an American city. But there are several options if you have an impulse toward after-hours entertainment. Most are open from 10 P.M. to 3 A.M. The music is taped, and all have wine licenses. The wine is reasonable. Some serve steaks and other staples, but not a full menu. Two of Dublin's most popular are:

* *Annabel's* in the Burlington Hotel, Upper Leeson Street (605222). Dimly lit with lively sound system. Admission includes a four-course buffet meal. Or if you prefer, there's an extra charge for carved roasts. Good value, especially on the evening scene. Open Monday-Friday 10 P.M. to 2 A.M. Saturday 8:30 to 1:00. Closed Sundays. All credit cards.

* *Raffles* in Sachs Hotel, 21 Morehampton Road (680995). A sprightly club in the basement of this old, but newly renovated, Regency hotel. Lively music, good foods, reasonable prices. Open Monday-Friday 10 P.M. to 2 A.M. Saturday 8:30 to 1:00. Closed Sundays. Full license.

THEATER

O'Casey, Yeats, Synge, Lady Gregory, Behan, Beckett, Shaw—and in recent times Brian Friel and Hugh Leonard—these and many others are the Irish theater, abounding in brilliance. The wealth of drama is truly astonishing for such a small country. Most Americans traveling to Ireland feel that an evening at the theater is a must. In Dublin there are a number from which to choose.

* *The Abbey Theater,* Lower Abbey Street (744505). World-renowned, this is Ireland's national theater and its most popular. It performs works by Irish

playwrights past and present. A fire destroyed the original Abbey in 1951, and the current house opened in 1966. Reserve tickets as soon as you can. Curtain is at eight o'clock sharp; if you're late you won't be seated until after the first act.

* *The Peacock Theater,* Lower Abbey Street (744505). This special smaller theater beneath the Abbey is an extension of the national theater group. It does such special productions as prose and poetry readings, one-man shows, luncheon theater, and children's theater—also hosts out-of-town companies. Evening performances at 8:00.

* *Project Arts Centre,* 39 East Essex Street off Dame Street (713327). Does works by contemporary and new playwrights. 8:00 P.M.

* *The Gate Theater,* Parnell Square (744045). Modern Irish drama as well as the best of the modern international scene. Curtain at 8:00.

* *The Olympia,* Dame Street (778962). Everything from operettas and variety shows to serious drama could turn up at this time-honored house. Check newspaper for schedule and times.

* *The National Concert Hall,* Earlsfort Terrace (711888). While concerts are held on a sporadic basis at other venues, this is Dublin's new and first concert hall. Mostly classical.

The Irish Times is a good source for checking other theatrical events.

Note that the cost of tickets for the Irish theater is extremely modest compared to those of most American houses. To make it even more appealing, the Irish Tourist Board, in conjunction with Irish Theatre Managements, is offering (for a very minimal fee) a booklet of discount vouchers to 17 theaters throughout the country, including those in Dublin. If you're interested, check with the Tourist Board in Ireland.

As mentioned earlier, Dublin usually holds its annual Theatre Festival during the first two weeks in October. Irish, European, and American theater people and aficionados attend the openings of Irish and international productions (many of them new). It can be a busy time, so it's advisable to reserve in advance (lodgings as well as tickets).

THE WONDERFUL WORLD OF DUBLIN'S GRAND OLD PUBS

Just as Ireland has a splendid legacy of theater, so it has a unique heritage of pubs. Certainly, they rank among the most captivating in the world. Even if you don't drink, you should make it a point to have a look at a few of them, for here you will see the Ireland of another day and sense the lifestyle of that time. Among Dublin's finest:

* *The Brazen Head* at 20 Lower Bridge Street is probably Dublin's oldest pub. As early as the 1600s (during the reign of Charles II), it was a popular haunt. In the late 1700s it became the meeting place of Irish freedom fighters. Such patriots as Wolfe Tone, Robert Emmet, and Daniel O'Connell crossed its cobble-stoned courtyard to frequent the pub's dim, lantern-lit bar and the ghostly parlors reached by a creaking staircase. In later years, James Joyce, Oliver Gogarty, and Brendan Behan attended it. (If you're looking for this place, you could easily miss the unmarked arch that leads to the courtyard entrance, but it's worth keeping careful watch.) The bar serves no draught stouts or lagers, and its trappings seem as old as the place itself. Patrons often sing late in the evening. However, this is mostly a conversation pub.

The Long Hall

* *The Long Hall* (more than 200 years old) at 51 South Great Georges Street is a long narrow bar with a cozy snug (which ladies used to frequent years ago so they wouldn't be seen drinking). Its splendid dark-wood bar trimmed with copper and gold plate, its magnificent stained glass panels, gilded mirrors, old crystal chandeliers, and grand pendulum clock (over 300 years old) qualify this pub as an historic monument. A must-see conversation pub. For more intimate chats, try the snug.

* *Mulligan's* at 8 Poolbeg Street (established in 1782) is another James Joyce haunt. A down-to-earth drinking man's pub with gaslights, dark woody trappings, and a fireplace in the back. This place used to attract a grand cross-section of Dubliners (truck drivers, dockers, actors, poets and would-be poets, businessmen, secretaries, college coeds), but unfortunately it has recently begun to draw a seedier youthful clientele along with the pseudo-intellectuals. Let's hope this changes. Regardless, it should be seen.

* *Doheny & Nesbitt* at 5 Lower Baggot Street near Merrion Row is a marvelous monument to Dublin Victoriana with its spectacularly intricate wood-trimmed bar and ceiling, marble tables, carved frame clocks, and snug. Thoroughly enjoyable.

* *Ryan's* on Parkgate Street (near Phoenix Park) is esteemed by many Dubliners as the finest of the old pubs. James Joyce, among others, was particularly fond of the place with its fine mahogany bar, ornate mirrors, graceful oil lamps, snug, and antique bar trappings. Definitely worth seeing.

* *The Bailey*, Duke Street (see Restaurants).

* *Davy Byrnes*, Duke Street (across the street from the Bailey) Like the Bailey this pub is mentioned in *Ulysses*. Bloom reflects on it as a 'nice quiet

O'Donoghue's

bar. Nice piece of wood in the counter.' These aspects may be the same today, as are the 19th-century murals, but the back snug, in what Bloom thought of as his 'moral pub,' has long since been modernized into a lounge, and the bare floors are now carpeted. Today it's one of Dublin's slicker pubs, attended by a well-dressed youthful crowd.

    * *Neary's* of Chatham Street is a turn-of-the-century pub with an elegant pink-and-grey-marble bar supporting enormous brass-stemmed global lamps. Its massive mahogany-framed mirrors, its paneled ceiling, and its cozy settees help make it one of Dublin's pleasantest pubs. Attended by a young to middle-aged well-off crowd.

    * *McDaid's* of Harry Street used to be thought of as the writer's pub. Dingy, bare (almost like an empty stage), this smoky room was once the setting for discourses from such literary lights as Brendan Behan. Unfortunately, the place has now been adopted by a pseudo-literary crowd and five minutes is more than enough (maybe too much).

    * *O'Donoghue's* at 15 Merrion Row is not the place to go if you're very thirsty—not in the evening, that is. Jam-packed with jeans-clad youth (and those not so young), it's virtually impossible to get anywhere near the bar. The main interest in this old pub is the impromptu entertainment; musicians drop by and start playing or singing. Sometimes there are several groups going at the same time, many of them excellent. So even if you can't drink, you can just stop in and listen.

    If you're still thirsty—and what's more important, if you're still standing—here are a few more pubs to add to your list.

* *Toner's*—Lower Baggot Street
* *Kehoe's*—South Anne Street
* *The Palace Bar*—Fleet Street
* *The Stag's Head*—Dame Court (and nearby is The Stag's Tail)
* *The Horseshoe Bar* in the Shelbourne Hotel, St. Stephen's Green (meeting place of trendy Dubliners as well as the International set)

Pub Notes: As in the rest of Ireland, drinks in Dublin are expensive because of high governmental taxation. However, prices are slightly lower at pubs than they are at the splashier grade-A* hotels. Today women frequent pubs (bar as well as lounge areas), which certainly was not always the case. Women's lib has arrived even in some of Ireland's staunchest male hangouts. However, in the real old-school men's bars, it's a rarity to see an unescorted woman.

A DUBLIN SHOPPING SPREE

Dublin has always been a city of pubs and shops, but now there are more of the latter than it knows how to sustain. With the openings of three new shopping centers within the city center area—the Powerscourt Townhouse Shopping Centre on William Street, The ILAC Centre on Moore Street, and The Irish Life Centre between Abbey and Talbot Streets—the city is rapidly approaching the day when there will be one shop for each member of the population. So as a tourist, *be wise:* don't attempt to cover them all, or you'll spend your entire vacation doing nothing else (and even then you won't have seen them all). As a rule of thumb, there are two major areas (along with a few off-shoots) of importance to the American tourist. All are within a stone's throw of one another. Most of the shops in these areas accept credit cards: AE, Visa, Master, some Diners.

* *The Powerscourt Townhouse Shopping Centre,* which covers the block from William to Clarendon Streets, is an exciting new shopping complex formed within the hollowed-out original structure of the vast four-story Georgian townhouse of Lord Powerscourt, which was built in 1774. The American counterpart of this center is Boston's spectacular Quincy Market in the Faneuil Hall (Cradle of Liberty) area. Powerscourt's magnificent plasterwork ceiling, which documents the country's transition from the rococo to the neo-classical period, and its grand exterior maintain its status as one of the country's finest examples of Georgian architecture. But the shops within—along with a few very pleasant and reasonable dining places (see Restaurants)—make this place a special treasure. There's a wonderful level of antiques (nine shops), including those with furniture, crystal, jewelry, home furnishings, silver, goldware, original oils, and maps. There's an entire level devoted to Dublin's young Irish craftsmen: woodwork, leatherwork, prints, batik fashions, stoneware, porcelain, jewelry. Beyond this, there are dozens of other boutiques featuring Belleek, Royal Tara china, Donegal tweeds, linens, tweed caps and hats, and gourmet foods (jams, smoked salmon, and trout, excellent Irish cheeses).

By all means, save several hours for Powerscourt, which is streets ahead of any other shopping center in Ireland. If you've any particular items in mind, you'll probably find them here. And while you shop or dine, you can listen to the Irish musicians who perform continuously for the public.

* When you're ready to leave Powerscourt, take the Clarendon Street exit. Cross Clarendon to Johnston Court, and meander down this small European-

style lane where aspiring young Irish musicians play tin whistles and violins; check the little antique jewelry stores as you move toward Grafton Street.

* When you come out on Grafton Street, you are in the heart of Dublin's next major shopping area. Here *Brown Thomas* and *Switzers* are opposite one another. Few Irishmen, or anyone who knows Ireland, would deny that these are two of the country's finest department stores. In them you'll find everything from Irish high fashions, tweeds, and knitwear to china, crystal, crafts, and gourmet food (new shop in Brown Thomas, the store to choose if you've time only for one,) Brown Thomas keeps changing, adding, improving— Ireland's answer to Bloomingdale's—without losing its national flavor.

* If time permits, you may want to check the rest of the Grafton Street shops (especially for apparel), maybe stopping off for coffee and sugary currant buns in Bewley's. Off Grafton Street are several other short, narrow streets of shopping interest: Anne Street, Duke Street, and Duke Lane. Here you'll find craft and antique shops, pubs, and the little cafes.

At the foot of Grafton Street's slope, you'll see Nassau Street. Follow it along opposite the gardens of Trinity College, and you'll pass the *Fred Hanna Bookshop,* with fine books of Irish interest. Keep going along Nassau Street to Kildare Street, and you'll come to *The Kilkenny Design Centre,* Ireland's showcase store for the country's top designs in pottery, crystal, knits, jewelry, linens, home furnishings, and furniture. There's a fine inexpensive restaurant upstairs (see Restaurants).

Backtracking a little down Nassau Street, you'll come to Dawson Street, which soon brings you to *Fergus O'Farrell,* a small craft shop with Irish pottery, ceramics, and a special emphasis on its famous carved wooden figures.

* Other places of interest slightly (and further) off this course:

Antiques

McDonnell Antiques, 15 Kildare Street (reputed to be Dublin's leading antique dealer). Dishes, glass, 18th-and 19th-century furniture, etc.

Kildare Antiques on Kildare Street near McDonnell's. Dishes and paintings.

Edward Butler, 14 Bachelor's Walk. Eighteenth-century paintings and fine furniture.

H. Danker, 10 South Anne Street. Silver, jewelry, some paintings.

J. W. Weldon, 55 Clarendon Street and 19 South Anne. Silver.

Greene's, on Clare Street. Old books (new ones too) dealing with Dublin and Irish folklore.

Try also; *Lawlor Briscoe Antiques,* 35 Ormond Quay (by the Liffey); *Ormond Antiques,* on Lower Ormond Quay; *Orken Bros.,* 33b Mill Street.

Irish Music

McCullough Piggott, Suffolk Street, has a vast range of records, cassettes, sheet music. And if you're really into it, you can toot your own whistle by purchasing a tin one. For those of you who'd like to slip an Irish harp aboard Aer Lingus for your return to America, they have those too.

Of Special Note: Shop at Jury's, Jury's Hotel, Ballsbridge (907181). Most hotel shops, like those at airports around the world, are mere conscience corners for guilty souls. Last-minute panic always puts these shops at an advantage, and a simple $25 silk scarf leaps to $50. Well, it's the way of the world—but not so at Jury's Hotel. The Shop at Jury's manager, Brendan

O'Rourke, prides himself on undercutting everyone. The tweed jackets are cheaper. So are the Blarney sweaters (even cheaper than they are at the Blarney headquarters), the fisherman knits (and of better quality), the Belleek china, in some cases even the Waterford crystal. The fine assortment of jewelry is several pounds lower than the Dublin shops. Also good books of Irish interest. This place is a real find because manager O'Rourke feels honesty is the best policy—and undercutting is even better. 'It brings in the trade—and it's better for me night's sleep.'

About a fifteen-minute walk, five minute bus ride from the St. Stephen's Green area, this place is well worth a visit if you're in a buying mood. Open 8 A.M. to midnight.

P.S. Most of the shops in these areas accept credit cards—AE, Visa, Master. Some Diners.

SPORTS

Certainly there's enough to do in Dublin to occupy the tourist for a month without even considering sports. But for those with an abiding interest, here's a listing of the possibilities.

* *Golfing*. There are literally dozens of golf courses (9- and 18-hole) within easy reach of the city center, many with caddy service and showering facilities. Popular clubs include: The Castle Golf Club, Rathfarnham; The Clontarf Golf Club, Clontarf; The Dun Laoghaire Golf Club, Dun Laoghaire; The Portmarnock Golf Club, Portmarnock; The Royal Dublin Golf Club, Dollymount. There are two public 18-hole golf courses in the area: Corballis, at Donabate, and The Public Golf Courses at the Deer Park Hotel, Howth. Clubs may be rented at St. Anne's Park, Raheny. Note: The Irish Tourist Board can provide you with complete listings of golf courses and further details.

* *Running*. The 2000-acre Phoenix Park within the city provides the ideal (and beautiful) terrain; many Dubliners run here. If you're really into running, you may be interested in the Dublin Marathon, usually held the day after the New York City Marathon in late October (but check The Irish Tourist Board). There are special, and very attractive, package-tour arrangements. Aer Lingus and Marathon Tours of Boston, Harvard Square, have done this in connection with the noted Irish runner Eamonn Coghlan.

* *Swimming*. There are dozens of seaside haunts near Dublin—north and south. Try Howth or Killiney.

* *Fishing*. For the fresh-water variety, the River Liffey (well outside its polluted city stretches) provides good grounds for salmon and trout, pike and perch. February to May best. The Clane area or Sallins and Leixlip are favored, but permits are required. You'll get them at the Dublin tackle shops. Check the phone directory's Golden Pages. Salt-water fishing: north, Howth; south, Dun Laoghaire and Greystones. Permits and bait at the Dublin tackle shops. Check Golden Pages.

* *Yachting*. This is one of the finest places in Ireland to do it. There are yacht clubs at Dun Laoghaire, Howth, Sutton, Malahide, Swords, Kilbarrack, Rush, Skerries, and Clontarf. Information from the Irish Yachting Association (800239), 87 Upper George's Street, Dun Laoghaire.

* *Hunting*. Many areas of County Dublin as well as nearby Counties Meath, Wicklow, and Kildare are the favored Irish hunting haunts. These hunt groups meet several times a week: South County Dublin Harriers, Naas Harriers,

Croke Park Hurling

Meath Foxhounds, Bray Harriers, Kildare Foxhounds, Ward Union Staghounds. Check The Irish Tourist Board for more details.

* *Polo.* Played throughout the summer in Phoenix Park, and at The Royal Dublin Society showgrounds during the Spring Show in May, the Horse Show in August.

* *Horse Racing.* The local courses are at Phoenix Park and Leopardstown. Thirty-five miles away in Co. Kildare is The Curragh, where most of the Classic Races are run. Punchestown, also in Kildare, is important in May, and The Fairyhouse, Co. Meath, is vital to racing fans at Easter.

* *Greyhound Racing.* This sport attracts well over a million patrons annually in the Irish Republic. It's held at Shelbourne Park, Ringsend, and at Harold Cross Stadium. Check the Irish Tourist Board for schedules.

* *Tennis.* The Fitzwilliam Tennis Club, Rathgar, is the bee's knees of the Irish tennis scene—or at least that's what its members think. There is a visitor's fee, of course.

* *Gaelic Football and Hurling.* These are two of Ireland's most exciting sports. You may wish to catch a match at Dublin's Croke Park.

DUBLIN'S STALWART LITERARY HERITAGE

Considering the relatively small size of the community, Dublin's literary heritage is one of the most impressive in the world. Here are some of the dozens of authors who have lived or worked in Dublin and a few of the literary landmarks associated with them.

* *Jonathan Swift.* St. Patrick's Cathedral (Church of Ireland), where Swift was named Dean in 1713 and was buried in 1745; Marsh's Library (the city's

first public library, opened in 1701), which Swift frequented and which today houses the oak table at which he penned *Gulliver's Travels,* along with his private book collection; No. 7 Hoey's Court, where Swift is said to have been born in 1666: only a plaque remains at the former site of the building.

* *James Joyce.* 41 Brighton Square West in the Rathgar section of Dublin, where he was born on 2 February 1882, marked by a commemorative plaque; 1 Martello Terrace, Bray, where he lived near the sea as a child and which figures strongly in *A Portrait of the Artist as a Young Man;* Joyce's Tower in Sandycove, an authentic Martello tower where Joyce spent a week in 1904 and which forms the setting for the opening of *Ulysses.* It's now a museum filled with bits of Joyceana. Open May-September 10 A.M. to 1 P.M. and 2 to 5:15 P.M. Monday through Saturday. Open Sunday 2:30 to 6 P.M. Very low fee.

Some real places in Dublin and environs that figure strongly in Joycean fiction: The Custom House, Mountjoy Square; the General Post Office, St. Stephen's Green; Grafton Street (Brown Thomas, Switzers); the National Library in Kildare Street; Eccles Street No. 7, fictional home of Leopold and Molly Bloom, which was the home of one of Joyce's friends in real life. Today the building is partly demolished, but its door is enshrined in the Bailey pub, Duke Street, which is across the street from the Davy Byrnes pub of *Ulysses* fame. Also Glasnevin Cemetery; The Ormond Hotel, Ormond Quay on the Liffey (now totally renovated); the Amiens Street (or Connolly) Station area, not what it once was—gone are the brothels of the Nighttown section of *Ulysses;* Bull Island off Dollymount, site of Joycean confrontations with the stormy sea; Howth Head, Howth, where Molly and Leopold first made love; Killiney Hill's cliff walk; Killiney, with its sweeping views of the sea; and Dublin and its suburbs.

* *Sean O'Casey.* St. Saviours Orphanage for Boys, 20 Dominick Street, was in O'Casey's time (the turn of the century) St. Mary's School, which he attended; nearby are Dorset Street, where he was born in 1880, and Henrietta Street, the northside tenement areas he captured so graphically in his plays.

* *Brendan Behan.* Mountjoy Prison, setting of his *The Quare Fellow;* and just about any old pub you can think of—McDaid's, Neary's, Sinnot's, The Palace, O'Donoghue's, The Lincoln Inn, and on and on.

* *George Bernard Shaw.* Torca Cottage, on Dalkey Hill, was his home from 1866 to 1874.

Beckett, Wilde, Thomas Moore, Lady Gregory, Yeats, Synge, and in current times Hugh Leonard and Edna O'Brien are only some of the many other authors who have touched down at least for a time in Dublin. And it would be remiss not to mention Trinity College and the Brazen Head Pub in this section, because they played an important role in the lives of so many of these illustrious writers.

Roots: During the present century there has been an enormous migration from the Irish countryside to Dublin, something like what happened in the United States in the 1850s, when everyone was heading for California, and motivated by the same dream—the pot of gold. In Ireland, the result is that nearly every Irish surname is now represented in Dublin.

Even so, the old names still run strong and outnumber most of the new arrivals. O'Kelly is one. The famous genealogy and history of the

O'Kellys, known as the *Book of Hy Many,* is at the Royal Academy in Dublin. The O'Kellys were a stately lot, producing many bishops and lords. One of the most famous was William Boy O'Kelly, who outlined the *Book of Hy Many* (a fertile Western plain and the original O'Kelly headquarters) which gives all the ancient details of this famous family. The name Doyle is derived from the Irish *dubh-ghall,* meaning dark foreigner, referring to Norsemen and the like who came to plunder and/or settle the eastern coastal area, especially around Dublin. So the Doyles are descended from a number of different but very distinct ancestors. Murphy, Smith, O'Brien, Kavanagh, and Byrne are all strong old Dublin names.

Fewer, but still well represented, are the names O'Neill, Reilly, Nolan, O'Connor, Walsh, Farrell, Carroll, Ryan, Moore, Cruise, O'Casey, Joyce, Delahyde, Plunkett, Talbot, Segrave, Sarsfield, Bagot, Luttrell, Harold, O'Ronan, and Malahide (owners of Malahide Castle, their family seat during the reign of Henry II).

Most of these families have their original roots in other parts of Ireland, but in recent times they have acquired a strong Dublin connection. It would be advisable to check other *Roots* sections of this book for further details on these clans and on their monuments and landmarks.

Legend: On Montpelier Hill, near the Rathfarnham section, are the ruins of Dublin's infamous Hellfire Club, an institution that generated so many different tales that it's hard to sift fact from fiction. But debauchery seems to have been the order of the day.

The Irish version of the Hellfire Club (which originated in England) was formed in 1720 by Richard Parsons, the first Earl of Rosse, and Colonel Jack St. Leger. Comprised of monied, boozy rakes with idle time, its activities included dressing up as Biblical figures for purposes of caricature and blasphemy. A mock Last Supper presided over by the devil and the Black Mass often figured in their pastimes, which reportedly included sexual orgies and the rape of local servant girls who were forced to dress up as nuns.

The club also met at the Eagle Tavern on Cork Hill, where a black cat alleged to be an intimate of the devil presided at the table. Someone dressed in a cowskin with tail and horns usually represented the devil at their orgies. The drink was the club's own local brew—scaltheen (whiskey and butter). When members met at the Eagle, they often soaked a cat in scaltheen, then set it ablaze and sent it shrieking into the streets to terrify the locals, who thought the devil had come for them.

Public outrage finally resulted in the break-up of the club around 1740, when, instead of a cat, a servant was set afire and killed. Shortly after that the building on Montpelier Hill burned to the ground. But tales of haunting persist to this day, and few have the nerve to go near this bleak, desolate place overlooking Dublin after dark.

AN OPTIONAL TOUR: THE BOYNE VALLEY

Full day from Dublin and return, approximately 90 miles. (Outdoor sites mandate good weather.)

YOUR PERSONALIZED BOYNE ITINERARY

This tour is on the must-see list of nearly everyone deeply interested in history; it is in the Boyne Valley area that you'll find some of Ireland's most venerated prehistoric sites and monuments. This is also the region where the Protestant King William of Orange defeated the Catholic King James II in 1690. The famous (or infamous, depending on how you look at it) Battle of the Boyne changed the course of Irish history, tragically, to this day.

Be forewarned, however, that this diversion, while only about 90 miles full circle from Dublin and back, will take you the best part of a day, preferably a fair one, on account of the many outdoor locations. If you're pressed for time but still interested, you could do only the Newgrange portion of the trip (mileage there and back—58).

★ Take the Dublin Airport-Belfast Road (don't worry, you won't come anywhere near Belfast or Northern Ireland on this trip). About nine miles out, you'll come to Swords. Make a brief three-mile detour here for Malahide, a popular seaside resort which houses one of Ireland's most famous medieval castles, *Malahide Castle*. Referred to as a castellated mansion, it was built in the late 12th century by Sir Richard de Talbot and was held by that family until the late 1970s, when the Dublin County Council acquired it as an historical site. There are nearly 300 acres of grounds, including lovely gardens. The castle itself, in excellent condition, contains a remarkable assortment of Irish period furniture along with a collection of oils belonging to the late Lord Talbot de Malahide. Dublin's National Gallery has also added some magnificent oils depicting Irish battles and sporting life. There are antique and craft shops here, as well as a restaurant. Open Jan.–Dec., Mon–Fri. 10A.M. to 5 P.M.; April 1–Oct. 31, Sat. 11 A.M. to 6 P.M.; Sundays and bank holidays 2 to 6 P.M. (Note: Sunday hours Nov. through March are 2 to 5 P.M.) Castle closes weekdays 12:45 to 2 P.M. if conducted tours are scheduled—best to arrive early morning. Admission very reasonable. For further information call (01) 452706.

Roots: Talbot

* Take the road back to Swords and rejoin the main Belfast road north to Drogheda or *Droichead Átha,* meaning Bridge of the Ford. This little industrial boom town traces its history back to the 10th-century Vikings, who established a fortified settlement and trading center four miles from the Boyne River's mouth. When the Anglo-Normans came into power, they built a bridge over the shallow estuary and two towns sprang to life on opposite sides of the river. During the reign of Henry IV they were united by charter. In the 14th century, Drogheda was walled for further protection and to enhance its trading position. Late in the century cruel Richard II forced the princes of Leinster and Ulster to submit themselves to him. The English Parliament held meetings here, and in the 15th century passed Poyning's Law that all laws originating in the Irish Parliament must be ratified by the English. An attempted capture of the town was staged by Sir Phelim O'Neill as part of the Rebellion of 1641, which sought full civil and religious rights for the Irish. The attempt failed, but in 1649 Cromwell took Drogheda with a massacre of over 2000 of the garrison and population. James II had control there when William of Orange began his fateful struggle—the outcome of which is all too well known.

Points of interest include:

* *St. Lawrence's Gate,* the only one of ten such gates that still survives. The structure of the 13th-century gate, with its two circular towers and a connecting wall, is one of the best-preserved examples in Ireland.

* *The Augustinian Abbey of St. Mary d'Urso* dates from the 13th century and is now in ruins; the central tower and dashing pointed arch remain. The Abbey was bilt on land said to have been sanctified by St. Patrick many years earlier.

* *The Dominican Friary,* which was all but destroyed by the ruthless Cromwell, still has its Magdalen tower with peaked arch.

* *Church of St. Peter* (Church of Ireland) in William Street stands high above the town and is rococo in decoration; inside is a magnificent medieval stone receptacle depicting the Baptismal scene of Christ and the Twelve Apostles. The church was built in 1748.

* *St. Peter's Roman Catholic Church* on West Street is Gothic in style and was built in 1681 as a memorial to the Irish Saint Oliver Plunket. An Archbishop of Armagh, he was hanged, drawn, and quartered at Tyburn, England in 1681 for his alleged involvement in the Popish Plot Affair (a fabricated story that English Catholics were plotting to take over the throne). His head was recovered and has been

preserved in a special shrine at this church, where pilgrims come to venerate him.

Roots: Plunket (actually first settled in Co. Meath in 12th century from Anglo-Norman origins; later descendants moved to Co. Louth—Drogheda—and Co. Dublin.)

* At this stage you might like to drop into the little *Gateway* restaurant at 15 West Street for an inexpensive lunch. A self-service place with good home-cooking, it was the town stables in the 18th century, now converted into a mews with patio. This is also the heart of Drogheda's shopping area. Visa, Master. Open 9 A.M. to 5:30 P.M. Closed Sundays, bank holidays. Wine license.

* If it's a beautiful day, you might like to ask your hotel to pack a picnic lunch (or stop at a grocer's and select your own items) and dine al fresco in the lush countryside.

* From Drogheda, continue on the Belfast road to *Monasterboice* or *Mainstir Buithe,* St. Buithe's Abbey (watch for turn-off signs). Here are the remains of a fifth-century monastic settlement founded by St. Buithe, about whom so little is known that even his origins are uncertain. Some say he came from what is now Wales, others insist on Scotland. Most agree that he was a missionary to the Picts, tribes that occupied the area now known as Great Britain and warred against the Romans. Buithe died around 521, according to legend, but remnants of the monastery remain to this day. The South Church, thought to be the oldest, has an oblong nave and the ruins of a chancel arch; the North Church also has an oblong nave and the remains of a round tower. The cross closest to the graveyard, St. Muireadach's Cross, is held by historians and geologists to be one of the finest examples of early Christian high crosses in Europe. Almost 18 feet tall, it is masterfully carved, with the Crucifixion on the west side and the Last Judgment on the east. There are two other crosses here as well as an ancient sundial.

* Another luncheon opportunity here—if you've held out. *The Monasterboice Inn* has very good food, moderate at lunch, expensive at night. L—12:30 to 3; D—5:30 to 10. Wine license. Visa, Master.

* After leaving Monasterboice, watch for (or ask for) the little dash of a road to the west that will take you to Collon and *Mellifont,* home of the first Cistercian order of French monks and nuns to settle in Ireland. Established by St. Malachy O'Morgair, Archbishop of Armagh, in 1142. Though widely opposed as foreign development, Mellifont was granted permission to build by Donough O'Carroll, Prince of Oriel (the bay of the nearby River Mattock). In the late 12th century Henry

II, during his visitation of Ireland, agreed to the 'painful submission' of the Irish chieftain O'Neill (probably unusually painful for O'Neill).

The Cistercian movement spread so rapidly in Ireland that the English monarchy felt threatened and suppressed the headquarters at Mellifont. The abbey then became the property of Sir Edward Moore, a descendant of the original Earls of Drogheda, who immediately turned the church into a fortified homestead. In 1539 Red Hugh O'Donnell, who had led risings against the English, stayed here upon his escape from prison in Dublin Castle at the request of Moore's son, Garret. During the siege of Drogheda, Phelim O'Neill gained control of the abbey, but the steadfast Moores regained possession and lived there until the early 18th century. What remains today are the ruins of the church and columns that once supported the belfry tower, a chapter house (where leaders of the church met) with its glazed, intricately designed floor tiles, the gate house tower, and the remains of a lavabo (lavatory) where monks washed their hands before meals.

Roots: O'Carroll, O'Neill.

★ From here, it's a very short drive over unclassified roads to *King Williams Glen* (if you have any difficulty, ask). In this wooded area on the banks of the Boyne, King William of Orange hid his forces in 1690 until he was ready to cross the river. When he did, he and his men stormed up Donore Hill to the medieval church where the exiled Catholic King, James II, and his men had their headquarters. After many losses, the Catholic forces retreated and finally surrendered.

★ After the Glen, take the road west for Slane. In a little less than a mile, there's an unclassified road to the left that will soon lead you to the ancient sites of *Dowth, Newgrange,* and *Knowth*—of which Newgrange is the most famous. Dating from the dawn of time, these three large cairns (tombs covered with pillared stone slabs and roofs) are truly Ireland's best-known prehistoric landmarks. Estimate has it that over 200,000 tons of stone slabs were needed for Newgrange alone. Note the finely calculated, swirl-patterned, decorative stones at the tomb's entrance, the passage of which is over 60 feet long and lined with upright stone slabs—many of them carved in decoration. Be sure to view Dowth and Knowth as well. This is a wonderful area for letting your imagination out for a run. What kind of people warranted such a burial? Where did they come from? Think of the earliest settlers—historical speculation suggests from Iberia or Brittany—sailing up the Boyne and stopping here to establish their homesteads, then their temples and their tombs. What were their lives like? Legend

Newgrange

says that they worshipped the sun, because the Newgrange tomb is situated so that the sun shines into the chambers on the shortest day of the year, December 21st.

* When you leave here, head for Slane and there take the road signposted Navan south to *Trim* or *Baile Atha Truim* (Elder-tree Ford). This lovely town, situated in a fertile area of the Boyne Valley, is one of the earliest religious settlements in Ireland. It sprang up around a Boyne ford, and legend has it that St. Patrick founded a monastery here. After the Anglo-Norman invasion in the 12th century, Norman Hugh de Lacy was appointed ruler of Co. Meath. Immediately he made his favored Trim its seat and erected Trim Castle in the latter part of the 12th century, to stand as a symbol of strength and safety for the entire county. Today, the relatively well-preserved two acres of remains include an outer wall with five surviving towers and a gate tower. A moat, which could be filled by the river's waters, surrounded the castle. Yet none of this stopped Cromwell's armies from roaring over the landscape in 1649 to seize control and massacre all the area's inhabitants.

* Looking across the river from the castle, you'll see the Yellow Steeple, which was once a dramatic feature of a 14th-century Augustinian abbey called St. Mary's. When Cromwell invaded, the citizens

thought it better to destroy the abbey than to let it fall into his merciless hands.

    * Leaving Trim, you'll take the road to Pike Corner, then to Kilmessan, and proceed a short distance to *The Hill of Tara*. This is a particularly exhilarating locale in which to end this journey into the past. Tara is just about as far back as you can go. When you arrive you'll see little more than a hill about 500 feet high, some remains of earthworks (earthen walls, either for defense purposes or as ritual entranceways), grave mounds, and a pillar stone. But when you think of the history and the legends—of all those who were or who may have been here before you—you're sure to sense the continuity of human life. Tara is best known for the period during the first centuries A.D., when it became the heart of all Ireland as the seat of the Irish high kings. At three-year intervals the leaders met, passed laws, planned fortifications, settled territorial disputes, considered ways to fashion peace. Tara was all-powerful until Christianity began to flourish. But its history reaches back further than this, and legends further still. Excavation of the Mound of Hostages at Tara revealed burial remains dating from about 2000 B.C.. Along with the remains of cremated bones, the find included pottery, jewelry, and weapons. The five-foot pillar stone called the *Lia Fail* is the source of a legend. In order for a king to be chosen at Tara, he must first have been acknowledged as the incarnation of masculinity. If a man was worthy, when he passed his hand between two tightly placed flagstones on Tara hill, the stones would open wide and *Lia Fail* (variously interpreted as the stone of destiny or the penis of stone) would shriek its approval so that all mortals could hear. It is interesting to note that manuscripts of these pagan times refer to Ireland as the Island of Fail or Fál and to its citizens as Fail's men.

    * From Tara, head for the Navan road and take it south back to Dublin. En route, the navigator might like to read the following bit of Tara folklore.

Legend (rendered as the Irish tell it): In the time of the royal kings of Ireland, King Cormac longed to have a husband for his beloved daughter Grainne, whose silken skin and blossoming beauty made her the most beguiling young woman in all Ireland. Though every king and hero in the land sought her hand, she refused them all, including aging Finn, leader of the Fianna, whom her father favored. But Grainne had already been smitten with the gallant young warrior Diarmaid. Lean and strong, he was of such superior masculine beauty that she was swept by longing.

When Cormac insisted that she marry Finn at Finn's behest, there was little she could do but honor her father's wishes. Yet even before their wedding day at Tara, Finn proved to be mean and spiteful to her, and her life was already a pitiful misery. Hope had all but died in her heart, save for the thought of the princely young man whom she'd heard tell was the best lover of maidens and women in all the world. The thought compelled her to scheme, and the fire of her passion summoned the courage to see her through with it.

After the wedding, at the feast in Tara's banquet hall, Grainne stealthily administered a sleeping potion to the drinks of all but Diarmaid (whom she had already favored with a love potion) and three of his friends. Diarmaid, although completely taken by her beauty, was reluctant to violate his trust with Finn. But his friends urged him to do so, saying he would be forever wretched if he didn't.

Finn and his Fianna gave chase, but the two managed to escape and lived as fugitives in a forest shelter built by Diarmaid, until one day they were surrounded by the Fianna. They were saved by Oengus, a Celtic god of love, who spirited Grainne away under his coat while Diarmaid leapt over the Fianna and followed after his love. Reunited and left alone, they wandered the forests, and Diarmaid quelled another attack by a branch of the Fianna who traveled by sea to slay him.

As overjoyed as they were at being together, they had not made love because of Diarmaid's fear of danger and destruction. But one day water splashed on passionate Grainne's leg, and with the longing flooding her, she told Diarmaid that his courage in battle was heroic, but with her the splash of water was more courageous than he was. With that, he could withstand her temptations no longer and surrendered to make her his wife. In the joyous days that followed the two were never long out of each other's anxious arms. Soon Grainne was pregnant. None was more delighted to see the wonder of this alliance than Oengus, who eventually quelled Finn's rage and helped foster peace between Finn and Diarmaid. This done, the two lovers were granted a gracious stretch of land in Connacht, where they lived in bliss bringing up a daughter and four sons.

One day when Finn was in the area, Diarmaid met him and the two went hunting the Wild Boar of Ben Bulben for the sport of it. Diarmaid slew the beast, not realizing it housed the spirit of his stepbrother. As he did, he wounded himself with one of the poisonous boar bristles. Only water that had dripped from Finn's hands, which were blessed with healing powers, could save his life. Just as Finn was about to administer the water, he remembered Grainne's beauty and let it slip through his fingers onto the ground, leaving Grainne to mourn Diarmaid as long as she was to live.

Note: To this day, there are various rocks and flat rock formations said to be the Beds of Diarmaid and Grainne. To approach them is to summon aphrodisia and fertility.

Literature: Mary Lavin, a short-story writer considered by many as equal to, if not better than, James Joyce in her medium, lives near this area in Bective.

II. THE HAUNTING JOURNEY FROM DUBLIN TO WEXFORD

Glendalough, Co. Wicklow

*The harp of the wood plays melody, its music brings
perfect peace; color has settled on every hill, haze on
the lake of full water.*

—from the Celtic, ninth century

YOUR PERSONALIZED DUBLIN-TO-WEXFORD
ITINERARY

Leaving Dublin for the southeastern countryside is a thrilling experience of dramatic seascapes and sweeping mountain vistas—even more exhilarating if Dublin was your first stop in Ireland and this is your initial view of the countryside. This trip encompasses about a hundred miles, via the most scenic route.

* Start as early as possible (having filled the tank the night before). If breakfast is a problem, remember that The Coffee Dock at Jury's Hotel, Ballsbridge (767511), opens at 6:00 A.M.

* Head south through Ballsbridge and Blackrock to Dun Laoghaire. The road is the N-11. If it's a good day, stop for a stroll on the famous Dun Laoghaire pier with magnificent views of Dublin Bay.

* Follow the road that hugs the sea from Dun Laoghaire (headed southeast). A short distance will bring you to Sandycove. Stop to have a look at Joyce's Martello Tower.

* Continue to follow the coastal road that is signposted Dalkey, then head for Killiney. Stop for its cliff walk and hill, with spectacular views of Dublin and suburbs and the dazzling sea.

* Follow on through Shankill and just before you come to the seaside resort town of Bray, turn right for Enniskerry on a road that passes between two slabs of granite, the Scalp. Slightly south of Enniskerry are the Powerscourt Gardens and falls. Plan a stop here if you're arriving after 10:30 A.M. when the gardens open.

* Take the road from Enniskerry to Glencree. At Glencree, turn to the left on the road for Laragh and Glendalough. Called the Military Road, this is one of the most spectacular in the south of Ireland. It takes you up through Sally Gap, affording you thrilling mountain and valley views. You might even like to plan a picnic—in advance, of course. Note: Be sure you have enough gas; this road is long, and there's nothing on it but the fabulous scenery and the mountain goats.

* At Laragh, where there's a gas station or petrol, follow the sign to Glendalough, a stone's throw away. Plan to spend an hour here where St. Kevin established his monastery in the sixth century. If you didn't picnic and you're hungry, there's the Grade-B* Royal Hotel, lunch till 2:30, which is inexpensive to moderate. (Closed November–March). Or back in Laragh, there's the Wicklow Heather, inexpensive

seafood (local rainbow trout etc.), open all day, wine license only. Closed
February–March.

* From Glendalough, go back to Laragh and make your way to Rathdrum along the beautiful road of the Vale of Clara beside the Avonmore River. A mile to the east of this town, visit Avondale, the home
of Charles Stewart Parnell, the famous Irish patriot. Then return to
Rathdrum and perhaps stop at the inexpensive Avondale Restaurant
and Craft Shop. Meat, seafood dishes, along with a good selection of
crafts. Take-away foods, wine license. Visa, Master. Open all day;
closed Wednesday from October to June.

* From Rathdrum drive through the Vale of Avoca to Avoca and
Woodenbridge, where you'll see the famous meeting of the waters,
as described by Thomas Moore.

* Continue on the Wexford road to Arklow, then on to Gorey. This
is the location of one of Ireland's finest country houses, Marlfield
House, where you can dine and stay (see below).

* From Gorey proceed to Enniscorthy. If you have time, drop into
the Enniscorthy Castle County Museum. Then on to Wexford. You
should arrive late in the afternoon, so you have time for a leisurely
dinner, a stroll around the harbor at sunset, and perhaps a stop at
a pub before calling it a day.

DETAILS ON THE SPECIAL PLACES ALONG THE WAY

* *Dun Laoghaire*, which is Irish for Leary's Fort, is seven miles from Dublin's city center. Its name comes from the fortress that was erected there in
the fifth century by Laoghaire, the High King of Ireland. In 1821 the name
was changed to Kingstown in honor of a visit by George IV, and the town
didn't regain its rightful name until 1920. Dun Laoghaire is famous for its
two enormous piers. The east pier is a promenade that stretches far out into
the Bay and is extremely popular with strollers for its glittering seascapes;
it's particularly awesome on a stormy day.

Dun Laoghaire is a major ferryboat port, with mail, passenger, and car
ferry service to England. This area offers yachting, fishing, and tennis, and
the famous Leopardstown Racecourse is three miles away.

* *Sandycove*, just southeast of Dun Laoghaire, is important for its Martello
Tower, one of many built during the Napoleonic Wars to guard against a
sea invasion. It is now called Joyce's Tower, because James Joyce stayed there
briefly in 1904 with Oliver St. John Gogarty before going into exile. The
setting is used for the opening of his *Ulysses*, which parallels Homer's *Odyssey*.
The tower has been converted into a Joycean museum housing some of his
letters, fragments of manuscripts, selected editions, and other items of Joyceana. Sometimes prose and poetry readings are held there. Below the tower
is the famous Forty Foot nude bathing place. The museum is open May through
September from 10 A.M. to 1 P.M. and 2 to 5:15 P.M. Sundays 2:30 to 6 P.M.
Very inexpensive, and there are fine views of the sea.

* *Dalkey and Killiney.* If you want panoramic views from hill-top heights,
these will provide you with the finest in this part of the country. Dalkey is

two miles south of Dun Laoghaire. Dalkey Hill is the spot here, and half way up the hill on Torca Road is Torca Cottage, where George Bernard Shaw lived from 1866 to 1874. A little south of Dalkey is Killiney. Looking down the sweep of Killiney Hill, you can see a lustrous crescent-shaped beach, and nearby are Big and Little Sugarloaf Mountains framing the forested Shanganagh Vale. From another point on the Hill, you can see across Dublin Bay clear to the dramatic Howth promontory. Somewhat closer, but equally spectacular, are the views of the River Liffey Valley and Dublin City and suburbs. Be prepared for the thrill you'll feel—because you're on top of the world.

On Killiney Hill itself are the remains of an ancient church and a group of stones forming what is known as the Druid's Chair, harking back to the pantheistic pre-Christian sect said to have practiced human sacrifice.

* *Enniskerry* is a lovely little town set among the dewy Wicklow Hills. Donald Davies, the famous Irish couturier, makes his headquarters here and has a tiny boutique on the main street that attracts many female visitors. But the main reason for visiting Enniskerry is Powerscourt. This 14,000-acre estate was one of Europe's finest. Tragically, fire gutted much of the mansion's interior in 1974. Restoration funds are being gathered—but it will be a long time. Built on the former site of the castle that housed the lords of the Glencullen River Valley, the O'Toole clan, the 18th-century mansion was constructed of granite. Its enormous reception hall served to entertain King George IV in 1821 when the monarch visited Ireland. Fortunately, many attractions have survived the fire: the magnificent gardens; the statuary collected from various parts of Europe; the two marble sarcophagi from a monastery near the Colosseum; the circular mosaic terraces and Triton Lake with its fountain; the Japanese gardens and grotto made from petrified sphagnum (bog moss); and the Bamberg Gate entrance, which once stood in the Cathedral of Bamberg, Bavaria. The gardens took over 30 years to complete and were the intricate work of the famous 19-century Irish landscape architect Daniel Robertson, assisted by a hundred men. The formal garden was finished in 1875, the Japanese garden in 1908. Roses, flowering shrubs (rhododendron, magnolia, azalea) and a vast variety of flora abound, including conifers from all over the world. The main drive to the estate (four miles from Enniskerry) is reminiscent of a Gothic-romance setting. It runs along a river through forests and landscapes of rare shrubberies to a deer park. On the way, you'll pass a 400-foot waterfall. The gardens are open daily from April to October 10:30 A.M. to 5:30 P.M. Drive and waterfall open year round 10:30 A.M. to 8 P.M. Picnicking permitted.

Roots: O'Toole.

* *The Military Road and Sally Gap.* If you yearn for solitude among rugged green mountains and lush, peaceful valleys, this is it. Once you leave Enniskerry, you may just feel you've left the world—all its people and troubles—behind. The expanses are so vast, so unpopulated (except for sheep and goats), you begin to wonder if you'll ever see civilization again. And before the journey's over, you wonder if you ever want to. It's no wonder that this area was for years a stronghold of the suppressed O'Tooles and O'Byrnes, who kept a leader of the 1798 uprising against the English, Michael Dwyer, hidden until 1803. The British found the area so problematic for their cause that they were forced to build a road (the Military Road) in from the Dublin area

St. Kevin's Tower, Glendalough

after 1798 to attempt to gain some semblence of control over the insurgents, which of course they never did. Even to this day, Wicklow has far too many hiding places. But what the British unintentionally produced with their expensive road through the mountains is a wonderful way to see this majestic area which might otherwise not have existed. The road from Glencree climbs swiftly upward (about 1600 feet) to Sally Gap, which is between the mountains of Kippure and Djouce (each over 2000 feet high). While these might not sound like dramatic heights compared to mountains elsewhere in the world, they take on sweeping proportions in a country as small and scenic as Ireland. From Sally Gap the road passes through stark moors and then moves down into the beautifully bright Glenmacnass Valley with its river and high walled mountains. From here, you drop into Laragh and the wonders of Glendalough.

Roots: O'Toole, O'Byrne.

* Glendalough, 32 miles from Dublin, is the beautiful valley where St. Kevin came in the sixth century in search of quietude and closeness to the beauty of the earth. It's easy to see why he found the place so congenial that he lived here for years—at first as a hermit. As time went by, he attracted many disciples and established a monastery and a center of learning. Thousands of students flocked here from all over Europe, making Glendalough a place of renown by the time of Kevin's death in A.D. 618. On the shores of the valley's two lakes are remains that go all the way back to Kevin's time. Some of the most interesting are:

* St. Kevin's Bed, a cave in a cliff 30 feet above the south side of the Upper Lake. It is thought to be here that Kevin slept when he first came to Glendalough and later returned when he craved renewed solitude.

* *Teampall na Skellig* (Church of the Rock). Kevin's first chapel, this is located near the Bed, but it must be reached by boat. The building is 25 feet by 14 feet, with doorways of granite slabs and a window carved from a single stone.

* Reefert Church (King's Burial Place). Now in ruins, this church served as the burial place for the O'Toole leaders and the ancient rulers who preceded them. There's a nave and a chancel connected by an arch. The windows are rounded at the top, and the old altar foundations remain.

* St. Kevin's Cell, shaped like a beehive, is in ruins now; this is where Kevin lived after he built the Reefert Church.

* Caher, on the eastern shore of Upper Lake, was the site of a Bronze Age stone fort.

* The Gateway was the chief entrance to the community that developed as a result of Kevin's charisma. Comprised of rounded arches of granite, it is located slightly east of Lower Lake.

* The Round Tower is linked to the Gateway by a flagstone causeway. The tower is well over a thousand years old and is one of the few remains in superb condition. It's over 100 feet high and more than 50 feet in circumference.

* St. Mary's Church where Kevin was buried is in this area. Nearby is St. Kevin's cross, a granite cross dating from the sixth century.

* Remains of the Cathedral, St. Kevin's Church, and St. Kieran's Church (discovered in the 1800s) are all to be seen as part of the ancient ruins.

In this majestic and historic Wicklow valley, you can still feel the inner peace that attracted Kevin centuries ago. Plan a quiet hour or so here, akin to losing yourself in the solitude of a California redwood forest. You discover that rare and wonderful feeling of a place where no time has passed. If you are fortunate enough to be there on a soft summer's evening with the lilting scent of heathered air, as you look up past the darkening velvet hills to the wash of moon and stars, you will feel—as Kevin must have—the real source of life.

Roots: O'Toole.

Literature: John Millington Synge, although better known for his Aran Islands (off Galway; see Aran), wrote of the area south of Glendalough, known as the Vale of Clara. Southeast of here, the village of Glenmalure served as the setting for his play *The Shadow of the Glen.*

* Avondale, a mile south of Rathdrum, is the site of the birth place of 19th-century Irish freedom fighter Charles Stewart Parnell (who fought diligently for Home Rule at Westminster). Several rooms of the fine old house, which dates from 1779, with embellishments including some exceptional ornamental plasterwork, are open to the public from May to September on Friday, Saturday, and Sunday afternoons, 2 to 6 P.M. The richly forested lands surrounding it are open year round.

Legend: If you've ever wondered where men like Ponce de Leon and Sir Walter Raleigh got the idea of searching for the fountain of youth, look no further. It was planted in their heads by the Irish and their wonderful Celtic folklore. One story involves the 12th-century Irish King, Laurence O'Toole, who was aging, to his great regret. Gone were the days when he could roam the forest and hill, glen and pass, hunting to his heart's content. Life was falling away, and he grew desperate for his youth once more. Folklore suggests that he found new sources of vitality in some of the herbs growing on the hills around Glendalough in Co. Wicklow, herbs that were said to have been planted by voyagers who had crossed many seas. The king flourished until the herbs were gone, when he began to age once again; this made it clear to all that a constant supply of such herbs could mean perpetual youth.

* The Vale of Avoca, 44 miles from Dublin is still another pastoral region that nurtures poetic inspiration, like that of the famous Thomas Moore, with its 'valley so sweet.' As you go south from Rathdrum, you see where the rivers of Avonbeg and Avonmore join at 'that vale in whose bosom the bright waters meet': the famous *Meeting of the Waters* below the dramatic cliffside site of Castle Howard. Like Kevin at Glendalough, Moore spent many hours of solitude here. Unfortunately, the castle area has been roped off now, and there are too many signs of erosion resulting from the depredations of souvenir hunters. But you can still form a good idea of how it once was.

The surrounding area is well worth a visit too; the waters meet again at Woodenbridge, four miles to the south. Imagine a sequestered valley with the blossoming wild fruit trees of early spring, the mountains around it, the gushing waters, the whistle of wind through the vernal landscape, and the scent of nature in bloom: now you have it.

Literature: Poet Thomas Moore.

* Gorey, a small town just inside County Wexford, deserves mention for one reason—Marlfield House. This is a lovely 35-acre estate with a Regency mansion, forest, and gardens owned by Mary Bowe. It's one of Ireland's best-known country house lodgings (of which you'll see others later). These places are special in that they give you (most important) a wonderful stay, and secondly, a perfect sense of 'the way it was.' Here you'll go back in time to the graceful, gentle values—the quietude long gone from the world. The moderately priced rooms (only 11, all with bath) are one of the best buys in the land. And the food, while verging on the expensive, is excellent, with vegetables home grown. Wonderful seafoods, especially mussels in wine cream sauce. Also rack of lamb, veal, roast beef Bearnaise, salmon specialties, and game-bird pies. The cheeses are of the best. Fine breakfasts, lunches too. Full license, but no credit cards.

On your first visit to Ireland you may not be able to consider a stay at Marlfield, on account of the time factor. But don't worry; there'll be other chances for such a stay along the way.

Entertainment at Gorey includes the Gorey Arts Festival, which is held for two weeks every August. It includes painting, photography, theater, traditional music, jazz, rock, and other activities.

* Enniscorthy or *Inis Coirthe* (Rock Island) is on the banks of the River Slaney and figured in many conflicts with the Anglo-Normans, including the Rising of 1798 when it was taken for several weeks by Irish patriots. In late June and early July the annual (and enjoyable) Strawberry Fair is held here, but the main attraction is Enniscorthy Castle. Some historians believe it was built by Raymond de Gros, one of the key leaders of the original Anglo-Norman invaders who landed in the 1170s. Others contend that it was built in the 13th century by the Prendergasts. Later it became the estate of the MacMurrough (variant of Murphy) and Kavanagh families, who eventually bequethed it to the Franciscans for a monastery. When the English outlawed monasteries, the castle changed hands several times. At one point the English poet Edmund Spenser, of *Faerie Queen* fame, lived here. Cromwell leveled his guns at the fortification in 1649, but though it was damaged, it survived to be used as a prison during the Rising of 1798. It wasn't until the 1800s that it became a residence again. One of the castle's square towers had to be rebuilt in 1586, and it is still in such perfect condition that it now houses a public museum. Here there are many items dealing with the Rising of 1798, along with others from the Easter Rising of 1916. There's also an old-fashioned still of the type a farmer might have (might still) use to make the illegal Irish brew, poteen. It's open June through September 10 A.M. to 6 P.M. and for the rest of the year from 2 to 5:30 P.M.

In Enniscorthy's Market Square is a 1798 Memorial by Oliver Sheppard depicting the patriot priest Father John Murphy and his brave pikemen (rebels against the throne). They took the towns of Wexford, Ferns, and Enniscorthy during the stormy rebellion, but were defeated on the town's eastern edge at the 390-foot Vinegar Hill by the British generals Lake and Johnson. Father Murphy managed miraculously to escape. He remained a fugitive until he was able to link up with French troops who were arriving to aid the rebels (too late as it turned out) in County Mayo. He fought on but was finally killed in Wexford's neighboring County Carlow. Later a song—*Boolavogue*—was written about the priest's heroic national exploits.

Roots: Kavanagh, Murphy, Prendergast.

Literature: Edmund Spenser.

III. WEXFORD

Wexford Town

Fine though you think the ale of Ireland, the ale of the Great Land is more heady; a wonderful land is the land I tell of, the young do not die there before the old.

—from the Celtic, ninth century

Wexford is a hauntingly beautiful town hovering on the banks of a gentle estuary and harbor. Now almost a city in size, this is one of Ireland's surprisingly special places; don't let it go without an overnight stop.

YOUR PERSONALIZED WEXFORD ITINERARY

Day One

* Arrive Wexford late afternoon. Check into your hotel. Try either *White's* or the *Old Wexford Coaching Inn,* which are close to the focal point of the evening walk outlined below. *Talbot's,* at the other end of the quays, is also good but will give you a longer walk.

* Dine at *Captain White's* in the Old Wexford Coaching Inn.

* Afterward stroll down either Monck Street or Charlotte Street to the waterfront. Then take the short walk across New Bridge (preferably at sunset). When you turn back, you will see the gentle harbor all shimmering in crimson and beyond that Wexford, with its hills and old buildings and quaint quayside. This soft-hued vision is an impressionistic painting come to life. It's the epitome of what you thought a European harbor town ought to look like—radiant and peaceful and born of the past. (Most such waterside towns today have had the past torn out of them, replaced by lifeless modern. So take some time to enjoy this setting—another that you'll not forget.)

* Once you've recrossed the bridge, you can either stroll along the quays or walk back up Monck Street and stop for a 'jar' in the fascinating old *Crown Bar.*

* At this stage it might be wise to think of calling it a day, so you can have an early start in the morning. But if you're still fresh, there's a section on evening entertainment below.

Day Two

* Rise early and eat at your accommodation. Check out.

* An hour-long walking tour (descriptions of the sights mentioned here are included in the longer optional itinerary which follows.)
Start at the *Old Wexford Coaching Inn* on North Main Street.

* Moving down North Main, you come to the *Bull Ring.*

* Then to *St. Iberius's Parish Church,* still on North Main.

* Continue on to *Keysers Lane* doorway and *Cromwell's Headquarters* (both on the left).

* When you come to South Main and Henrietta Street (again on the left), follow Henrietta to the *John Barry Memorial.*

Return to Main Street and cross it. Take Allen Street to High Street and *St. Patrick's Church.*

* Continue down High Street to the *Immaculate Conception Church.* Then you'll come to *Market House* or Town Hall.

* Move from *Cornmarket* to Abbey Street past the newer White's Hotel to *Selskar Abbey.*

* Continue around the Abbey to the *West Gate* ruins.

* Prepare to depart for Waterford and Cork.

An Optional Day-Two Tour of Wexford

Designed for those on extended Irish stays and planned in conjunction with a tour of old Kilkenny.

* Rise early and eat at your accommodation. Check out.

* A morning walk of 1½ hours–3½ if you lunch and shop. (You should be ready to leave Wexford by 1 P.M. for your journey to Kilkenny.) Although the streets are twisted and hilly in true European style, Wexford is relatively easy to get around in once you've acclimated yourself. As you travel the following route, take time to stop into a few of the fine Wexford shops, some of which will be listed later.

* Start at the northern section of town by the railway station. Across the way is the *Redmond Monument* in honor of John Redmond, a key early 20th-century Irish political leader who fought in the British House of Commons for Home Rule like Charles Stewart Parnell before him. In 1914 Redmond won the battle.

* Follow the street left of the Monument—Selskar Street—which runs into North Main Street. On your right is the *Old Wexford Coaching Inn,* formerly Old White's Hotel, which was founded in 1779. This building now includes as part of its expansion the birthplace of Sir Robert McClure, the man who discovered the Northwest Passage.

* Moving on, you will soon be in the *Bull Ring,* scene of the ancient sport of bullbaiting (a horrific pastime of jaundiced Norman nobles comparable to the cockfights held by America's Southern gentry). The savagery of these events was overshadowed by Cromwell in the grey chill fall of 1649, when he ruthlessly slaughtered several thousand citizens in this square. There is also a statue by Oliver Sheppard here, the Pikeman, which was erected in 1905 to commemorate the brave Rebellion of 1798. Country market stalls were established in this area in 1871 for the sale of goods and foodstuffs, which continues today on Tuesday, Friday, and Saturday mornings. Across the street, in the building that now houses Diana Donnelly's shop, Oscar Wilde's mother was born.

★ From here move to the left and continue down Main Street. You'll soon come to *St. Iberius's Parish Church,* which was built in 1760 and is said to be reminiscent of the architecture of St. George's in Hanover Square, London. The church stands on the site of a building dedicated to St. Ibar, the prepatrician missionary who is credited with bringing Christianity to Wexford.

★ A little farther along Main, you'll come to Anne Street on the left. At the end of Anne Street, on Custom House Quay, is the *Maritime Museum.* It's housed in the *Guillemot*—an old lighthouse ship—and contains many fine mementos from Wexford's old seagoing days. It's open daily in the summer months from early morning to 9 P.M.

★ Return to Main Street and enjoy the wonderful smell of fresh baked goods from all the different bakeries as you progress—a difficult scent to resist. If you don't succumb, move along South Main till you reach a small door on the left which leads to *Keysers Lane.* Established in Viking times, it led the way to the wharves and was for the sole use of the Vikings. A few steps away from this doorway is a Woolworth store converted from an old building that served as *Cromwell's Head-quarters* while he was ensconced in Wexford during the 17th century.

★ Farther down South Main on the left is Henrietta Street, named for Queen Henrietta, wife of King Charles I. As you follow this street toward the harbor, you'll pass the *Irish Tourist Board* office. Straight ahead is the dramatic statue of a stalwart man with a rapier facing out to sea, a monument of particular interest to Americans. The *John Barry Memorial* was presented to Ireland by the United States Government in September 1956 in memory of 'the Father [founder] of the American Navy,' who was born ten miles from this harbor at Bally-sampson, Co. Wexford. When the American Revolution broke out in 1775, he became the navy's first commissioned officer as captain of the American ship *Lexington.* In 1797 George Washington, who was impressed with his maritime feats, named him Commander-in-Chief of the growing navy. He died in 1803 in Philadelphia. Two American presidents have visited this Wexford memorial to Barry—Dwight D. Eisenhower and John F. Kennedy.

★ As you face the harbor, turn right and follow the quayfront to the V formed by Trinity Street and Lower King Street where you will find the *Talbot Hotel,* built on the site of the former townhouse of a prominent Wexford family. The Talbots were also relatives of the Duke of Tyrconnell and the Earl of Shrewsbury and Waterford.

★ Stop for a pub luncheon (if you're hungry) at the Talbot's fine *Tavern Bar.*

★ From the Talbot, move up Lower King Street to where it meets Barrack Street on the left and South Main Street on the right. On the Barrack Street corner, where St. Doologue's Parish now stands, there was once a church built by the Danes in 1035. Nearby is *Kelly's Pub*, a rough-and-tumble workingman's bar today; this building was the birthplace of *William Cody*, the father of Colonel William Cody, better known as Buffalo Bill. Wexford's ancient South Gate once stood near here, and the site of the present military barracks was a Danish fort in A.D. 850.

* Head back to Main Street and on the left you'll come to Bride Street. At the top is the Roman Catholic *Church of the Assumption*, an awesome example of modern Gothic design by Richard Pierce. Its identical twin (right to the 225-foot steeples), the Church of the Immaculate Conception, stands in Wexford's Rowe Street. The foundation stones of both were laid on the same day in June of 1851.

* Turn right and walk down Roches' Road, through St. Peter's Square and straight on to School Street. Here there are some fine examples of Georgian architecture. Further along on the left is the *Franciscan Friary,* which has a stirring history. It was first established in 1230, but Henry VIII suppressed it and finally confiscated it in the mid-16th century. When the Friars resumed use of one of the chapels secretly in 1622, they passed unnoticed until 1649 when Cromwell found out, flew into a rage, and sacked the place. Rebuilt in 1691, it served as a parish church until the new twin churches were created. The Friary was redecorated in the late 1800s.

* Facing the Friary is Mary's Street; walk down it to High Street and turn to the right. At the end of the street are the ruins of 12th-century *St. Patrick's Church,* and in its graveyard repose the remains of the brave, slaughtered like animals by Cromwell in the Bull Ring and silenced again by the British in 1798—this time because the promised French aid didn't arrive on time.

* Walk on down High Street until you reach the *Church of the Immaculate Conception* on the left at the Rowe Street crossing. Then you'll come to *Cornmarket*. At one stage (Norman times) all area produce had to be traded here. By the *Market House* or Town Hall, with its sweeping arched entryways, is Wexford's contemporary Arts Center. And across the way, the *Thomas Moore Pub* (see Pubs) was the townhouse birthplace of the poet's mother.

* Move from Cornmarket to Abbey Street and follow it past the newer White's Hotel to *Selskar Abbey*—probably the town's most famous site. The name Selskar is an anglicized version of St. (or Holy) Sepulchre. The Abbey once covered great tracts of ground, but only portions remain today. Underground, there are vast passageways and streams that run to the far side of town and show just how vast a complex spread out from Selskar. The Irish-Norman conflict was re-

solved by a treaty in 1169. When Henry II murdered Thomas à Becket, he did a Lenten penance here in 1172. Later Strongbow's daughter married Raymond Le Gros, a powerful Anglo-Norman leader, here. The Abbey was destroyed by Cromwell in 1649, but the old bells were salvaged and can be found in River Street Church, Liverpool.

* Continue around the Abbey from Abbey Street to Temperance Row to *Westgate*. You're now in back of Selskar Abbey at the ruins of Wexford's ancient West Gate, which will give you a true sense of what was considered security in the past. The Irish built walls like those of the Chinese (some of the older Leinster ones around Tara may even be pre-Chinese). When you walk these grounds in this pleasant little historic town, your feelings are engaged whatever your nationality.

* If at this point, you still haven't lunched, do so before you start for Kilkenny—about 50 miles away.

WEXFORD'S HISTORY

Wexford goes back to the dark reaches of prehistoric time. What the few area findings—flints, stone axes, and other artifacts—indicate is that a community or communities existed here around 2000 B.C. whose inhabitants grew barley for trading. About A.D. 150 the Egyptian geographer Ptolemy marked this area on his map as Menapia, or *Lough Garman* as it becomes in Gaelic. In the ninth century, Viking sailors were so smitten with the locale that they claimed it as their own. Hating the native name, they changed it to Waesfjord or the Harbor of the Mud Flats. Actually it was then two villages: the Viking stronghold with its own barracks, churches, and burial grounds, and to the north, but completely separate, the Gaelic community living in crowded dwellings around Selskar Abbey, their center of worship in both pre-Christian and Christian times, with their burial grounds.

As strong as the Viking warriors were, they weren't prepared to withstand the attack of the Anglo-Normans in 1169. Led by Robert Fitzstephen, Maurice de Prendergast, and Robert de Barry, they entered the country at sandy Bannow Bay at the base of what is today Co. Wexford and marched north. There were helmeted knights in mail—flexible armor—archers, and foot soldiers bearing axes, swords, and javelins. Having joined the warrior king of Leinster, Dermot MacMurrough, they undertook to seize Wexford. MacMurrough sided with the Anglo-Normans because of his bitter feud with the warrior king of Breifne, Tiernan O'Rourke, the result of a triangular love affair. This affair was to profoundly affect the course of Irish history—as will be seen below. In 1649 Cromwell seized Wexford and slaughtered every member of its population not fortunate enough to escape.

In 1798 Wexford again figured prominently in Irish history, when courageous Irish patriots made their first attempts to withstand English tyranny (strangely enough, inspired and aided by the French, who had once been English allies). Moving into the 19th century, the sun shone on Wexford in the form of a booming economy via sea trade. It was at this point that Wexford turned into a smaller Belfast, with its own ship-building industry. It also became a center for farm machinery production.

Legend (A love triangle that affected the course of Irish history):
In the mid-12th century, Ireland saw internal battles for political supremacy. King against king, they fought, raided, plundered. Two characters stand out to this day: the warrior king of Breifne, Tiernan O'Rourke, and his opponent, Dermot MacMurrough of Leinster. Their power struggle was enough to make them enemies, but another factor would soon turn their hatred into blind rage.
The year was 1152, and the factor was Tiernan's wife, Devorgilla, whose growing fancy for the tall, formidable, and gallant MacMurrough soon flamed into passion. Bowing to temptation, she sent a note to Dermot confessing her desire and proposing that he abduct her. Immediately, he sped to her on horse-back and swept her away, making Tiernan a cuckold and a laughing stock throughout the land. Although he retrieved his wife from a brokenhearted Dermot a year later, the rage and enmity between the two grew greater.
By 1166 MacMurrough was all but wiped out. Forced to flee the land, he went to France with his profound bitterness and met with Henry II, King of England. Together they hatched a plan (which would involve Henry's English, French, Scottish, and Welsh subjects) for the Anglo-Norman invasion of Ireland. Thus it was that Dermot MacMurrough bartered his country to soothe his rage—a rage that changed Ireland irrevocably.

LODGINGS

* *Ferrycarrig Hotel,* Ferrycarrig Bridge (22999), is a modern B* accommodation with 40 rooms, all with bath and phone. It's nestled in peaceful countryside on the banks of the Slane estuary about five miles from Wexford on the Enniscorthy-Dublin road—N-11. Tennis court. Moderate, and the breakfast is included.

* *County Hotel* (Grade B) on Anne Street (24377), is an old abode with 13 rooms (no private baths). Pleasant. Inexpensive.

* *Kincone Lodge,* The Bridge, Wexford Town (23611), is a B* just across the New Bridge of Wexford Harbor. A small, new hotel with a pleasant little coffee shop. Moderately inexpensive.

* *The Talbot Hotel,* Trinity Street (22566), is a grade-A hotel with 116 rooms (92 with bath), all with direct-dial phone. Located in town, it has its own leisure center adjoining the hotel with heated pool, saunas, solarium, squash court, exercise equipment, table tennis. A beauty therapist is on hand to assist you. Moderate. Special low-price weekend packages available.

* *The Old Wexford Coaching Inn* (formerly Old White's Hotel), North Main Street (24002), is a marvelous old (1779) place. British militiamen stayed here in its early days, and after the Rebellion of 1798 guests began arriving by stagecoach, having braved the highwaymen in traveling the dirt roads from Dublin, Cork, or the western counties. Recently renovated, it still retains its old flavor. There are 22 rooms, and those without bath have washbasins. All have direct-dial phones. The drawing room has TV. Inexpensive and centrally located in town.

* *White's Hotel,* Abbey Street (22311), is a grade-A hotel with 100 rooms (60 with private bath), most with color-TV and direct-dial phone. Good service

and fine accommodations for moderate prices. And it's centrally located in town.

Guest Houses

* *St. Aidan's Mews,* John Street (22691), is a 17th-century home with seven rooms (none with private bath) located in town. It's cozy, clean, and inexpensive.

* *Whitford House,* New Line Road (22576/24673), is two miles from the town off the Duncannon Road. It has 22 rooms (12 with bath). Comfortable, clean, and bright. There's even an indoor pool. Inexpensive.

RESTAURANTS

* *The Bohemian Girl,* North Main Street (23596), is an interesting Tudor-style pub with beer-keg seats, homemade soups, hearty meat platters, salads. Incidentally, the place was named after the operetta by William Balfe, who lived nearby. Open 10:30 A.M. to 11:30 P.M. But no food on Sunday or Thursday nights. Moderate. Full License. Visa, Master.

* *Michael's Restaurant,* North Main Street (22196). Cozy little wine bistro serving pleasant grills, salads, fish dishes, omlettes, etc. Open noon to 12:30 A.M. Moderate.

* *Nagle's Coffee Dock,* North Main Street, is the Bewley's of Wexford (Bewley's being Dublin's grande dame of coffee-based dining places) with its bustling activity, its wonderful homemade cakes and baked goods. Like Bewley's, the place also serves good hearty meals—roast rib of beef, chicken, ham, ham salad, plaice, rainbow trout. All with a fine array of vegetables. Not posh, intimate dining—but good value (amazingly inexpensive). Open 8 A.M. to 6:30 P.M. Closed Sunday.

* *The Old Granary,* Westgate Street (23935), is a pleasant Tudor-style restaurant with very tasty Irish meat and fish dishes. Quaint and quiet with intimate dining booths. Open 10:30 A.M. to 11:30 P.M. Closed Sunday. Full License.

* *Captain White's Seafood Restaurant* in the Old Wexford Coaching Inn (23591). Intimate firelight dining and a private bar. A fish aquarium announces the house specialty. Although there are some meat dishes, the long menu puts the emphasis on the *poisson.* A fine starter is the fish chowder. Grilled black sole and the bass dishes are especially good entrees; also turbot flamed in Pernod and trout stuffed with walnuts, as available. The chef's recommendations are worth heeding. L—12:30 to 2:30, moderate. D—7 to 10, expensive. Closed Sunday. Full license. AE.

* *The Coffee Shop* of the Old Wexford Coaching Inn (23591) serves full Irish or Continental breakfasts till 10 A.M.; coffee and cakes all morning; seafood platters and open-faced sandwiches at lunch. Also afternoon tea and full meals in the evening. Open 8 A.M. to 9 P.M. Good and inexpensive. Full license. AE.

* *Forth & Bargy Bar* in the Old Wexford Coaching Inn (23591) is named after two of the Norman baronies of Wexford. It's a dark, woody old Irish-style pub serving very inexpensive food. Especially good are the baked Wexford ham and Irish cheddar-cheese sandwiches. Open 10:30 A.M. to 10 P.M. AE.

* *The Guillemot Restaurant* of the Talbot Hotel (22566) is an elegant, candlelit dining room with good fresh seafood and fine meat dishes as well. L—

12:30 to 2:45. D—6 to 8:45. Breakfast served here from 8 to 10:30. Expensive. AE, Diners, Master, BankameriCard.

* *The Pike Grill* of the Talbot Hotel (22566). Fast service and excellent food, especially steak and seafoods (sole, salmon, lobster). Open 12:30 P.M. to 11 P.M. on weekdays and Saturday, 1:30 P.M. to 10 P.M. on Sunday. Inexpensive to moderate. AE, Diners, Master, BankameriCard.

* *The Tavern Bar* of the Talbot Hotel (22566). A wonderful place for pub food is this Tudor-style tavern. There's an excellent hearty homemade pâté served with brown bread. Do try the Kilmore crabmeat sandwich (enormous and delicious). But the menu has still more to offer: mussels, oak-smoked salmon, Rossmore oysters, trout mayonnaise salad, Kilmore lobster mayonnaise or sandwich. There are a few non-seafood entries, along with a succulent rhubarb cream pie. L—12:30 to 3. D—6 to 9 weekdays and Saturday. On Sunday lunch ends at 2:45. Inexpensive. AE, Diners, Master, BankameriCard.

* *Tim's Tavern.* South Main Street (23861) is yet another Tudor-style pub. This one even has thatching over the bar. The fare includes pleasing soups, salads, sandwiches, curries, steaks. Open 10:30 A.M. to 11:30 P.M. Inexpensive to moderate.

* *The Selskar Restaurant* in White's Hotel (22311) has an elegant Old-World atmosphere and fine seafoods, meats (especially beef), and poultry. L—12:30 to 2. D—7 to 10. Also serves breakfast 8 to 10. Expensive. AE, Diners.

* *The Shelmalier Bar* of White's Hotel (22311) serves good sandwiches and pastries. 10 A.M. to 10 P.M. Inexpensive. AE, Diners.

PUBS

* *The Crown* on Monck Street, once an old stagecoach stop, is one of the country's oldest pubs, and it's still owned by the original Kelly family. Drift into one of the rear lounges for a pint, and you'll be captivated by the array of memorabilia, including all sorts of military equipment (rapiers, dueling pistols, pikes from the Vinegar Hill massacre, gun collections, Norman armor) and some excellent old prints. At quiet hours, the place is more like a museum than a pub. Should be seen.

* *The Cap Con Macken* at the Bull Ring is one of the strangest pubs in that it combines an old bar with a grocery store, a spirit shop, and an undertaking establishment. Name your poison. Come to think about it—maybe there's method in their madness.

* *Andy Kinsella's* on South Main Street, with its frosted windows, old brass lamps, and massive mahogany bar is one of Wexford's oldest, and it's in the heart of the shopping area.

* *Mooney's* on the Quays is a loungey youth haunt.

* *The Thomas Moore Tavern*, Cornmarket Street is another very old pub. Done in Tudor fashion with two floors, it was the birthplace of the poet Thomas Moore's mother. Very popular with the young set, often mobbed. But you should see it.

* *Forth & Bargy Bar* in the Old Wexford Coaching Inn, described under Restaurants.

* *The Wavecrest Bar* on the Quays is a raw, rugged place with nightly traditional music and a young crowd.

* *The Tavern Bar* in the Talbot Hotel, described under Restaurants.

ENTERTAINMENT/ANNUAL EVENTS

There is something in the traditional music vein going on practically every summer's night at either the Talbot Hotel or White's Hotel. Young people seem to gravitate to The Barn (once a hotel stable) in White's. If you're lucky and there's a *Seisiún* group in town (government-sponsored evening of traditional song and dance), it's very enjoyable and educational—often held at White's. The Talbot offers The Talbot Irish Cabaret Show (music and comedy) Wednesday—Saturday nights from the end of June to mid-September. 7:30 P.M. dinner and cabaret. Moderate. Or 9:30 P.M. for the show only at a special low price.

* The Wexford Art Centre, Cornmarket (23764), has summer performances.
* The Wexford Mussel Festival, inaugurated in 1980, is a three-day event held at the end of August to celebrate the home of Ireland's mussel industry. Events include a fishing competition, a tennis tournament, speedboat racing, para-gliding, water-skiing, and a dance.
* The Wexford Opera Festival, held each year at the end of October (for about a week and a half), has become world famous since its inception in 1951. Its policy is to produce rarely performed classic operas. Make reservations early: the Theatre Royal is small.

Note: Check The Irish Tourist Board for the exact dates of these events, and if your visit coincides with these popular festivals reserve your lodging well in advance.

SHOPPING

* Crafts Center. On North Main across the street from the Old Wexford Coaching Inn. Irish food products, coffees, crafts, woven baskets, sugan chairs, ornaments.
* The Book Shop, Charlotte Street. Good selection of books on Ireland, especially those concentrating on County Wexford.
* F. J. Hynes, South Main. Irish glass, silver, Claddagh rings.
* Joyce's China Shop, South Main. Fine selection of Waterford crystal, especially glasses.
* Barker's, South Main. Sizable stock of Waterford and Belleek china.
* The Wool Shop, South Main. Irish crafts, woolens, especially sweaters, sheepskins, souvenirs.
* Wexford Art Centre, Cornmarket Street. Young Wexford artists sell their own paintings. There's also an inexpensive coffee/luncheon room here.
* Bridge's, Selskar Street. Fishing equipment.

SPORTS

If you are planning a longer stay here, swimming, golfing, riding, and fishing are all within easy reach. The Irish Tourist Board can fill you in on the details.

Literature: This is a town of writers' ancestors rather than writers themselves—Oscar Wilde's mother (see *Bull Ring*) and Thomas Moore's mother (see *Thomas Moore Tavern* under Pubs).

Roots: Redmond (Redmond Monument); McClure (the Old Wexford Coaching Inn); Barry (Barry Memorial); Talbot (Talbot Hotel); Cody (Kelly's Pub); Murphy or MacMurrough; Fitzgerald/Grogan/Esmonde (each

owners at different times of Johnston Castle three miles south of Wexford—grounds may be visited by the public each day); Kennedy (the
John F. Kennedy Memorial Park and the Kennedy ancestral home, six
miles off the main Wexford-New Ross Road, N-25. Open year round 10
A.M. to 5 P.M.).

AN OPTIONAL JOURNEY THROUGH THE NORE
VALLEY TO KILKENNY
(50 miles)

* In the early afternoon, leave Wexford and drive the pleasant 23 miles of inland countryside on the N-25 to New Ross. This is one of those neglected towns that most travel guides forget to tell you about because it's on the way to a more important destination (Kilkenny or Waterford), but do have a look at it. It's a lovely ancient town on a hill that dips to a waterfront of picturesque old buildings on the River Barrow, just a little south of its junction with the River Nore. It is said to have been founded in the sixth century by St. Abban. (Don't linger here too long because you'll want to arrive at Kilkenny by three o'clock.)

* Take the road (T-20) from here to Thomastown and Kilkenny— 27 miles in all. Thomastown, the headquarters of the Kilkenny Hunt, is another attractive old town situated on the banks of the River Nore.

Roots: Walsh. Thomas Fitz-Anthony Walsh, who was the Seneschal of Leinster, built a wall around the town and erected a castle and a church in the 13th century. Ruins of these may be seen, along with some fine monuments of that period.

* Drive on to Kilkenny so as to arrive at mid-afternoon.

IV. KILKENNY

Kilkenny Town

The roots from which they grow destroy them.
—from a Celtic reference to the witch of Kilkenny

YOUR PERSONALIZED KILKENNY ITINERARY

* Arrive Kilkenny mid-afternoon. You will be staying overnight here (suggestions later), but to save valuable time do not check into your hotel. Instead proceed directly to *Kilkenny Castle,* which you'll see on your way into town. It's open only until 4:30, and its very much worth a visit. If you're interested in shopping at the Kilkenny Design Workshops, which are across the street in the castle's old stables, leave it until later, as the workshops are open till six o'clock.

Kilkenny Castle is, as you would expect, by far the most imposing building in the town. This monumental fortress makes it easy to see why there were so few military confrontations here: the castle is so formidable it would scare off Darth Vader. Even Cromwell was said to have quailed before launching the only successful attack on the castle in 1650. Pure fury over the Kilkenny Confederation and its chicanery, which included the manipulation of King Charles I, drove him to storm the castle with the power of a madman. And because of what he considered the deceit of the monied Catholic landowners and their brutality (exaggerated) against the Protestant plantation of Ulster, he was so possessed with the cause of Anglo-Aryanism that he prevailed.

Since the castle was in much disarray (needless to say) after Cromwell finished with it, it was a bright moment when the Butlers regained control and restored its French styling in the reign of Charles II. The Butlers owned the castle for centuries more, and through its courtyard passed such luminaries as King George and Queen Mary (1899) and King Edward VII and Queen Alexandra (1904). In a state of decline by 1967, it was turned over to the people of Kilkenny as an historical monument. Much restoration has been completed and a continuing program is in effect.

The visitor sees first the monumental entrance gateway erected in 1708, then the grand hall and picture gallery with its twin white-marble fireplaces, marble tables, and magnificent wood-paneled ceilings. The portraits in oil are of those associated with the castle over the years, especially the Butlers. Other attractions include the paneled dining room in one of the towers, fine woodwork throughout, and a skylight ceiling in the portrait gallery. The basement houses an art gallery and the castle's stalwart old kitchen, which is now a restaurant.

* Shop the *Kilkenny Design Centre.* Then drive to your hotel for check-in. Try the *Newpark* on Castlecomer Road or the *Rose Hill* on College/Callan Road. Both are on the fringes of town about five minutes from town center.

If you have arrived in Kilkenny before mid-afternoon, do go to *Rothe House* on Parliament Street. Now a museum, it was once the house of Elizabethan merchant John Rothe. Built in 1594 and preserved as it was, it will give you a splendid idea of how such a merchant lived. Open Sundays year round from 3 to 5 P.M. Open weekdays from April 1 to October 31, 10:30 A.M. to 12:30 P.M. and 3 to 5 P.M.

You should also see *St. Canice's Cathedral* on St. Canice's Place, erected in the 13th century by Norman bishop Hugh de Rous on the site where St. Canice founded a monastic order in the sixth century. In 1866 the Cathedral was restored, and The Round Tower outside the building is all that remains from St. Canice's day.

* If it should happen to be Friday, it's *Kyteler's Inn* on St. Kieran Street for dinner. This place has a lurid history (see *Legend*). Each Friday there's a Witches' Banquet that recalls the days of Dame Alice Kyteler. Even if it's not Friday, you can partake of a meal at Kyteler's Inn (with less panache). Or if you like, you can stay right at your hotel and dine at one of the fine places mentioned at either. (See Restaurants for details.)

* After dinner, if you're outside of town, drive in and stroll the old streets with such names as Pennyfeather Lane, Sweet Butter Slip, and Pudding Lane . . . here is a true sense of the Middle Ages.

* Before you call it a day, drop into *Tynan's Bridge House Bar* off John's Bridge at 2 Horseleap Slip (see Pubs).

* Turn in early for the long day's journey to Waterford and Cork.

KILKENNY'S HISTORY

Kilkenny or *Cill Chainnigh* (Canice's Church or the Cell of Canice) dates from the sixth century, when St. Canice founded a monastic settlement and a church here. Little remains of them except for the round tower at the present-day St. Canice's Cathedral. What makes this town important today is that it is the finest example of a medieval town in Ireland, virtually intact.

In pre-Norman days Kilkenny was one of the capitals of the country. When Strongbow invaded, he handed the growing town over to his son-in-law William le Mareschal (Marshall) who granted it its first charter in 1207. During the 14th century Kilkenny hosted many sessions of parliament and rivaled Dublin in importance. At the same time, the Anglo-Normans and the original Irish settlers found themselves increasingly attracted to one another. As intermarriages and love affairs began springing up audaciously right and left, right under parliament's nose, the incensed leaders dropped a bomb on the whole situation by passing the infamous 1366 Statutes of Kilkenny, which they enforced with the will of a Hitler. It was high treason for the original Irish to mix in any way with the Anglo-Normans. They weren't even allowed to enter the walled section of the town, let alone to live there. The Anglo-Normans were forbidden to speak the Gaelic tongue, to give Irish names to their new-

born, or to wear any Irish-made clothing (including even underwear). Needless
to say, this caused more than mild consternation, with many families literally
torn apart by the edicts.

It was years before there was any relief, which came when the descendants
of le Mareschal sold the massive walled fortress to James Butler, the third
Earl of Ormonde. The Butlers had accompanied Henry II to Ireland when
the Anglo-Normans took the country. They were a strong Catholic family,
obviously rather more lenient toward their subjects than their predecessors
had been (a little too much so in Anglo eyes). Despite their feuds with the
monarchy, they maintained the castle, and over the next century their wealth
and power grew—much to the discomfort of an enfeebled England, which
was moving to the brink of Civil War.

By the early 17th century, the Catholic population was so abused that after
the Ulster Rebellion of 1641 a Confederation of Kilkenny was formed to represent original Irish and Anglo-Irish Catholics. For six years this parliament
governed Ireland, striving for religious and civil rights. At one point Pope
Innocent X sent the Confederation some 6000 arms and 20,000 pounds for
the cause. The Confederation was finally dissolved in 1648, and after Cromwell's seige in 1650, a treaty was signed which allowed the Irish army to
surrender with full honors. However, considerable damage was done to the
property of the wealthy. St. Canice's Cathedral was sacked, its stained-glass
windows smashed, and the invaders' horses stabled in the church aisles. By
now, it was becoming evident that England was not worried about the Irish
armies or the poor; they could control them. It was the burgeoning wealthy
Irish Catholic population that had to be quelled.

Once Cromwell gained control, every member of the previous Confederacy
was in dire straits. Many of the leading families of Kilkenny lost their lands
and belongings when they were banished to the west of the country. Despite
the penal laws that followed, the city's cultural revival flourished. Today the
town is popularly known as Marble City, because of the fine black marble
quarried in the area.

Legend: The intriguing story of Dame Alice Kyteler and Kyteler's Inn on
Kilkenny's St. Kieran Street stems from the early 14th century, so many of
the details are obscure; here's what is known.

Dame Alice's family was of the prosperous money-mad Anglo-Norman kind.
Her father died when she was a young woman, leaving his banking business
to her. It is said that he had taught her well the value of power and money,
so well that she developed an insatiable desire for both. This and her voluptous
beauty would prove to be her downfall. Many powerful men were drawn to
her doorstep, and she was passionately attracted to four of them in turn. After
whirlwind courtships and brief marriages, three of these men widowed her,
painfully and mysteriously, as it was said. When she married the fourth, still
building her fortune, gossip and envy flamed. Dame Alice was now the largest
moneylender in the land, and while masquerading as deeply concerned for
the needy, she raised her rates of interest to usurious heights. When a fourth
husband began sliding toward oblivion, public outcry reached epidemic propor-
tions, and Dame Alice's Waterloo was close at hand.

By now she had become so jaded and self-involved that she scarcely noticed
the case building against her. Idleness had led her to the proverbial devil's
work, as it would the Irish gentry of a later time who formed their own counter-

part of England's Hellfire Club. She had begun worshipping the devil in the form of a great black dog about the time husband number one was expiring. It is said that by now her desire for money far outweighed her attraction to this man or any other. A few witches' potions laced with poison brought on a slow agonizing death and another inheritance. It is said that after each death she took to the ritual slaughter of animals, and her innocent serving girl, Petronilla, believed her tale that they were diseased, just as she had believed in and joined the Dame's mourning.

But the townspeople and the Bishop of Ossory weren't tricked. A long-time foe of her money-lending practices, the Bishop now demanded that she be tried for witchcraft. Even though Dame Alice's powerful friends, led by seneschal Arnold le Poer, had the Bishop imprisoned, he was a determined man. Soon released, he insisted on the trial, at which her children by her first three husbands gave evidence against her. Found guilty, she was sentenced to burn at the stake. Through the aid of her friends, she fled the country the evening before her scheduled execution, leaving humble Petronilla to be the scapegoat who would rid the town of the devil and witches' curses. Dragged screaming through the streets of Kilkenny, she was set ablaze and went to her death in prayer. To this day, her spirit is said to haunt Kyteler's Inn and the streets of Kilkenny.

LODGINGS

* *The Newpark Hotel,* Castlecomer Road (22122), was once a stately Victorian home on the edge of town. The house has been saved, but the newly added wings are very modern. You might want to ask for one of the older Victorian rooms, even though they don't have private baths, as do the 38 modern rooms. All rooms have TV, direct-dial phone. Located on the northern fringe of the town, it's the only A-rated (Tourist Board) hotel here. Moderate.

* *Rose Hill Hotel,* College/Callan Road (22603), is an old Grade-B* Regency-period hotel (built by the man who rebuilt Kilkenny Castle as it stands today—William Robertson). But the bedrooms are modern. There are 60, all with private bath, direct-dial phone, TV with in-house films. A health and leisure center includes an indoor pool, saunas, sunbeds, hot tubs, gyms, tennis court. Located on the northern fringe of town. Moderate. Master only.

* *Club House Hotel,* Patrick Street (21994), is the largest hotel within the town, with 30 rooms (four with bath). A very old hotel dating back to Georgian times, it has a pleasant bar, old-fashioned dining room, and a B rating from the Tourist Board. Inexpensive.

* *Springhill Hotel,* Waterford Road (21122) looks almost like an American motel. With a B* rating, it's clean and tidy and offers 44 rooms with bath, phone, TV with in-house films. Located on the southern fringe of the town. Moderate.

* *Hotel Carmel,* John's Bridge (22235), is another very old hotel within the village. Because none of its 14 rooms has a private bath, it rates only a C. But it is pleasant and inexpensive.

RESTAURANTS

* *Fitzpatrick's,* Parliament Street, is a very old pub offering good pub food at low prices. Salads are its specialty. Open 10:30 A.M. to 11 P.M. Inexpensive.

* *Kyteler's Inn,* St Kieran Street (21064), spells eerie dining because ghosts haunt the place, which dates back to 1324 (see *Legend*). Fine meat and seafood

dishes nightly, but on Fridays the Inn goes to town with its famous Witching Banquet and *Seanachai*. A witch will greet you at the door with a glass of mulled wine and usher you into the courtyard. Later you'll dine in the scary dungeon-like basement area with its flickery candles (four-course meal with very tasty meat and fish entrees.) Then you'll move to the Inn's Tudor Room for an evening of traditional Irish music and a special *Seanachai* (storyteller), topped off by a complimentary Irish coffee to ward off the ghostly chills. Dinner from 6 P.M. Moderate and pleasant, but make a reservation. There's inexpensive pub food (very good) during the day. Full license.

* *Mulhall's Restaurant,* Pudding Lane (21329), is reached through a small arcade at 6 High Street. There's a snack bar, a grill bar, and a regular dining room in this new restaurant that retains, through native wood and stone, the architectural feeling of the area. Meals include good beef, pork, sole, and salmon dishes. Fine scones and cakes for snacks. Breakfast is served here as well. Open 9:30 A.M. to 7 P.M. Monday through Wednesday and 9:30 A.M. to 10 P.M. Thursday–Saturday. Closed Sunday. Inexpensive to moderate. Wine license. Visa, Master.

* *The Grill Room* at the Newpark Hotel, Castlecomer Road (22122), offers good grills and roasts, with veal, chicken, and ham specialties. Open 10 A.M. to 11 P.M. Monday–Saturday and 1 P.M. to 11 P.M. Sunday. Moderate. AE, Visa, Master, Diners.

* *The Main Dining Room of the Newpark Hotel,* Castlecomer Road (22122), is an elegant room in the old Victorian section of this hotel, the rest of which is very modern. Wonderful Gaelic steaks, racks of lamb, fine seafoods. Great place for a quiet romantic rendezvous. L—12:30 to 4. D—6:30 to 9:30. (Breakfast served here, 7:30 to 10). Moderate. AE, Master, Visa, Diners.

* *The Coffee Dock* of the Rose Hill Hotel, College/Callan Road (5994), has a menu ranging from light snacks to full meals, including breakfast. Open 7 A.M. to 11 P.M. Closed Jan. 1–March 31. Inexpensive to moderate. Master.

* *The Main Restaurant of the Rose Hill Hotel,* College/Callan Road (5994). Crabs and prawns are excellent in this modernized Regency room. So are some of the French and German specialties. Breakfast is served here as well. Open 7 A.M. to 3 P.M. D—6 to 11 P.M. Moderate. Master.

* *The Rothe Inn,* High Street (22718), is a quaint Tudor-style pub with a wide variety of pub foods ranging from sandwiches to casseroles cooked in lager. Inexpensive.

PUBS

* *Tynan's Bridge House,* 2 Horseleap Slip, off John's Bridge. This pub has everything to suggest its antiquity—a carved, marble-topped bar with brass-globed oil lamps, gilt mirrors, spice drawers, and anachronistic bar trappings. There's also an ancient clock, a fine front snug, brass scales, and wonderful impressionistic Irish landscape paintings that are almost Monet-like. Don't mistake it (or miss it); this is one of Ireland's finest old country pubs.

* *Fitzpatrick's,* Parliament Street (see Restaurants).

* *Kyteler's Inn,* St. Kieran's Street (see *Legend,* Restaurants).

* *Marble City Bar,* High Street. Just have a look at its magnificent marble front. The interior is not as impressive.

SHOPS

* Kilkenny Design Shop, across from Kilkenny Castle (22118). This is supposedly the finest design shop in the country. The truth is—it isn't. But there

The Hunt

are wonderful designs from all areas: silver, crystal, wood, knits, textiles, furniture, etc. Many fine things, but the Kilkenny counterpart shop in Dublin is far superior, and better stocked.

★ Roberts' Books, St. Kieran's Street, has wonderful antique prints, books, paintings, maps. Just under Kyteler's Inn, this is one of the city's finest shops.

★ The Book Centre and Kilkenny Book Store, both on High Street, offer wonderful Irish history books, including area books on Kilkenny.

★ P. T. Murphy, High Street. Antique silver and jewelry.

★ The Monster House Department Store. Traditional Irish clothing and crystal.

★ Liam Costigan, Colliers Lane off High Street. Finely crafted silver jewelry.

★ Rudolf Heltzel Gold and Silversmith, Patrick Street. Beautifully fashioned contemporary jewelry in gold and silver, some with precious stones.

SPORTS

For those staying longer in this area, available sports include hunting, fishing, hurling, golf, tennis, squash, and running. The Irish Tourist Board will give you further details.

ENTERTAINMENT/ANNUAL EVENTS

The New Theater Group of Kilkenny presents two or three three-act plays a year. It also does short plays at its lunchtime pub theater in the Club House Hotel. *Seisiún* (program of traditional Irish music and dance) is held Wednesday evenings at the Newpark Hotel.

The Kilkenny Arts Week, usually held at the end of August/beginning of September. Irish arts and crafts brilliantly displayed, along with fine classical music and theater presentations.

Literature: Jonathan Swift, George Farquhar, and William Congreve attended Kilkenny College. William Butler Yeats celebrated the life of Dame Alice Kyteler in his poem "1919."

Roots: Marshall; Butler (Kilkenny Castle); Rothe, Archer (Rothe House); Shee (the Tudor Almshouse founded by Sir Richard Shee in 1582 on Rose Inn Street); O'Shea, derived from Shee; Palmer (St. Francis Abbey just off Parliament Street: the tower and chancel remain, along with a seven-light east window commissioned by Dame Isabella Palmer in 1330); Grace (Kilkenny Courthouse, where once stood a castle built by the Grace family as its living quarters). Other prominent Kilkenny names over the years have included: O'Brennan, Shortal, Walsh, Tobin, Murphy, Ryan, Byrne, O'Carroll, Delany, Comerford, Dowling, Maher, Cantwell, Kelly, and O'Brian.

V. A LONG DAY'S JOURNEY
TO WATERFORD AND CORK

Cork farm

Smooth is its lowland—pleasant its fields . . .
—from the Celtic, 12th century

YOUR PERSONALIZED ITINERARY TO WATERFORD AND CORK

This trip comprises between 108 and 124 miles, depending on the route you take.

★ If you have taken the optional tour with an overnight in Kilkenny, rise early and breakfast at your lodgings. Check out by 9–9:30. Drive the 30 miles down the N10 (which later becomes the N9) to *Waterford.*

★ If you're doing the shorter itinerary and heading directly to Waterford and Cork from Wexford, see the highlights of Wexford, finishing by 9:30 or 10 at the latest, and proceed down the N25 the 39 miles to Waterford.

★ Cross Redmond Bridge into the city of Waterford, and park your car for a walking tour. Just past the bridge on Bridge Street are the ruins of the *Dominican Friary,* which was founded in 1226, making it one of the oldest in the country. In 1541 the crown suppressed and confiscated it. Queen Elizabeth presented it to Sir Anthony St. Leger (whom she is said to have fancied) in 1599. The finely fashioned square tower and belfry remain intact.

★ Walk back and explore the handsome quays overlooking the peaceful *River Suir.* Centuries ago, the merchant princes set up their guild halls, townhouses, and commercial exchanges here. Many of these buildings are still extant as stores, restaurants, and other establishments.

★ Stop at the Irish Tourist Board office and make reservations for an 11:45 A.M. tour of the *Waterford Glass Factory,* about 1½ miles from Waterford on the Cork Road. (Note: Factory closed either the latter part of July or the first three weeks in August when employees vacation.)

★ Next you will come to the *Granville Hotel,* which is of particular interest to Americans. This fine building was one of Waterford's grand old Georgian mansions. Built during the reign of George III by the Quan family, it was here that Thomas Francis Meagher (whose mother was a Quan) was born in 1823, in what is now called The Thomas Francis Meagher Room. He became a determined member of the Young Ireland Party and a founder of the Irish Confederation. He was captured by the British and sentenced to death for treason for his involvement in the failed 1848 Uprising, but his sentence was commuted to lifetime exile. In 1852 he escaped to America, where his burning desire to fight for a cause led him to form The Fighting 69th of the Confederate Army, which fought with distinction at Fort Sumter, Bull Run, and Fredericksburg. 'Never were men so brave,' cheered General Robert E. Lee of Brigadier General Meagher and his men. His battle flag of the Irish Brigade, sword, and uniform are on display farther down the road at the Council Chamber of Waterford City Hall, on the Mall just above Reginald's Tower. Meagher of the Sword, as he was known, later became Governor of Montana. This was shortly before his death by drowning in 1867 in the swift deep waters of the Missouri at Fort Benton.

* Moving on you will pass by the *Clock Tower,* which the captains of the great merchant ships checked anxiously so they could bring their cargo in on time. The tower served a dual purpose in that the landlocked could water their horses at the watering troughs which formed its base.

* As you stroll on, you'll come to the ruins of the old *French Church* built in 1240 by Sir Hugh Purcell and suppressed in the 16th century, as was the Dominican Friary. It then became a hospital and its grounds a cemetery for Waterford's most prominent families. In the late 17th century it was a refuge for the religiously persecuted French Huguenot exiles.

The Mall's buildings, especially City Hall, are fine examples of Georgian architecture; a little farther to the right is *Christ Church Cathedral,* an excellent representative of the style. This and many other edifices in the area were designed by the native Irish architect John Roberts.

* By 11:45 A.M. you can take to the Cork Road, N-25, for the mile-and-a-half trip to the *Waterford Glass Factory* (half-hour tour at 11:45 A.M.). Thousands of people converge here each year to see the most renowned crystal works in the world, whose products have made their way into the wealthiest international households. (When Jacqueline Kennedy was in the White House, all the cognoscenti waited breathlessly to find out which pattern she would select next.) The first plant produced the wonderful Old Waterford successfully from 1783 to 1850, when an onerous British law levied such a tax on the crystal that no one outside the country could buy it. The envious English would have rejoiced at the demise of the Waterford works, but in 1947 the Irish had the sense to revive this flagging business. The crystal's quality ensured its renaissance: nothing has stopped it since. The half-hour tours are conducted at 10:15, 11, 11:45, 2:30, and 2:50. *Make reservations.* In accordance with Irish labor practices, the factory is closed during part of the summer: either the last week in July and

the first two weeks in August, or the first three weeks in August. Note that you cannot buy Waterford at the factory, nor are there any sales of seconds.

* From here, you'll reach the end of the quays and Waterford's most historic monument—*Reginald's Tower.* This fascinating old edifice consists of a circular fortification with a cone-shaped roof and walls ten feet thick. The Norsemen built it in the 11th century in the name of Reginald McIvor, the governor of Waterford. It connected with the old city walls (parts of which are still visible) and formed part of the town's earliest defense system. The despised Anglo-Norman Strongbow captured the tower in 1170; in its upper room his daughter, Eva, married the Irish warrier king who arranged the Anglo-Norman takeover of the country—Dermot MacMurrough. The tower is now a museum housing a perfect compendium of Irish history: open at 9:30 A.M.

* Just across the street is a statue of *Father Luke Wadding,* the renowned historian and philosopher, who was educated in Lisbon and ordained here in the early 17th century. An Irish linguist and writer of distinction in the late 16th and early 17th centuries, he presented thousands of Roman manuscripts to Irish colleges. He was also a major supporter of the Confederation of Kilkenny, which opposed the throne in the cause of Irish civil and religious rights—until Cromwell put a stop to it.

* If you're not taking the Waterford Glass Tour, you might like to stop in at the *Stonecourt Gourmet Restaurant* on Waterford's O'Connell Street, or at one of the other places noted in Restaurants, for a quick early lunch ending around 12:30.

* Proceed south from the glass factory the 25 miles to *Dungarvan,* a small town on Dungarvan Harbor, site of the ruins of one of King John's castles (1185) along with those of the town wall and keep.

Roots: McGrath (Abbeyside Castle or McGrath's Castle, with a ruined tomb inscribed *Donald McGrath 1490*).

* Continue along the Cork road about five miles until you come to *Seanachie,* a traditional bar and restaurant where those who haven't eaten should stop. It's a restored thatched farmhouse serving good Continental and Irish food in the inexpensive to moderate range. Full license.

* Now drive the 19 miles on the Cork Road to *Youghal,* which is pronounced as an American Southerner would drawl *you all.* This fine seacoast resort town just over the Cork border harks back to the days of Sir Walter Raleigh—poet, adventurer, explorer—who

brought Ireland its first potato along with its first smoked tobacco—
both from North Carolina. Raleigh was mayor here from 1588 through
1589, after his attempts to colonize America. (Brief history of Youghal
follows.)

 * Here take a stroll through the town, which is built on a hill,
and see (starting as you enter from the Waterford side) the 13th-cen-
tury *Dominican North Abbey* remains with lower church walls and
a gable to the right. Farther along and off to the right is *Myrtle House,*
the fine Elizabethan home where Sir Walter Raleigh is said to have
lived during the time he was mayor here, but which is not open to
the public. Behind it, at the end of William Street, is *St. Mary's Collegiate Church.* This is one of the oldest and largest medieval edifices
in the country, built by Thomas, eighth earl of Desmond, in the 15th
century. The church fell into disrepair, and parts of it were roofless
for centuries. Restoration reclaimed it in the 1800s. The eloquent interior architecture is worth a visit, including some of the original oak
ceiling and arches and the enormous pulpit with its canopy of carved
bog-petrified oak. The church's interesting monuments include the
finely sculptured tomb of Richard Boyle, a lawyer who became the
first earl of Cork in the early 17th century.

Farther down South Main Street on the right is the *Red House,* a
good example of an early 18th-century home. Opposite it on the left
are the remains of *Tyntes Castle,* built by the Walsh family, with
parts of its 15th-century tower (a later addition) still intact. Beyond
it on the right is *St. John's House and Abbey.* Only a chamber of
this Benedictine priory remains as evidence of St. John the Evange-
list's foundation of 1360. Next is the *Clock Gate,* with its 18th-century
clock tower. On the right is *Water Gate,* built in the 17th century
and restored in the 19th. Cromwell passed under it in 1649.

 * From Youghal proceed back north to the Waterford road; slightly
out of town is the left-hand turn to Tallow, 14 miles away. There
pick up the northwesterly turn for Fermoy (13 miles). At Fermoy,
take the N72 to Mallow (19 miles). Here you should plan to spend
the night and dine at one of Ireland's musts: the 18th-century *Longueville House,* one of the country's finest elegant country houses (see
description under Cork Lodgings). To miss it would be to lose the
material for one of life's most rewarding memories.

Important: Since this is one of Ireland's very special out-of-the-way
places, you may have trouble obtaining reservations. Do so long in
advance, so you won't be disappointed. If it's bad news, you should
know before you leave Youghal, in which case take the alternative
route to Cork on the major N25. Eleven miles down the road, you'll
come to Castlemartyr. If you're still keen on lodging and dining in

one of the fine old country houses, you can take the turn for Ballycotton and go nine miles to Shanagarry, where the 17th-century *Ballymaloe House* is located. Again, be sure the owners can accommodate you first, as this is another lovely and popular place. While here, be sure to see the ruins of the ancient home of the *Penn family*—one of whose members founded the state of Pennsylvania.

Roots: Penn.

* If neither Longueville nor Ballymaloe House is available, continue along the N25 from Castlemartyr to Cork City (another 20 miles), where you can select from a variety of accommodations. *The Arbutus Lodge* in the Montenotte section is highly recommended. *The Imperial* on the South Mall, and *The Metropole* on McCurtain Street are both good and centrally located (see Cork Lodgings section for details on all of these).

Happy Faces Along the Way

WATERFORD'S HISTORY

In Irish it is known as *Port Lairge,* which means Lairge's Landing Place. Situated on the south bank of the River Suir, it was established as a settlement called Vadrefjord by Sitric the Dane around 850. The Danes were converted to Christianity and lived peacefully until the arrival of the Normans under Strongbow in 1170. With the aid of Raymond le Gros, Strongbow took the town and later married the Irish warrior king Dermot MacMurrough's daughter (see *Reginald's Tower,* Itinerary). From this point on, Waterford rivaled Dublin as the country's finest fortress. In 1171 King Henry II arrived with pomp and circumstance to survey his newly acquired domain, and the citizenry offered its allegiance. King John thought so much of the city and its people that he granted Waterford its first charter in 1205 (ten years before he granted the Magna Carta to his own English nobles at Runnymeade). He revisited the city in 1210 and strengthened its fortifications. It's noteworthy that in 1487 Waterford was the only Irish city to vehemently oppose the Yorkist pretender to the throne, Lambert Simnel, and the city closed its gates again in 1495 to Perkin Warbeck, another pretender. For this loyalty, Henry VII rewarded the Waterford citizenery with 1000 marks and a motto that praised their fidelity: *Urbs Intacta Manet Waterfordia.* This is still used today on the city's coat of arms, along with its Sword and Cap of Maintenance.

By the 16th century, in the wake of great religious persecution, the citizens finally began to rebel against English supremacy over their religion. Even though they stood by Great Britain in civil matters, it wasn't enough to please the throne. The city lost its charter, and members of the corporation were either fined or imprisoned. In 1649 Cromwell encountered major opposition in his attempt to take the city and had to abandon the seige. It wasn't until the following year that Waterford fell. The Catholic King James II was received in the city after his defeat at the Battle of The Boyne, en route to Kinsale where he would attempt to regain the crown and, failing, would exile himself to France. The city was soon forced to surrender to the new Protestant King, William III, to whom the citizens later became loyal subjects.

During the next century, Waterford enjoyed affluence and industrial development. The highly valued and now priceless antique Waterford glass was produced during the latter part of the 18th century.

Roots: Walsh, Power, Bulter, Ryan, McGrath, Sullivan, Tobin, McCarthy, Murphy, O'Brien, Morrissey, Kelly, Flynn, Foley, Whelan, Meagher (Granville Hotel).

If you're planning a longer Waterford stay, here's a brief listing of the high points. Check Restaurants if you'd like to have lunch here, especially if you're not taking the Waterford Glass Tour.

WATERFORD LODGINGS

Ardree Hotel (modern, 100 rooms overlooking the town, moderate to expensive, phone 3491); *The Granville Hotel* (a fine old place to stay on the River Suir at the Quay, centrally located, 50 rooms, extremely pleasant, moderate, phone 55166); *Dooley's* (modernized old coaching inn, centrally located at the Quay, pleasant, 42 rooms/25 with bath, moderate, phone 3531); *The Tower*

Hotel (modern, 81 rooms centrally located on The Mall across from Reginald's Tower, moderate, phone 75801).

WATERFORD RESTAURANTS

Ballinakill House (two miles outside Waterford off Dunmore East Road, splendid dining in front of a large romantic fire in a room that dates back 350 years, all dishes are local produce with game and wildfowl in season, homemade ice cream/desserts, AE/Visa/Master, expensive lunch/dinner); *Beer & Bite* (in town in a little lane just off Baroncourt Street, fast but good, mainly sandwiches, inexpensive); *George Chapman* (on the Quay, deli/grocer/ restaurant, pleasant lunch with sandwiches, salads, heartier roast chicken or steak and kidney pie, also Irish and Continental breakfasts, very inexpensive); *Eagan's Lounge Bar* (on Barronstrand Street, inexpensive to moderate pub food from sandwiches to hot monkfish and scampi, steaks and chicken, salmon and fish salads served in a Tudor setting); *Galley Cruising Restaurants* (at quays, daily except Sunday and Monday you can cruise the river for two hours while you have your afternoon or high tea, good food, moderate); *The Granville Hotel* (on the Quay, has the expensive but elegant and romantic Sword Restaurant with excellent racks of lamb, Steak Béarnaise, and seafood plus the inexpensive to moderate Bianconi Grill with snacks to full grill meals, AE, Visa, Master, Diners); The *Reginald Grill* (beside Reginald's Tower, with fine grills at moderate prices and open till 11 P.M., AE, Visa, Master, Diners); *Sitric* (also near Reginald's Tower, Edwardian, superior fresh fish dishes including—in season—superb sea trout, expensive, dinner only, AE, Visa, Master, Diners); *The Tower Hotel* (excellent sandwiches and grills across from Reginald's Tower, moderate, all credit cards); *Stonecourt Gourmet Restaurant* (centrally located on O'Connell Street just behind the quays, a very old store converted into a miniature tropical paradise with violin music and everything from American hamburgers to steak and good fish dishes, lunch moderate, dinner moderate to expensive, AE, Master, Visa).

WATERFORD PUBS

T. H. Doolan's (on George's Street, a must-see old Irish pub with authentic Tudor decor, snug booths, and carved wooden bar and ceilings, traditional music and singing Wednesday, Thursday, and Saturday nights); *Egan's* (Barronstrand Street, described above); *Reginald Lounge* (near Reginald's Tower, has a cozy turf fire burning for your welcome and sporadic musical interludes; you can see sections of the original fortress walls nearby).

WATERFORD SHOPS

Joseph Knox (on Barronstrand Street, probably one of Ireland's finest Waterford glass shops, with a large selection. Remember that you can't buy Waterford—not even seconds—at Waterford Glass Factory, so this is a good place to shop for it); *Shaw's Department Store* (on the Quay, also has Waterford crystal plus Aran knits and Irish silver); *Waterford Craft Centre* (on Michael Street, a fine array of Irish crafts, besides the crystal); *The Book Centre* (on Michael Street, offers a fine collection of books on Ireland, fine photographic essays as well); *O'Neil's* (on O'Connell Street, for antiques); *Nicholl's* (on The Mall near Reginald's Tower, also antiques).

SPORTS

Within the area—sailing, tennis, squash, golfing, fine running, greyhound racing, horse racing, pony trekking, river cruising.

ENTERTAINMENT/ANNUAL EVENTS

Professional Irish touring companies do frequent productions at the city's magnificent old *Theatre Royal,* which was built in 1788. Jenny Lind appeared on this stage.

For the past quarter-century Waterford has held the annual Light Opera Festival at the end of September or the beginning of October.

Besides these, there are the *Seisiún,* on which the Tourist Board can advise you of the where-and-whens.

YOUGHAL'S HISTORY

Eochaill or Yen Wood is an ancient fishing port and marketing town beautifully situated on the banks of the Blackwater River estuary. It was probably an established settlement under the Danes in the 8th century, but most of Youghal's known history dates from the 12th century with the arrival of the Normans. Its town walls, probably the best-preserved in the country, go back to the 15th century. The spirited English adventurer Sir Walter Raleigh helped the Tudors conquer Ireland and was rewarded with 42,000 acres of land in Youghal, where he served as the warden and mayor in 1588–89. It was during this time that he met the English poet Edmund Spenser and helped him edit his great *Faerie Queene.* Raleigh was so much in favor with Queen Elizabeth at the time that he was able to get financial aid from the monarchy to support Spenser's literary efforts. Just before this period, Raleigh had made the first British attempt to colonize America in what is now the North Carolina area. Even though it failed (largely because of American Indian opposition), it augmented the British attraction to the New World, which would end in a bloody Revolutionary War.

Raleigh later sold his Irish estate to Sir Richard Boyle, who became the Earl of Cork. In the 1600s Cromwell made it his Youghal headquarters for his southern Irish campaign.

Roots: Desmond (St. Mary's Collegiate Church); Walsh (Tyntes Castle); Fitzgerald (Franciscan Friary, commemorated by the South Abbey thoroughfare, which was founded by Maurice Fitzgerald in 1230); Boyle (17th-century tomb of Richard Boyle in the Church of St. Mary).

Literature: Sir Walter Raleigh, who added writing to his activities as an adventurer, explorer, colonizer, and politician. Among his best-known excursions was a surprisingly dour look at life called *A History of the World,* in which he suggested that the world was merely a prison from which several were called to their executions each day.

PUBS

Moby Dick Lounge, just around the corner from the Clock Gate, has a seafaring motif and got its name when John Houston filmed his version of *Moby Dick* in the area around Youghal.

Aherne's Pub & Seafood Bar on North Main has excellent locally caught seafood (open all day, full license, expensive, AE, Visa, Master, Diners).

The Bush Courtyard on Quarry Road offers romantic candlelit dining—Irish and continental—in the converted stables of an old country house (wine license, moderate).

SHOPS

Youghal Pottery on Quarry Road has a showroom shop offering fine hand-made Irish pottery, which it will ship to America if you like.

VI. CORK

Cork City

When my heart was as light as the wild winds that
blew,
Down the Mardyke through each elm tree
—Irish ballad

The spreading Lee encloseth Corke with his divided
flood . . .
—Edmund Spenser

YOUR PERSONALIZED CORK ITINERARY

Day One

* Check in and since it's been a long day, perhaps plan to eat at your lodgings (descriptions provided in Restaurants.) If you're staying at one of the old country houses, enjoy the luxury of coffee or an after-dinner drink at leisure in one of the grand sitting rooms. Before retiring, you might enjoy an evening stroll around the grounds. If you're staying in Cork City, you could drop by a pub for your after-dinner drink and perhaps take a brief stroll in town. Or you might prefer some theater (details later).

Day Two

* Have breakfast at your lodging and check out. Prepare for a walking tour of Cork City. (For details of the walk and lunching facilities, follow the tour as outlined in the Optional Day-Two itinerary.)

* After lunch proceed to Blarney, then west and finally north to Kenmare in County Kerry, where you'll spend the night (a distance of about 70 miles in all). At Blarney, which is five miles north of Cork on the L69, what remains of *Blarney Castle* is very handsome indeed, as are the grounds. And of course there's the castle's Blarney Stone, which you may want to stop and kiss so you'll be blessed with the gift of gab. While here, you could visit the fine *Blarney Woolen Mills and Shop*, which offers the regional Blarney sweaters as well as other Irish and European crafts.

* From here it's 30 miles to *Macroom,* whose castle was the scene of many sieges during the 16th and 17th centuries. It was once the property of Admiral Sir William Penn, the father of William Penn, who founded Pennsylvania. Nearby amid towering cliffs is a lake, *Gougane Barra,* whose tiny island served as the hermitage of St. Finbarre, Cork's patron saint. In one of the houses near the lake lived the marvelous Irish storyteller Timothy Buckley, who was a tailor by trade. During the late Thirties and early Forties, he and his wife, Ansty, held court at their fireside with such notable local authors as Frank O'Connor and Sean O'Faolain.

Literature: Under the name of The Tailor, Timothy Buckley wrote daringly about the humorous aspects of the sexual lives of the Irish country people. This was in easier times—before the establishment of the English language in this part of the country. Once the Irish Free State and the Church became more firmly entrenched, the book written from 'The Tailor's' fireside chats was banned, and two puritanical priests forced him and his wife to burn the manuscript in the hearth which had kindled so many cheery—if earthy—tales. Even today many say that this was the cruelest adventure of the early Irish Free State. But shortly after 1943, when the tailor and his wife had died in disgrace, this wonderful book was released to the general public and became an enormous success.

★ From here move on to *Ballingeary,* a small town in the heart of the Kerry Gaeltacht. Continue through the Pass of Keimaneigh—a spectacular two-mile stretch—to Ballylickey and Glengarriff (see below). From here you go north to Kenmare.

An Optional Day Two in Cork

For those on longer stays, and planned on conjunction with a tour of southwestern County Cork.

★ Have breakfast at your lodgings and check out.

★ Drive to the village of Blarney, which is five miles north of Cork and within easy reach of the country guesthouses mentioned. Blarney Castle opens at 9:30 daily, so spend a half hour there before proceeding to Cork for a walking tour.

★ Begin at the center of the city, called *the Flats* or Flat of the City, an island surrounded by the north and south forks of the River Lee. Once a marshy area, it was filled and paved in 1789. *St. Patrick's Bridge,* one of the major bridges spanning the river, serves as a good starting point. This bridge replaces the one that was swept away in the great Cork flood of 1853. In front of the bridge on Patrick Street is the *Father Matthew Statue.* This work by the 19th-century Irish sculptor John Henry Foley depicts Father Theobald Matthew, the apostle of temperance and a superior of the Capuchin Order. He worked diligently to better the conditions of the poor in Cork, especially during the famine.

★ Patrick Street, the city's main artery, takes you to Academy Street (on the right) which leads to Emmet Place, where you'll see the 18th-century red-brick *Crawford Municipal School of Art* and its *Gallery.* Here are exquisite examples of 20th-century Irish paintings, especially the haunting landscapes. An exceptionally quiet, peaceful little museum to visit—9:30 to 5:30 Monday–Friday and 9 to 1 Sunday.

★ From the museum, it's a short walk via Paul Street to the *Church of Saints Peter and Paul,* which is a late 19th-century Gothic revival building in red sandstone.

★ Return to Patrick Street and follow it to a right turn which leads to Cornmarket Street and the open air *Coal Quay Market.* This flea market (open daily except Sunday) is interesting to visit, but not nearly as grand and colorful as it once was.

★ Go back to Patrick Street and follow it to the *Grand Parade,* which stretches to the South Mall. On the Grand Parade, you will find an entrance to the *English Market.* This is Cork's answer to Dublin's Moore Street Market (or what Moore Street used to be), only this one's roofed over with cast iron and glass. Fruits, vegetables, meat, and fish are available, and it's fascinating to watch the proceedings and listen to the intriguing Cork accents.

★ Continuing along the spacious Grand Parade, you will come to Washington Street on the right. Here you will see the *Holy Trinity Church,* which was erected in 1720 on the site of a medieval church, and the *Court House,* which was designed with Corinthian porticos and built in the mid-1800s. This area, known as *the Marsh,* is the oldest part of the city.

★ Backtracking a little, you'll notice, *North and South Main Streets* off Washington Street. At the ends of these streets once stood the main gates of the walled medieval city: North Gate Bridge and South Gate Bridge. Today they are lined with interesting food shops and fragrant bakeries. On South Main is the 18-century Protestant *Christ Church,* built on the ruins of another church that dated back to Norman days. This is thought to be the site of the marriage between English poet Edmund Spenser and his Irish bride, Elizabeth Boyle, in the 1500s. Off North Main Street is Adelaide Street, which leads to Henry Street and *Mercy Hospital,* built in the 18th century as the vast townhouse of the mayor of Cork. Its Sardinian architect, Davis Ducart, brought a strong Italian influence to its design, including the fine stucco-work ceiling to be seen in the lobby.

★ From here move around to *Bachelor's Quay,* which features some lovely Georgian homes and promenades.

★ Return to the Grand Parade via Washington Street, and pass the Berwick Fountain and the Cork Lending Library; at the Parade's end is the *National Monument* to the Irish patriots from the period 1798–1867, including Wolfe Tone, Thomas Davis, Michael Dwyer, and O'Neill Crowley. Nearby are some splendid examples of the bow-fronted houses of the 1700s.

★ As you leave the Grand Parade and move down the South Mall, you come to the memorial of the *Royal Munster Fusiliers,* heroes who fell to the Germans during the First World War. On the left is the main office of the *Allied Irish Bank,* whose six interior marble pillars are from the old St. Paul's Cathedral in London. Off to the right of the Mall is Father Matthew Street, leading to the *Father Matthew Memorial Church*—a Capuchin friars' church dating from the mid-1800s and commemorating Theobold Matthew for his strong leadership in the unpopular cause of temperance. Today he is hailed as one of the major Irishmen of the 19th century.

* Backtrack a little to Parliament Bridge, cross it, and turn to the right. Follow Sullivan's Quay, then Proby's Quay, to Bishop Street and *St. Finbarre's Cathedral*, which towers over the city. It occupies the site of the sixth-century church established by the city's patron saint. As a result of heavy damage in the Siege of 1690, the original church was razed and a new one erected in 1735. This was later replaced by the present fine French-Gothic church built between 1865 and 1880 from the designs of English architect William Burges (who designed the quadrangle at Yale University in New Haven, Connecticut). Its sweeping twin spires are its most notable feature, but the elaborate recessed doors and stained-glass window are also striking. On the heights behind the Cathedral is Elizabeth Fort, off Barrack Street, whose massive 17th-century walls remain.

* From the Cathedral walk directly back to Parliament Bridge; instead of crossing it, turn down Mary Street to the *South Chapel*, which is one of Cork's oldest parishes. Hidden among the houses here is the tower of the Augustinian *Red Abbey*. During the Siege of Cork in 1690, the Duke of Marlborough made the Abbey his headquarters and stationed a cannon on the tower so he could fire on the old city walls. From this point, it's a short walk back to Parliament Bridge and the South Mall, which will deliver you to the Grand Parade and Patrick Street with some fine shopping areas along the way (see Shopping).

* Lunch time is near, and the suggestion is the *Arbutus Lodge* in Montenotte on the city's north side, which you can explore afterward. Located on one of Cork's San Francisco-type hills, the Lodge gives a true perspective of the city. Details under Restaurants, but let's note here that it is expensive. Like Dublin's Le Coq Hardi, however, it is thought to be one of Ireland's finest. There is also a cheaper—and good—pub lunch here served at the bar or, on fine days, on a terrace overlooking the majestic sweep of Cork City below. Make reservations.

* If you're still of able body afterward, stroll down the very steep hill toward Patrick's Bridge, reminiscent of San Francisco and Boston; here you can sense the profound impact of the Irish immigrants on American development. The contours of the homeland were translated through community planning and architecture to the New World; in America, Ireland is never far away. This, as you walk down the hill, especially if you have Irish ancestors, is very moving. You can almost see the many desperate people who thronged through the city of Cork to the port town of Cobh from whence they sailed away—

leaving behind a world impoverished and oppressed by monarchy, giving up all for freedom. And yet so haunted were these people by their land that they refused to let their heritage die. And this is truly both America's gain and her reward.

★ From here, those interested in church architecture will have a field day. When you reach Patrick's Bridge, move along Camden Quay and follow it to Pope's Quay for the *Dominican Church*. This porticoed edifice was built in 1852 from a design by Cork's best-known architect, Kearns Deane. See the 14th-century carved ivory madonna inside.

★ Move on to Shandon Street which leads to *St. Mary's Pro-Cathedral* dating from 1808. After a fire in 1820, the interior was remodelled. Fine figures of 27 apostles and saints, as well as a relief of the Last Supper, may be seen here.

★ Follow Roman Street to Eason's Hill and turn right till you come to St. Anne's Church of Shandon, best known as the subject of the

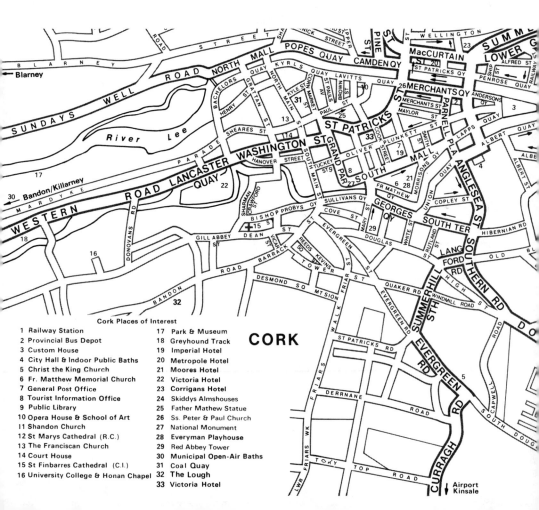

Cork Places of Interest

1 Railway Station	17 Park & Museum
2 Provincial Bus Depot	18 Greyhound Track
3 Custom House	19 Imperial Hotel
4 City Hall & Indoor Public Baths	20 Metropole Hotel
5 Christ the King Church	21 Moores Hotel
6 Fr. Matthew Memorial Church	22 Victoria Hotel
7 General Post Office	23 Corrigans Hotel
8 Tourist Information Office	24 Skiddys Almshouses
9 Public Library	25 Father Mathew Statue
10 Opera House & School of Art	26 Ss. Peter & Paul Church
11 Shandon Church	27 National Monument
12 St Marys Cathedral (R.C.)	28 Everyman Playhouse
13 The Franciscan Church	29 Red Abbey Tower
14 Court House	30 Municipal Open-Air Baths
15 St Finbarres Cathedral (C.I.)	31 Coal Quay
16 University College & Honan Chapel	32 The Lough
	33 Victoria Hotel

CORK

poem 'The Bells of Shandon' by Francis Sylvester Mahony (Father Prout) in the mid-19th century:

> *'Tis the bells of Shandon*
> *that sound so grand on*
> *The pleasant waters of the River Lee.*

The church was built between 1722 and 1726. Its fine square steeple (two sides in red sandstone, two in white limestone) with tiered top and weathervane is what many people remember when they are far from this city: the bells, clock, and weathervane of St. Anne's have come to represent Cork over the years. Father Prout's grave may be seen in the churchyard near the tower.

* In the late afternoon take a leisurely drive out past Cork Airport and south to Kinsale 18 miles away, where you should spend the night.

Note: There is an alternate route (L66 and L67) to Kinsale which is slightly longer and takes you through *Passage West,* a former dockyard town on a narrow passage of water which joins Cork Harbor and the sea. Here the first steamer to cross the Atlantic—the *Sirius*—set sail on its 18½-day voyage to America in 1838.

CORK'S HISTORY

Cork, from *Corcaigh*, meaning marsh, is Ireland's third largest city, with a population of 130,000 and a history that goes back to the sixth century. St. Finbarre established a church and school here in a marshy area on the south bank of the River Lee, and part of the city is still known as the Marsh. As the school developed and thrived over the next two centuries, a town grew up around it, until Norsemen sailed up the Lee in 820 and burned the village. A few years later, they returned to establish an exclusive fortified settlement between what are now the North and South Gate Bridges on the Lee. As time passed their exclusivity waned, and the Norsemen merged with the native Irish population. In 1172, when the city was invaded by the Anglo-Normans, Cork was basically a Danish fortress. But after the fierce invasion, the Normans won control and forced Dermot MacCarthy, the native chieftain of South Munster (of which Cork is a part), to marry a Norman woman. They also ordered him to pay homage to King Henry II of England, who established the fortress in Cork and gave the city its first charter. Eventually, as with the Danes, the Anglo-Norman inhabitants were assimilated by the Irish. British laws remained in nominal effect, but it was the edicts of Cork's wealthy businessmen that ruled as time went on. In fact, the citizens demanded and obtained an unusual degree of independence from British authority for the period. This was taken a step too far in 1492 when Perkin Warbeck, the pretender to the throne, visited Cork. The mayor and the leading citizens were taken with Warbeck, and the situation became a *cause célèbre* when they accompanied the Pretender to Kent and proclaimed him Richard IV, the true King of England. As a result, all were executed at Tyburn and Cork lost its charter.

In later years, when war broke out between King Charles I and parliament, Cork remained loyal to the throne. When Cromwell came along in 1649, the city surrendered to him peacefully. In 1690 King William III's army laid siege to Cork, and five days later the citizens found themselves surrendering their garrison once again. This time the army destroyed all walls and fortifications.

In the 19th century, Cork rebelled again against injustice. The Fenian movement began here in 1858 with the formation of The Irish Republican Brotherhood, whose sole purpose was to overthrow the British government in Ireland. The group was named after the *Fianna*, a legendary band of rovers whose only interests in life were warring and hunting. The Brotherhood was a major factor in Ireland's War of Independence from 1919 to 1921; during these years much of the city was burned to the ground and two of its mayors were killed.

Legend: Five miles north of Cork is the village of Blarney, which anyone with even a mild interest in Ireland has heard of. Kissing the Blarney Stone is a major item on the agendas of most Americans visiting Ireland, according to the Irish Tourist Board. It's questionable why it has assumed such importance, considering all that Ireland has to offer, but to say more than this would appear heretical in some circles. Blarney is, in fact, a pleasant village with a fine woolen factory and shop. And the surviving portion of Blarney

Castle, which houses the Stone, is a formidable example of an ancient fortification. Even more fascinating is its legend.

The castle was built in the 15th century and heralded as the strongest in all Munster, with walls that were over 18 feet thick and a gigantic square tower or keep with battlements 83 feet high. Originally it was a fortress for the powerful MacCarthy family. During the reign of Queen Elizabeth I, Cormac MacDermot MacCarthy was the Lord of Muskerry. He was both a procrastinator and a despiser of the throne. Time and again, the queen's Deputy, Carew, asked in her name that he refrain from the old practice of electing a chief of the clan and instead swear total alliegence to her. Using fair words, soft speech, and charm, MacCarthy lulled Carew, and months went by without the promised compliance. Elizabeth became so enraged that she made a laughingstock of her deputy. Carew responded to this by sending her yet another of MacCarthy's promises. She received this news upon rising early one morning and not in the best of spirits. Her reaction was to contort her face, shake her head wildly, and shriek 'B-l-a-h!' Then she crumpled the note and threw it across the room, shouting 'This is all blarney! What he says he never means!' From then on, Muskerry Castle became known as Blarney Castle, and its lord was the Lord of Blarney, which came to be defined as charming, lilting talk calculated to deceive but in a totally disarming way. The connection between this and the custom of the stone is a little cloudy, to say the least. One story has it that a stone bestowing the gift of heavenly oratory in return for a kiss was brought to Ireland from the Holy Land during the crusades and placed in the battlements of Muskerry Castle. This was embellished by the legend that MacCarthy later rescued from drowning a woman who turned out to be a witch, and who rewarded him by whispering the forgotten secret of the castle's magic stone.

To this day, it is said that if you kiss the stone you'll receive the gift of blarney. Blarney! But thousands of people still pay their admittance and climb the tower's 127 steps to do so. In the late 18th century, the Scottish novelist Sir Walter Scott visited here, and later Father Prout put the story to verse. If you choose to kiss the stone, you'll get a certificate verifying the fact! Open daily 9:30 A.M. to 8:30 P.M. and Sunday till 6—summer hours. Open only till 4 P.M. in wintertime.

Roots: In 1703 the castle was purchased by the Jeffreys family, whose descendants still own it.

LODGINGS

★ *The Arbutus Lodge,* Montenotte (northern hilly section of the city) (501237). This lodging boasts one of the highest-rated restaurants in Ireland—and it deserves its rating. But the accommodations are something special too. There are only 20 rooms (all with bath), fairly small but very cozy. And with each comes your own terry-toweling bathrobe and private wine/liquor chest with mixers. So after an exhausting day, you can draw a bath while savoring your favorite beverage, then drift down to a memorable meal—of which see details in Restaurants. Major credit cards. Expensive.

★ *Ballymaloe,* Shanagarry (about 20 miles from Cork City) (62531). This truly old Irish house has its roots in several pasts. The main part of the house dates from the 17th century. Another section consists of a 14th-century Norman tower that was once part of a castle owned by the Fitzgerald family.

An archaeological dig on the grounds here produced elk antlers preserved in bog which date from around 15,000 B.C.; they now hang over the front door. William Penn was so fond of Ballymaloe that he made several visits before sailing away to America to found Pennsylvania. Even Oliver Cromwell dropped by for a leisurely respite from his stormy life. Ghosts are said to haunt Ballymaloe, but none of the wretched types rumored to linger around places like Kytler's Inn in Kilkenny. These are said to be very pleasant, unbothersome ghosts who think of Ballymaloe as a paradise on earth and miss it too much to leave it forever. And it's easy to see why. Besides the lovely house and courtyard with its 28 comfortable guest rooms (22 with bath), there are 400 acres to this medieval farm estate, including verdant lawns, beautiful floral terraces, and peaceful rolling farmland. Other features include a swimming pool, golf course (9-hole), tennis court, and trout pond. And we still haven't mentioned the food. Because this is still a working farm, all the ingredients are grown or raised here—vegetables, spices, fruits, meats, and even some of the fish. (See Restaurants for more about this wonder.) Major credit cards. Moderate.

* *Corrigan's* MacCurtain Street (501620). Very inexpensive old hotel with just 20 rooms, none with private bath. Centrally located.

* *Imperial Hotel*, South Mall (965333), is Cork's grande dame. On a par with Dublin's Shelbourne Hotel, it ranks with the finest of the old days. Now 80 rooms with 80 baths—but it still retains its distinguished heritage, which goes back to the 1700s. Well worth its moderate to expensive cost.

* *Jury's*, Western Road (966377), is Cork's best modern hotel with 140 rooms, all with bath, TV, and phones; heated pool, saunas, and a gym for exercise fans. For all its modernity, the hotel still has a pleasant Irish ring to it—similar to Jury's in Dublin. Expensive.

* *Longueville House,* Mallow (about 22 miles from Cork) (27156). There would be more than enough justification for staying at this Georgian manor house in the restaurant alone. But happily, there's so much more. If you're at all romantically inclined, this splendid estate set out on a hill overlooking the rich Blackwater River Valley is a must. Whether sipping a drink in front of a carved wood fireplace in a sitting room elegantly appointed with antique (but comfortable) furniture, or having coffee at twilight in the conservatory, or strolling by moonlight some of the 500 acres of grounds, you'll experience peace and pleasure. Try for one of the front antique-furnished bedrooms, from which you can look down the sweep of hill and across to the spectacular ruins of Dromineen Castle, the ancient home of the O'Callaghan family, overlooking the Blackwater River. The castle is flanked on either side by majestic oak trees planted in the formation of the English and French battle lines at Waterloo. Watching a sunset over this area is unforgettable.

The Longueville manor house was built in 1720 by the Longfield family on land granted by Cromwell, who had snatched it from its original owners, the O'Callaghan family, when he attacked Dromineen Castle in the 1600s. When Richard Longfield was dubbed Baron Longueville in 1795, he promptly dropped the house's Gaelic name, *Garamaconey,* in favor of Longueville House. Shortly after, he was named a Viscount for his support of the British Act of Union and received a huge sum of money as compensation for his loss of a parliamentary seat. Spurred by the money and the pride of his titles, he set to work renovating in the splendid Georgian tradition. Two enormous wings were added on either side of the house, along with the marvelous stone parapets and the pillared porch. Other features still to be seen today are the dramatic half-door entrance with its fanlight, the Portland-stone-floored entrance hall, the ornately decorated plasterwork ceilings, the white marble Adam fireplace with its carved relief of Neptune, the massive inlaid mahogany doors, and the grand staircase. In 1866 a genteel Victorian conservatory was added, complete with a wrought iron facade and curved glass panels. The house also has a collection of antique Irish silver, old Waterford chandeliers, excellent paintings of Irish patriots and presidents, and some memorable landscapes, including a stunning pastoral of haystacks and limegreen fields.

The fascinating thing about Longueville is that after years of displacement the O'Callaghan family remained attached to its beautiful landscapes (some say the finest in the country). Senator William O'Callaghan, the father of the present owner, purchased the property back from its illegal heirs in 1938. The Senator's son, Michael, and his charming wife, Jane, have turned the estate into one of Ireland's most romantic homesteads, complete with its own vineyard and farm. And the O'Callaghans truly love the tourist business. They care about the people who stop at Longueville. Overheard: 'Let me give you a good map of Cork and be sure to follow it. We've seen people head off there and with all the bloody one-way streets, they haven't been heard of since. . . . You've got all that planned for today? Oh, that's far too much. And this place isn't even there anymore. Let's sit down and plan out an itinerary. You're wasting too much time with this.'

The produce for the dining room's splendid cuisine is all from the Longueville farm, including some of the wines. Mrs. O'Callaghan engineers the cooking and the preparation of preserves, honey, and sausages. And this is only a sneak preview; see Restaurants for the full details. *No* credit cards accepted. Moderate.

Legend: There are those in Ireland who believe that a member of the O'Callaghan family from Dromineen Castle discovered America before Columbus. As evidence, they point to the transcript of a diary which is now housed in the archives of the Maynooth (a suburb of Dublin) Library. Purportedly written by an O'Callaghan in America in the years before Columbus, it contains a detailed account of his earlier life in Dromineen. Found by members of an Indian tribe, the original is said to have circulated among various educational institutions, where at some point a transcript was made. The original is now thought to be at an American university, and a search continues.

* *Metropole*, MacCurtain Street (508122). Another of Cork's beautiful old hotels, this is a handsome red-brick Victorian structure, but the whole interior has been modernized. There are 125 rooms, all with direct-dial phones and color TV; 100 rooms have baths. Centrally located on the north bank. Moderate.

* *Moore's*, Morrison's Island. (227361). It's centrally located, has 35 cozy, comfortable rooms, 31 with bath. Moderately expensive.

RESTAURANTS

* *The Arbutus Lodge*, Montenotte (northern hill section of the city) (501237). The Arbutus dining room remains one of the finest for French cuisine in Ireland. A sampling of the wonders appearing on the extensive menu include:

Arbutus Lodge

sautéed lobster with fresh fennel, sea bass with Pernod sauce, ris de veau in a lemon/cream shallot sauce (succulent), medallions of venison with fried aubergine, wine-poached sole and turbot, beef ribs in a Beaujolais and marrow sauce, and a delicious vegetable platter for vegetarians. You'll find it hard to make a selection in this Victorian room that's a kind of Irish Paris. The wine list is exhaustive—and the prices (in many cases) are far below those of Dublin. The view is spectacular, conjuring thoughts of a European San Francisco. L—1 to 2 (can be a little hectic if it's busy—but still worth it). D—7 to 9:15 (very leisurely). Closed Sundays. Expensive. Major credit cards.

* *The Yeats Room of Ballymaloe House,* Shanagarry, about 20 miles from Cork City (652531), boasts some of the best paintings of Jack Yeats, brother of William Butler Yeats. The food served in this ancient house is remarkably good, mainly because it is all farm-grown locally (except for the fish which comes from the nearby Ballycotton Bay). Fish chowder, wonderfully fresh crudités, hot crab pâté are suggested starters. Main courses include lobster served in the shell, casserole of roast pork with mustard sauce, crisp duckling, roast ribs of beef Béarnaise, rack of lamb, and tarragon calve's liver sautéed in whiskey. The desserts are equally fine and all freshly baked. Full license. L—1 to 2. D—7 to 9:30. Expensive.

* *Bianconi Grill,* Pembroke Street off the South Mall, is a dark paneled restaurant, comfortable and quiet, which offers sandwiches, curries, salads, shepherd's pies, plus snacks. Open 10 A.M. to midnight. Inexpensive.

* *Cafe de Paris,* Queen's Old Garden Shopping Centre, The Grand Parade (962426). This very pleasant restaurant is another that will turn your thoughts

to the Continent. With its gentle background music, its sepia prints of Paris, its excellent French staff and cuisine, you could be in Montparnasse instead of Cork. Quiche, fish, game, fowl, cheese, and delicious desserts from which to choose. Wines are available at very reasonable prices. Open 9 A.M. (Continental breakfast of freshly baked croissants) to midnight. Closed Sunday lunch. Inexpensive to moderate.

* *La Duchesse of the Imperial Hotel,* South Mall (965333), is an intimate rendezvous-type restaurant that offers both elegance and live (but subdued) piano music nightly. The French cuisine is good. L—12:30 to 2:30. D—6 to 9:30. Closed Sunday and Monday. Expensive.

* *The Pembroke Grill of the Imperial Hotel,* South Mall (965333). A fast-food grill that's very popular and offers fresh, tasty beef, lamb, and pork dishes along with meat sandwiches. Hearty breakfast also served. B—7 to 10. L—12:30 to 2:30. D—6 to 10:30. Moderate.

* *The Fastnet Restaurant in Jury's Hotel,* Western Road (966377), is similar to the Kish in Jury's Dublin, with its pavilion complex overlooking an indoor/outdoor swimming pool and garden. The food is good, but not as good as the Dublin location's. D—6:30 to 11 (10 on Sunday). Expensive.

* *The Glandore Room of Jury's Hotel,* Western Road (966377), is a less expensive version of the Fastnet but with equally good food, both meat and fish dishes. Breakfast is also served here. Open 7:30 A.M. to 11 P.M. (10 on Sunday). Moderate.

* *Longueville House,* Mallow, about 22 miles from Cork City (27156). This grand Georgian dining room is decorated with portraits of Irish presidents, and its tables are adorned with some of the finest food in the country. The creamy salmon mousse pâté is so delicious that you're addicted immediately. Jane O'Callaghan is responsible for this addiction, as she is for so many others. For entrees, you'll be forced to choose from free-range crispy duckling, escalop of salmon in cibolette (chive) sauce, roast leg of Longueville lamb and rack of lamb (the finest in the country), heavenly black sole on the bone, succulent pink trout baked in herbs, veal in Stilton sauce (very rewarding on a chilly night), veal kidney in mustard sauce, poached salmon hollandaise, pickled oxtongue, apple-stuffed roast pork, fresh turbot in prawn sauce, prawns in garlic butter, and veal sweetbreads in wine sauce. Not to mention the Veal Terrine, the avocado with prawn filling, the farm-fresh vegetable soup, the equally fresh Blackwater trout, and the monktail salad with artichoke hearts. Desserts are also superior, often incorporating the farm's own fruits; cheeses are pleasing too. And for breakfast, there are specially prepared honey, jams, sausages, and breads. This is a memorable place, partly because Jane darts off in slow season to bone up at places like London's Cordon Bleu and the French Moulin de Mougins, while her husband Michael travels in search of new wines. (This consummate wine buff has his own vineyard on the Longueville estate.) The prediction: Once you've spent an evening here, you may well want to revise your itinerary so you can stay longer. D—7 to 8:30. Closed Sunday and Monday to non-residents. Full license. No credit cards. Expensive, but well worth it.

* *Lovett's,* Churchyard Lane off Well Road, Douglas—Cork suburbs (294909). French cuisine, especially seafood, is served in this grand Georgian-period house owned by Dermot Lovett. L—12:45 to 1:45. D—7:30 to 9:45. Wine license. Major credit cards. Closed Saturday lunch and all day Sunday. Expensive.

* *Mary Rose's,* Savoy Centre, Patrick Street (507766), offers snacks and light meals in the lobby of a converted movie theater. Open noon to 9 P.M. Inexpensive.

* *Murphs,* Savoy Centre, Patrick Street (504059). Seafood, hamburgers, steaks and salads are the order of the day at this cousin of the Dublin Murphs. Located in what was once the mezzanine of an old movie house, it attracts a rather young crowd. It also offers American beer, in case you're missing it. Open noon to midnight. Closed Sunday and bank holidays. Full license. Inexpensive.

* *The Oyster Tavern,* Market Lane off Patrick Street (22716). This is a very popular steak house that also has good seafood. But you may have to wait a while at the bar before you're seated. Open 12:30 P.M. to 10:30 P.M. Full license. AE, Diners, Visa, Master. Moderate.

* *The Pavilion,* Patrick Street (509059). Everything from snacks to full meals is offered in this self-service restaurant that was once the balcony of a movie theater. Especially good are the steaks and chicken. Open 10 A.M. to 7:30 P.M. Closed Sunday and bank holidays. Full license. Inexpensive.

* *Upstairs Downstairs,* Oliver Plunkett Street (24752). Morning coffee, light lunches, snacks, afternoon tea, light evening meals, both meat and seafood. Open 9:30 A.M. to 11:30 P.M. Closed Sunday all day, Monday night, and bank holidays. Full license. Visa, Master. Inexpensive to moderate.

PUBS

* *The Gateway,* Barrack Street, is across the river on the south side near the old Fort Elizabeth. It's the oldest pub in Cork, going back to the early 1600s when such notables as the Duke of Marlborough imbibed in its dusky clime.

* *Le Chateau,* Patrick Street, established in 1793, is a grand old Cork bar a little reminiscent of Dublin's Davy Byrnes—but with less panache.

* *The Old Bridge Tavern,* Patrick Street, now has tasty grills, full meals, and fine carvery roasts. It's one of Cork's old standbys, with a very masculine decor.

* *Rearden's Cellar Bar,* Washington Street, was a popular 1800s haunt and remains so today. Not a cellar at all, its wine-keg and wooden-stool bar attracts the legal profession from the Cork Court House across the street. Some very good pub-food luncheons at very reasonable prices.

* *Shandon Tavern,* Lavitt's Quay, notable for inexpensive pub food.

SHOPPING

* James Mangan, Patrick Street. Crystal, pottery, silver and jewelry—all Irish style—in this elegant and stately old Cork establishment.

* Cash's Department Store, Patrick Street, stresses Irish crafts, crystal, clothing in a setting comparable to Dublin's famed Brown Thomas.

* Queens Old Castle Shopping Centre, Grand Parade and Patrick Street, once a department store, now converted to Cork's finest and most interesting shopping mall, where you'll see all the Irish crafts and find a lovely French/Irish cafe—Cafe de Paris. Worth some time.

* Savoy Centre, Patrick Street, is a strange mixture of past and present. The past—the old 1930s Savoy movie house; the present—it's been converted into a maze of shops and restaurants. Here find some special Irish craft shops.

* Saville, Oliver Plunkett Street. Fine men's wear.

Sailing in Cork Harbour

* Antiques. Cork has a fine selection of shops. The antique market on Tuckey Street is a good place to start. Notable here is Parade Antiques, with everything from furniture to silver, old brass, fine porcelain, and old English/Irish jewelry. Also noteworthy are the many antique shops on the little side streets crisscrossing between Patrick Street and the South Mall: fine old silver and jewelry to be found here. Also check out Marlboro Antiques on Marlboro Street.

SPORTS

For those on longer stays, there's an abundance of golf courses, fantastic sailing in Cork Harbour, riding, running (many experienced runners love to accept the challenge of the Cork hills). Spectator: Hurling and Gaelic at Páirc Uí Chaoimh Stadium, Marina Walk; Rugby and soccer, University Grounds, Mardyke Walk. Check *Cork Examiner* for times.

ENTERTAINMENT/ANNUAL EVENTS

* The Cork Choral Festival is held in May and draws choirs from many Western countries.
* The Cork Jazz Festival, held in late October, is a relatively new but popular event.
* The Opera House, Emmet Place (20022), stages operas and ballets by the Irish Ballet Company.
* The Everyman Playhouse, Father Matthew Street (26287), emphasizes Irish plays.

* The Entertainment Centre, Grand Parade in back of the Irish Tourist Board office (23251) does lunchtime theater during July and August. Monday through Friday, one-act plays by Irish writers. A light lunch is served from 12:45; performance from 1:10. Very inexpensive.

The Centre also presents an evening program Monday through Friday during July and August. Different events each night include: *Oíche Chéilí*—an evening of Irish music and dance in which the audience rises to perform with the cast; *seisiún*—lively program of Irish traditional music, folk music, and ballads; *rinceoil chorcaí*—traditional musicians play a wide range of Irish music and do some *ceili* dancing. Curtain is at 8:30 or 9, depending on the program. Phone in advance. Very inexpensive.

* The Mall Room, Imperial Hotel (965333), holds folklore discussions June through August, Tuesday and Thursday, 5:30 to 6:30.

* Mr. Bojangles, The Savoy Centre, Patrick Street, is a popular night club for with-it youth and hopeful middleagers.

Literature: Frank O'Connor, the famous short-story writer: Shandon Hill and Blarney Street (where he was born), Summerhill and environs on the north side. Sean O'Faolain, another notable short-story writer: Half Moon Street, his birthplace, and the Flats (city center). English author William Makepeace Thackeray, Grattan's Hill (where he and his mother-in-law composed *Vanity Fair*).

Roots: McCarthy (Blarney Castle); Matthew (Father Matthew Statue, Patrick Street, and Church, Father Matthew Street); Mahony (Shandon Church); Fitzgerald (Fitzgerald Park, Cork, and Ballymaloe House, Shanagarry); O'Callaghan (Longueville House and Dromineen Castle, Mallow); plus a strong showing for the names O'Sullivan, Murphy, O'Brien, O'Donovan, O'Connor, Regan, Walsh, O'Leary, Collins, Crowley, O'Connell, O'Driscoll, Buckley, Daly, and Barry.

VII.   KINSALE AND ENVIRONS

Kinsale Harbour

And the sea went down, so that there was a bright fair calm; and there came a warbling of unknown birds.

—from the Celtic, 14th or 15th century

YOUR PERSONALIZED KINSALE TO KENMARE
ITINERARY

This 92-mile journey begins with an optional overnight in Kinsale
and takes you thence through Clonakilty, Rosscarbery, Skibbereen,
Ballydehob, Bantry, and Glengarriff to Kenmare. If the Beara Peninsula is included, the trip becomes 142 miles.

Day One

   * Arrive Kinsale early evening and check into your hotel. *The Blue
Haven* is a strong suggestion, if available. If not, try *Acton's,* or one
of the other listings under Lodgings.
   * Now comes the hard part: Kinsale is considered Ireland's gourmet
paradise. And justly so, even though the whole country is now moving
in this direction (which was definitely not the case in the past). Again,
the suggestion is the *Blue Haven,* but there are other very good dining
places under Restaurants. Some prefer a kind of restaurant crawl,
analogous to a pub crawl: an appetizer or two here, an entree or two
there. It's advisable to starve yourself in advance, unless you plan
to diet later on. But don't miss out on an excellent dinner here, and
perhaps a pub or two.

Day Two

   * Breakfast at your lodgings, check out.
   * Stroll around Kinsale village, which is easily covered within a
short time. *The Church of St. Multrose* is worth noticing, a 12th-cen-
tury building, on Church Street with a dramatic tower and a handsome
transept. The ominous English pillory is preserved here. Then there's
the *Carmelite Friary* on Friar's Street, a 14th-century edifice. Legend
has it that somewhere underground in this area is a secret passage
leading back to St. Multrose, said to have concealed Irish activists.
Desmond Castle on Cork Street was once known as the French prison,
because this 16th-century townhouse was used to imprison the French
during the Napoleonic wars. Today it's a museum housing Kinsale
memorabilia. While you're strolling, notice the lovely old stone Georgian buildings as well. Within easy walking distance of the town, but
across the Bandon River, is *James' Fort,* a key point in the attempt
of James II to recover the crown from William of Orange after the
Battle of the Boyne.

* Prepare to depart for Clonakilty in your journey to Kenmare, the southern start of the Ring of Kerry. There are approximately 92 miles to go. After Clonakilty comes Rosscarbery and then Skibbereen. The latter was the scene of many deaths during the terrible 19th-century potato famine. The coastal scenery around this area is especially attractive.

* At this point, you might like to stop at *Liss Ard House Hotel* (a Georgian mansion set in 70 acres of parkland) for a light meal. Open from noon, it specializes in fresh seafoods. AE, Visa, Master. Inexpensive to moderate.

* On to Ballydehob, then inland and northward to *Bantry*—a total of 26 miles. In 1689 Bantry was stormed from its harbor by the French in their attempt to join the Catholic James II in his battle with William of Orange. The French instigated another invasion in 1796, but were eventually dispersed by sea storms. The first Governor General of the Irish Free State, Tim Healy, was born here in 1855.

Bantry is a pleasant little seaside village surrounded by peaceful hills and with a fine harbor. Beside the town and at the head of the bay is the stately mansion *Bantry House*. Built in the mid-18th century, the south front was added so the earls could expand their splendid collection of tapestries and European artwork. This stone-and-red-brick structure is considered one of Ireland's finest historic houses and is open from 9 A.M. to 6 P.M. daily (open till 8 P.M. in spring and summer). Inexpensive and truly rewarding. If you haven't eaten, there's a tearoom here that's open from 10 A.M. to 6 P.M.

* Drive the 11 miles to Glengarriff or *Gleann Garbh,* which is Gaelic for Rugged Glen. The village is located in a glen that was once surrounded by sheer rock. All that has changed through forestation, and now oaks, pines, elms, holly, yew, floral arbutus, and fuschia abound here. Glengarriff's harbor is protected by mountains and hills and is one of the most beautiful in the west of Ireland. This is a wonderful area for water sports, running, and walking. Be sure to take the two-minute pathway walk west of the post office to see *Poulgorm* (Blue Pool) Cove.

Note: For those with plenty of time, the route west of here—the L61—leads you through the majestic Healy Pass, named for Tim Healy (mentioned above), and to the spectacular Beara Peninsula. You can cut all the way across the pass to Laragh and up to Kenmare (your destination for the evening), seeing the whole of Beara from the mountainous heights of the Pass. Or you can double back halfway across the Pass and do the full circle of the Beara Peninsula, a distance of 67 miles from Glengarriff to Kenmare. If you take this route, you'll pass through Castletownbere on the sweeping southwestern tip of the peninsula. About two miles from the town are the ruins of *Dunboy Castle,* the fortress of the O'Sullivan Bere family who were lords of Bere. They were the last in the Munster region to hold out for the forces of Philip of Spain, in the hope that he would save the land from the dreaded British rule. But in 1602 their castle was reduced to rubble for their refusal to surrender to the British. Off to the left here is Bere Island where there are two Martello towers, built at the time of Napoleon when Ireland expected to be invaded by that ambitious ruler.

Legend: This part of the country is said in folklore to be the land of fertility, perhaps because it is one of the warmest, most tropical areas. Paganism was reputedly rampant here, with sexual exploits at their wildest. In later times, a voluptuous Spanish princess, whose father was plotting with the Irish nationals to free Ireland of the British, fell madly in love with an Irish warrior prince. Her name was Beara and his, Eogan. At the dawn of Irish history, this couple lived one of Ireland's most passionate love stories. Their union reportedly produced the ancestors of the nation's strongest freedom fighters. The peninsula later became known as Beara, after the beautiful Spanish princess.

★ If time is a limiting factor, it is possible to take the most direct route from Glengarriff to Kenmare—the N-71—a distance of 17 miles.

Roots: Healy (Bantry and Healy Pass); O'Sullivan (Dunboy Castle, Castletownbere); Lynch (a common name in the area, including one scandalous representative named Eliza Lynch, an alleged native who zipped off to even more heated climes and became the lover of the dictator of Paraguay in the early 19th century).

KINSALE'S HISTORY

Kinsale or *Ceann Saile,* meaning Head of the Tide, is an exceptionally attractive old European community set into the slopes and furrows of Compass Hill, overlooking the Bandon River estuary and its short rush to the sea. On a warm summer's day, with its ancient whitewashed stone buildings and the deep blue waters at its feet, Kinsale takes on a Mediterranean air. It is thought that the town was first settled by the Anglo-Normans around 1177. Edward III granted Kinsale its first charter in 1334, and the settlement so prospered that it became one of the chief ports of the English Navy until the 18th century, when its docking area became too small to keep up with the vast trade expansions and larger ports drew ahead of it.

The years of prosperity were not trouble-free, however. Trade was frequently disrupted by pirates. Then there was the big siege of Kinsale, 1601–02, when the Spanish forces took over the walled town. Upon hearing this, the Irish forces under the leadership of the Earl of Tyrone and the Earl of Tyrconnell (Red Hugh O'Donnell and Hugh O'Neill) rushed down from the north to lend the Spanish their support. But 12,000 Englishmen under Lord Mountjoy and Lord Carew overwhelmed the Spanish and repossessed the town, forcing the Irish earls to flee to the European mainland to save their necks. This marked the last attempt of the medieval chiefs to withstand British tyranny. After this, the English ejected all Irish from the walled town, a ban that was enforced until the late 18th century. James II made his last feeble attempts to recover the throne from William of Orange in Kinsale after the Battle of the Boyne; in 1691 he fled from here to France in defeat.

KINSALE LODGINGS

* *Acton's Hotel,* Cork Road (72135), is a modern but somewhat disappointing grade-A hotel. Its lobby, along with some of its 59 rooms (38 with bath) are on the gloomy side. But it does have the advantage of overlooking spectacular Kinsale Harbor. Moderate.

* *The Blue Haven Hotel,* Pearse Street (72209), is one of those cozy old places that people just love. There are only 12 rooms (just one with bath). The Tourist Board gives it a B*, and it's centrally located in the village. Another advantage of staying here is that it has a wonderful restaurant and pub (see Restaurant). Inexpensive to moderate.

* *The Folk House,* Guardwell (72328). Old, pleasant place with equally pleasant bar. There are 18 rooms, none with bath. A B rating from the Tourist Board. Full license. Inexpensive to moderate.

* *.Trident Hotel,* Kinsale Harbor (72301). Very modern, almost motel-like. Overlooking the harbor, it has 40 rooms with bath. Moderate.

* *Perryville House,* Long Quay. (72731). An old Regency townhouse with a special dining place—The Four Seasons (see Restaurants). There are 10 rooms, all with bath. Full license. Inexpensive to moderate.

RESTAURANTS

* *Acton's Hotel,* Cork Road (72135), specializes in good fresh seafood. Open L—12:30 to 2:30. D—7 to 9. AE, Diners, Carte Blanche. Moderate.

* *The Bistro,* Guardwell (72470). An intimate candlelit restaurant that emphasizes its elegance and its original oils. Tasty international cuisine includes, oysters, mussels, black sole, salmon, fish casserole poached in white wine, rabbit Provencal braised in red wine, roast quail with juniper berries, steak filet stuffed with fresh oysters and flambéed in cognac. Open 7:30 to 10:30 P.M. Closed Monday and bank holidays. Wine license. Visa, Master.

* *The Blue Haven,* Pearse Street (72209) When Bloomingdales, New York, planned its huge Irish promotion in the fall of 1981, Brian and Anne Cronin, owners of this fine establishment, were wisely chosen to do a presentation of Irish cuisine. Start with the seafood pancake, the smoked mackerel and salmon pâté, the creamy shellfish chowder, or the fresh soup of the day. Then you can choose from poached salmon hollandaise, filet of brill with shrimps and capers, shellfish casserole, sole stuffed with mussels and shrimps. In the meat area, you'll relish sautéed beef with mead sauce, fileted chicken in Irish whiskey, mushroom, and cream sauce, steak au poivre with brandy sauce. And for dessert try the coupe Blue Haven—a mixture of assorted homemade ice creams, fresh fruits, grated chocolate, and whipped cream. The restaurant is small and intimate, and the oak-paneled bar has a fine fireplace. L—12:30 to 3. D—7 to 10:30. Full license. Visa, Master. Moderate to expensive.

* *The Four Seasons* in Perryville House, Long Quay (72731). This Georgian restaurant prides itself on basic Irish beef dishes and fresh seafood. Open 7 to 11:30 P.M. All major credit cards.

* *Man Friday,* Scilly (72260). A wonderfully romantic candlelit restaurant with stone and pine walls. Its seafood dishes are highly recommended. Try the prawn dishes or the turbot. Open 7:30 to 10:50. Closed Sunday. Wine license. Visa, Master. Moderate.

* *Max's Wine Bar,* Main Street (72443). A tiny beamed cottage with an open fireplace, offering homemade soups, quiche, salads of prawn and crab, filet steaks, Stroganoff. L—12:30 to 2:30. D—7:30 to 11. Closed Tuesday. Wine license. Inexpensive to moderate.

* *Skipper's Restaurant,* Lower O'Connell Street (72664). Another fine seafood restaurant, especially for salmon, prawns, lobster, mussels. Open 7:30 to midnight. Closed Monday. Wine license. Major credit cards. Moderate.

* *The Vintage,* Main Street (72502), is another tiny cottage-type restaurant. Neat, clean, tucked away from the world. The baked crab appetizer is a worthy starter, or the mussel soup. A sampling of the entrees: sweetbreads with oysters, veal with sausages, monkfish in blackberry butter sauce, roast leg of lamb served with a jug of herb juices. Open 7 to 10:30. Closed Tuesday and Wednesday. Wine license. Visa, Master. Moderate to expensive.

PUBS

* *The Folk House,* Guardwell, is a pleasant, dark, woody old place abounding in chat and story telling.

* *The Shanakee,* Guardwell, is a lively spot across the street from the Bistro restaurant with traditional music Monday and Saturday nights.

* *The Spaniard,* edge of village, is a very popular fisherman's pub overlooking Kinsale Harbor with beamed ceilings, fishing nets, and other atmospheric touches. Good conversation here, and occasionally professional Irish singing groups drop by for a spontaneous sing-song. Pub food available.

* *The Stowaway Bar,* Kinsale, is a clean, cozy little place that offers inexpensive curry dishes.

SHOPS

* J. Cronin, Commercial Hall, for Kilkenny stonewear, Mullingar pewter, Kilkenny design dishware, Irish crystal, rugs, mohair shawls, sweaters, sheepskins, turf ornaments, Kinsale T-shirts and sweaters.

* The Craft Shop, Commercial Hall (across the street from Cronin's), has a large selection of Irish crafts, particularly pottery.

* Angling Center, Pearse Street (next to the Blue Haven Hotel) for rental of fishing equipment.

ENTERTAINMENT

* The Kinsale Gourmet Food Festival is a very popular event held each year in early October. Book well in advance.

VIII.   KENMARE AND THE RING OF KERRY

Kerry Cliffs

The loveliness of the place to which we had come was unbounded.

—14th century ballad

YOUR PERSONALIZED KENMARE ITINERARY

Day One

* Check into your lodgings in the late afternoon. The strong suggestion here is the truly elegant *Park Hotel,* situated on a hill overlooking Kenmare Bay just outside the village. Expensive, but it's worth it. See *Lodgings* for details.

* Dine in the impressive old dining room of the *Park Hotel* even if you aren't staying here.

* After dinner, stroll around the hotel's beautiful 11-acre grounds. Then perhaps come back via the French doors to the charming bar or the sitting room for an after-dinner drink. If time permits, you might then like to take a walk in the pleasant little village. But the suggestion here is to leave it till morning and just have a relaxing evening where you are—the Park Hotel is well worth your time.

Day Two

* Eat at your lodgings and check out.

* Prepare to tour the Ring of Kerry, starting in Kenmare and ending in Killarney—a distance of 88 miles of scenic beauty. (Note: A Ring itinerary follows). You will spend the next night in Killarney.

LODGINGS

* *The Park Hotel,* outskirts of town overlooking Kenmare Bay (41200), is truly one of Ireland's most beautiful hotels. From its majestic stone exterior commanding a verdant sweep of hills overlooking the sea to the splendor of its richly furnished interior, you'll go far to find its peer in Ireland, America, or anywhere else for that matter. Built in 1897, the hotel now has more period furniture and oils (in both bedrooms and public rooms) than most museums. Yet there is no museum stuffiness here. The French doors are often open to the gentle, refreshing bay breezes. And the place is immaculate, even to the public restrooms (which also house beautiful antiques). The bar and sitting rooms are so charming you'll hate leaving them. The dining room's food is as appealing as the view (see Restaurants). There are 50 rooms, all with bath. You might like to try for one with a mahogany four-poster bed. But whatever you do, take time to enjoy the antiques and paintings. A stroll of the grounds (at least some of the 11 acres) is a must. Just about every sport imaginable may be found in the near vicinity. Very expensive—but what a way to live.

* *Kenmare Bay Hotel,* Sneem Road (28180), is a modern grade-A hotel with 100 rooms, all with bath and phone. Inexpensive to moderate.

* *Riversdale House,* just outside Kenmare overlooking Macgillicuddy's Reeks mountain range (41200), has 40 rooms, 30 with bath. Inexpensive.

Kerry Sunset

If you are economizing, try the very inexpensive Lansdowne Arms or the Wander Inn—both Grade B.

RESTAURANTS

⋆ *The Park Hotel,* outskirts of Kenmare overlooking Kenmare Bay (41200), is everything you could possibly want in dining. The twilight sea spread out beneath velvety hills is the view from your window table, a fit setting for the dinner in store. Guests grow lyrical about the crabmeat salads, veal sweetbreads, poached turbot with salmon stuffing, lamb salads, seafood in light lime sauce, beef entrecote in red wine sauce. Enjoy. L—1 to 2. D—7 to 9. Full license. All major credit cards. Expensive.

⋆ *The Purple Heather,* Henry Street (41016) is a small elegant cafe offering wonderful seafood specialties. All served in a comfortable bar setting. L—12:30 to 2:30. D—6 to 8:30.

⋆ Two other popular dining places in Kenmare are the *Pantry* on Main Street (good, cheap light lunches, open all day) and the *Old Dutch Bistro,* Henry Street, (steaks, Dutch and German foods, light lunches). Open 12:30 to 11:30 P.M.

SPECIAL EVENTS

⋆ Town Fair held on Main Street every Monday during the summer. The bargain here is Irish handknit sweaters sold at far less (20%) than the usual prices.

⋆ The Fruits of the Sea Festival held here every September is said to rival Kinsale's Gourmet Festival.

Staigue Fort

YOUR PERSONALIZED RING ITINERARY

* Start in Kenmare (*An Neidin,* which is Gaelic for Little Nest). This beguiling village, set where the Roughty River flows into the Kenmare estuary and eventually Kenmare Bay, is surrounded by some of the finest hills and mountains in Kerry. In and around the town are several key historical points.

* *Cromwell's Fort* is at the northern end of New Bridge and was held by English troops during the Cromwellian wars.

* *Cromwell's Bridge* is a footbridge across the River Finnehy. A short distance northwest of the town, it was built to provide access to St. Mary's Holy Well north of the bridge.

* *The Druid's Circle* is nearby in the area known as the Shrubberies. It consists of 15 vertical stones with a diameter of 50 feet. At its center is a dolmen (a megalithic tomb topped with a roofing or capstone).

* *St. Finan's Holy Well* nearby has a reputation for healing those suffering from both physical and mental anguish. Here too are the ruins of the ancient St. Finan's Church.

For the active, there's swimming in sheltered coves west of the town. Excellent fishing in both the rivers (brown trout and salmon) and the sea. There's also a nine-hole golf course, and if you're a runner or a cyclist, any part of the Ring will provide you with a thrilling (but often very strenuous) course.

* As you leave Kenmare and move along the Ring road toward Sneem, you will be following the beautiful Kenmare estuary toward its seaward connection. Across the river are the stalwart Caha and Slieve Miskish Mountain Ranges; on the right are the mountains of Letter South and Knockanaskill. On this route are several medieval castles. The first is *Dunkerron Castle,* with Dunkerron Island just opposite it in the estuary. Then there's *Cappanacuss Castle,* where the O'Sullivan family once resided. After the village of Tahilla, located at the mouth of Coongar Harbor, comes *Derryquin Castle* with the little island of Rossdohan opposite it.

After passing through Sneem, another charming little village surrounded by mountains with a church dating from Elizabethan times, you will come to one of Ireland's most enchanting vacation spots: *Parknasilla.* The scenery of this area, where the Kenmare River meets the sea, has everything from mountains and unspoiled forests to islands, sea views, and riverscapes. Because of its location on the Gulf

Stream, you'll find tropical flora and—believe it or not—palm trees. Even the winter months are mild here.

Many visitors are so taken by Parknasilla that they decide to stay on and cut back on the rest of their itinerary. And who could blame them, in view of the region's ideal facilities for swimming, waterskiing, boating, sailing, running, golfing, fishing, tennis, riding, and pony-trekking. Beautiful walks abound along the beaches or through the woods, with small bridges to mark where the sea pools flow.

If you do decide to stay on, the *Parknasilla Great Southern* (45122) is the only hotel here. And an impressive place it is, especially if you like the feeling of going back in time. This grey stone mansion overlooking the sea has 200 acres of grounds and a winding forested drive adorned with flowers. Sixty rooms with private baths and some suites. There's an indoor heated pool with saunas. Tennis and golf course (nine-hole) on the grounds. Good seafood. Expensive.

* After leaving Parknasilla, the Ring road moves inland for a short distance through rugged mountainous scenery until it rejoins the coast and reaches the peaceful beaches of Castlecove and Westcove. From here, an unclassified road leading off the Ring road for about a mile takes you to the ancient *Staigue Fort,* considered one of Ireland's best archaeological sites. The fort is fashioned of crude stones which were perfectly laid without the use of a drop of mortar. The stones form a circle 90 feet in diameter and the walls are nearly 15 feet thick and about 18 feet high. A little doorway leads inside, where there are several staircases of equally fine construction.

* Back on the Ring road, you will come to the village of Caherdaniel near the shore of Derrynane Bay. Here you can get directions to visit *St. Crohane's Hermitage,* an ancient structure amazingly carved from solid rock. Near here are the remains of Kilcrohane Church and a fort similar to, though smaller than, Staigue Fort. *Derrynane House* is about two miles southwest of Caherdaniel. This is the former home of Daniel O'Connell (1775–1847), called the Great Liberator of Ireland. O'Connell brought an exciting new concept and spirit to his time, emphasizing emancipation. He dreamed of an Ireland united as a single nation, but was opposed to any form of violence in achieving this objective. The home of his politically active years is now beautifully restored and contains a museum housing O'Connell's effects, including his furniture which provides a fascinating study of the period's style. It is open all year round. Nearby are the remains of *Derrynane Abbey* and a prehistoric ogham or inscribed stone, formerly underwater and now brought to road level for viewing. Archaeologists are hard put to decipher the primitive Celtic inscriptions of the ogham stones.

* As the road ascends, it passes the mountains of Cahernageeha

(1640 feet) and Farraniaragh (1549 feet). Looking seaward, you will have a breathtaking view of Scariff Island and the Deenish Islands. Soon after, the road crosses through the Pass of Coomakista, 700 feet above sea level. To the left is Benorourke Mountain (1017 feet). Here are more awesome panoramas: Ballinskelligs Bay, the Skelligs Rocks, and mountains rising over 1600 feet, as you descend to the resort village of Waterville.

* Waterville or *An Coirean* (the Little Whirlpool) is on a tiny thread of land that separates Ballinskelligs Bay from Lough Currane. The Lough is fed by the River Cummeragh, which originates in the purity of mountain tarns. Thus the lake is said to be one of Ireland's finest for fishing. One of its lovely islands, *Church Island,* has the ruins of a 12th-century church which was dedicated to St. Finian in the sixth century. South and east of the lake, mountains rise from its shores to heights of 2000 feet. It is easy to see why the late Charlie Chaplin chose Waterville as the site of his vacation-house retreat.

Like Parknasilla, Waterville seems to have everything for the sports-minded: swimming, snorkeling, boating, sailing, fresh- and salt-water fishing, golf, tennis, riding, mountain climbing, and running.

Note that if you want to stay on here the *Waterville Lake Hotel* is a thoroughly enjoyable lodging, from its panoramic views of lake, sea, and mountains to its championship 18-hole golf course. There are plush suites and rooms (all with bath) and lounges, but the restaurants offer only acceptable cuisine. The hotel operates its own luxury cruising boat, the *Anna Maria,* to take guests on picnic outings along the Kerry coast. It also boasts an indoor heated pool, saunas, a sunbed, and a games room. Riding, fishing, and tennis facilities are available. But you'd be better off dining elsewhere on the Ring (see Restaurants). High tea is very disappointing, other meals somewhat better. Run by the owners of Ashford Castle, Co. Mayo. Expensive.

Waterville has other less expensive hotels. Among the best is the *Butler Arms,* which overlooks the Atlantic, has 43 rooms (21 with bath), and offers guests an 18-hole golf course and horseback riding. It's a stately old resort hotel. Moderate.

The *Bay View* is a fine Grade-B (Irish-Tourist-Board rated) hotel with 29 rooms, eight with bath. It faces the Atlantic. Inexpensive.

* Shortly after Waterville comes the tiny village of *Ballinskelligs,* which ornaments the head of Ballinskelligs Bay. This mainly Irish-speaking community attracts many students of the language who come here to improve their skills. It's one of the few places in the country outside of localized areas in Galway and Donegal that still struggles to preserve the haunting beauty of the Irish language.

Outside of Ballinskelligs village is a four-mile stretch of beach with some beautiful coastal scenery. To the west are the remains of an ancient castle that belonged to the McCarthy family in olden days. Boats may be rented here for trips to Puffin Island and Derrynane Bay, or the Skelligs Rocks; they are also available for sea fishing trips.

* The road from Waterville moves inland through mountainous vistas for about 11 miles, until it comes to Cahirciveen at the foot of Bentee Mountain (1245 feet), overlooking the beautiful Valentia Harbor. Here the Roman Catholic church was built in 1888 as a memorial to Daniel O'Connell, The Great Liberator. The arched keystone (from the house of St. Clement in Rome) and the cornerstone were presentations of the pope. Close by on the Glenbeigh road are the ruins of O'Connell's birthplace.

* Two miles from Cahirciveen is the village of Kimego West, where you will see *Fort Leacanabuaile* standing on a rocky hill. Finds from this site indicate it was used to protect the area as far back as the sixth century. The immense circular fort has several sets of stairs on its interior walls, plus chambers and secret passages.

* Also near Cahirciveen, but some distance off the Ring road, is *Valentia Island,* which is connected to the mainland by a bridge. (You may wish to visit it if you have the time). Seven miles long and two miles wide, it has the distinction of being one of the most westerly points of land in Europe. The surface is rough and rocky, with Geokaun Mountain (880 feet) at the northern end and Bray Head Mountain (792 feet) at the southern. The views from either are spectacular, and the island is also a deep-sea fisherman's paradise. Ten miles off Valentia are the *Skelligs Rocks.* The Great Skellig is a gigantic rock mass rising straight out of the sea to a height of nearly 800 feet. On this the largest Skellig are the ruins of an early Christian monastary, with churches, oratories, and crude crosses. Pilgrims once came here to do penance.

* The Ring road north from Cahirciveen is perhaps the most spectacularly scenic portion of the entire Ring of Kerry. It moves through the broad valley to Kells for a dazzling view of Dingle Bay, across from which is the lonely jutting of the Dingle Peninsula, where *Ryan's Daughter* was filmed. Kells was once the center of the ancient kingdom of *Ossory.* There are still some fragments of the ancient town walls, but nothing remains of the castle built here after the Anglo-Norman invasions in the 12th century.

* From Kells, the road rolls high above the bay past the Drung Hill and then moves down to *Glenbeigh,* a tiny village arching to Dingle Bay with a backdrop of sweeping mountains and hills, referred to by locals as the Glenbeigh Horseshoe. Here where the River Behy rushes into Dingle Bay, there are many beautiful mountain walks guaranteed to bring serenity back into your life. If you're a climber, no more need be said. If you're a fisherman, the fresh-water trout are said to abound. And for beach lovers, there are sandy miles of it.

* Leaving Glenbeigh, you pass through several miles of the Windy Gap along the River Caragh to Glencar, a mountain-climbing must. There's also most promising fishing in the lengthy four miles of the heather-banked Lough Caragh.

* Next comes *Killorglin* at the northern end of the Ring. This little village stands near the headwaters of Castlemaine Harbor and its connecting estuary, the River Laune, where salmon run. At Killorglin the annual Puck Fair is held in August. Attended by thousands, it lasts for three days and nights, as described below.

Legend: This should be called Legends Plus, for by now everything but the kitchen sink has been thrown in along with the outlines of this originally pagan event, still presided over by a he-goat obtained from the nearby mountains of MacGillicuddy Reeks. The first day is Gathering Day, when the captive goat is trimmed with red ribbons and rosettes and hauled through the streets to be crowned by a beautiful maiden. After the ceremony in the town square, the goat is lifted by a pulley system to the top of a three-tiered platform, signaling the start of dancing and revelry. On the second, or Puck's Fair Day, all the business is conducted, including the sale of livestock. The third day, Children's or Scattering Day, is a time for more music, dancing, and merrymaking, as the goat is dethroned by the children, led again through the town, and set free. During the days of the fair, which resembles a kind of Irish Mardi Gras, the shops, pubs, and restaurants never close.

Is all this an excuse to throw a big party, or perhaps a clever ploy to drum up more business? Perhaps in part, but there seems to be much more to it. Some feel Puck's Fair is associated with the ancient August festival of Lughnasa—one of four great pre-Christian harvest festivals celebrated in Ireland. It was also called Garland Sunday, which ties in with the goat's rosettes and ribbons. Others recall that the goat was a pagan symbol of good fortune and therefore an object of worship. In medieval times the sound of stampeding goats warned of the approach of invading armies, giving the citizens an opportunity to fight or flee.

* Around Killorglin you will see many reminders of the Ice Age— cutbacks, incisions, and molds in the earth and rock, as well as tarns slashed out of mountainous sections.

* From Killorglin, drive the 14 miles to Killarney where you will stay the night. You should arrive here by mid-afternoon.

RESTAURANTS

Many find the scenery so enchanting that they would rather pop into a grocery store in one of the villages and pick up the makings of a picnic than waste time eating indoors. And there are so many possible sites for a memorable picnic that it's probably easier to let your stomach decide on one.

Of course if the weather's inclement or al fresco dining is not your style, most of the hotels along the Ring offer tasty lunches, and many of the pubs have good and inexpensive food. Some of the hotels were mentioned earlier. Other Ring restaurants open for lunch include:

* In *Sneem,* Paddy's Seafood Restaurant is a quaint, clean little cafe with wine bar. Moderate.

* In *Waterville,* the Huntsman offers fine French cuisine and seafood specialties in an oak dining room with sea views. Wine license, Visa and Master. Moderate. And the Smugglers Restaurant on Cliff Road, also overlooking the sea, has comparable seafood and French dishes. Snack menu available. Wine license, AE, Diners. Inexpensive to moderate.

* In *Cahirciveen, Teach Culainn* Bar and Restaurant serves traditional Irish food (Irish stew, bacon and cabbage, etc.) in an old-time atmosphere. Full license. Inexpensive.

* In *Glenbeigh,* the Falcon Inn Hotel serves both snacks and meals in a country-inn setting. AE. Inexpensive to moderate. The Glenbeigh Hotel offers snacks and hearty meals in its old tavern inn. Moderate. The Towers Hotel offers fine seafood and curry dishes, including soups, and also has tasty roast beef. AE, Master. Expensive.

SHOPPING
* * In Kenmare, the Craft Shop on Main Street.
* * In Sneem, the Homestead Craft Shop in New Street and Marshall's on North Square (which also has a tea room).
* * In Castlecove, Castlecove Pottery and Craft Shop.
* * In Glenbeigh, Carragh Crafts.
* * In Killorglin, Crowley's, the Square, and *Sheeóg* on Upper Bridge Street.

Roots: O'Sullivan (Cappanacuss Castle, near Kenmare, was a residence for part of the family); O'Connell (Derrynane House in Caherdaniel was the home of Irish liberator Daniel O'Connell, and the ruins of his birthplace are at Cahran, close to Glenbeigh); O'Mahony (Dromore Castle, six miles from Kenmare on the Ring road, once the O'Mahony fortress); McCarthy (the castle in Ballinskelligs—now in ruins—was the McCarthy family home). Other names with roots in this area include: O'Connor, O'Shea, Murphy, Walsh, and Fitzgerald.

Literature: George Bernard Shaw loved this part of the country and often stayed at the Great Southern in Parknasilla. In fact, he wrote some of *Saint Joan* there.

IX. KILLARNEY

Killarney Lakes—and lonely nearby streams

> *The calm black lakes are sleeping in the mountain*
> *shadow, and on the water's canvas, bright sunshine*
> *paints the picture of the day.*
>
> —Irish ballad

overleaves—

> *The silver of yesterday is the soul of tomorrow.*
>
> —from the Celtic, fifth century.

YOUR PERSONALIZED KILLARNEY ITINERARY

Day One

* Arrive mid-afternoon and check into lodgings. Possibilities range from the elegant and expensive *Europe Hotel* on the outskirts to the more centrally located *Great Southern Hotel* (moderately expensive), to the *Three Lakes* (moderate) or the *International* and the *Arbutus* (both inexpensive). You might also wish to choose from the area's many fine farmhouse accommodations. If so, the suggestion is *Tullig House* in nearby Beaufort. It is very inexpensive and pleasantly colorful.

* Prepare for a stroll around Killarney village before dinner. As you take in some of the fine old shops and perhaps a pub or two (see below), you might have a look at *St. Mary's Cathedral* on New Street, a fine example of early English-Irish architecture. Built in 1855 to a design by Alexander Pugin, this awesome structure, verging on the austere, conveys a sense of serenity while exemplifying a strong religious philosophy.

Legend: Alexander or Augustus Pugin became an Irish legend in his time. Although he was of English-French extraction, the son of another famous architect, he came to love Ireland deeply. He lived for only 40 years (1812–52), yet he was responsible for a major medieval-Gothic revival in Ireland; his ecclesiastical works can be seen in many areas. He did so many impressive things in such a short time that he was a kind of architectural George Gershwin. Pugin's purpose was to establish, and hopefully to prove, the existence of a divine spirituality that transcended all life as we know it. Fear, love, peace, and inspiration were said to have been his worksheets and mortar.

Another site worth visiting is the *Memorial of the Four Kerry Poets* on College Street, across from the Gothic Franciscan Church with its fine old intricate woodworking. This is an impressive monument by Seamus Murphy to four Kerry poets: Pierce Ferriter, an Irish patriot who was executed in 1653; Geoffrey O'Donoghue, (d. 1677); Aodhgan O'Rahilly (d. 1728; and Eoghan Ruadh O'Sullivan (d. 1784). The woman sculpted on the memorial, called the Skywoman of Kerry, is an allegorical symbol of Mother Ireland. Some say this is the nation's greatest sculpture, portraying as it does love, despair, hope, fear, and peace in a single work of art.

* The dinner suggestion is *Gaby's* on High Street, an outstanding Mediterranean-style seafood restaurant and certainly one of Ireland's best places to dine (see Restaurants).

Day Two

* After breakfast at your lodgings and check-out, there are several choices of a morning itinerary.

* One is a trip through the spectacular Gap of Dunloe, which can be accomplished in part or entirely by pony trap. (The first part of the journey may be made by car.) Leave the town via New Street and you will soon glimpse the dazzle of the lakes, with the mountains in the background. After you cross the River Laune, you'll see *Dunloe Castle*. Although much of the edifice has been modernized, the original castle walls are those erected by O'Sullivan More in the 13th century to defend the entrance of the Gap of Dunloe. The castle was the site of many sieges, including the Insurrection of 1641, and fell only to Cromwell's forces. Today there are 3000 acres of grounds abounding in beautiful flora.

Nearby is the fascinating *Dunloe Cave,* a man-made souterrain, or what's left of one. It's composed of mortarless field stones, several of which bear inscriptions and are known as ogham stones. Ogham is an alphabetical script with 20 letters formed in strokes on a transverse line, an archaic form of the Irish language probably dating from the 5th to the 10th centuries.

South of here is the famed *Gap of Dunloe,* a four-mile gulch carved by glaciers. The setting is enhanced dramatically by the Purple Mountains on the left and Macgillicuddy's Reeks on the right. *Kate Kearney's Cottage* is at the entrance to the ravine.

Legend: Supposedly the cottage was named for an Irish beauty whose appearance drove men wild with desire. The original cottage was long the headquarters of bootleggers, who sold the illegal Irish beverage poteen to the tourists as they passed through to marvel at the scenery. A few swigs and everybody had a joyous trip through the gap. Unhappily for the tourist, this spirited service has gone out of style and been relegated to the dustbin of history.

Near the cottage, all travelers by car continue the journey either by transferring to a jaunting car, bike, or pony, or by walking. The trip through the gap itself can give you an eerie feeling, as the boulders rise high on either side and several seemingly bottomless tarns converge to form a surging stream that runs alongside the road. All sounds echo in the canyon, and you seem to be back in the Ice Age.

Legend: As you move up toward the head of the gap (795 feet above sea level), you will pass Black Lough, another glacial tarn that legend claims is without fish because St. Patrick drowned the last Irish serpent in its waters.

From the top of the gap, the views are breathtakingly compounded of purple mountains, the Upper Lake, and the Cummeenduff (Black Valley) rolling into the hills.

Descending from the gap to the shore of Upper Lake, you'll see an old hunting lodge called *Lord Brandon's Cottage*. This is a wonderful area for a picnic lunch. (Note: There is an optional continuation of this tour which takes you by boat through the lakes of Killarney— but it will take you the rest of the day to do it. Since many will not have the time, this will be covered later under Kerry's Optional Travels). For those holding to the shorter itinerary, it is now time to backtrack by jaunting car to Kate Kearney's Cottage and then into town. But first you might like to stop at the cottage for an Irish coffee. Yes, it still houses a bar, even though poteen is no longer available. There is also an Irish crafts shop here and a place where you can buy passable sandwiches and tea or coffee.

It is worth noting that the Gap of Dunloe, after all its years as a tourist attraction, has not become overly commercialized. The emphasis is still where it should be: on the haunting beauty of the locale.

Another possible half-day tour is that of the Muckross estate, including *Muckross Abbey, Muckross House,* and *Torc Waterfall.* The journey can be made by car or by jaunting car. Three miles outside Killarney on the Kenmare Road is the entrance to Bourne-Vincent Memorial Park, which takes you by way of the Lower Lake shore to Gothic Muckross Abbey. (Some walking is required for those driving themselves). Donal MacCarthy founded the abbey in the mid-15th century for the Franciscan monks. In 1542 it was suppressed by the English, but the monks valiantly lived on here until the Elizabethan soldiers drove them away in 1589. Their determination was so great that they returned to repossess it and remained until Cromwell's army burned the abbey in 1652. Still undaunted, the monks refused to leave the area. Their former home, although partly in ruins, is considered one of the best-preserved examples of religious architecture in the country. Slightly farther down the road is *Muckross House* and *Gardens,* a truly impressive 19th-century manor with a Portland stone exterior. Here you'll see exhibits of Kerry folklife, including ancient forms of harvesting, cobbling, and printing, along with such crafts as stone carving, basket-making, pottery, and weaving—to say nothing of the hand-carved period furniture. The subtropical gardens and the nature walks offer a fine example of the beauty and serenity of the country. From here, you'll come to the sweeping 60-foot *Torc Waterfall*, fed by the Devil's Punch Bowl on Mangerton Mountain. If you follow the road farther you'll come to a majestic view of the lakes, *Ladies View*. There's a fine craft shop here called Ladies View Industries, and a snack shop and bar. From here, you'll follow the main road back to Killarney.

    ★ A third classic half-day tour, which can be made shorter if you forego the jaunting car and drive, is to *Aghadoe Hill*. Moving out of Killarney on the Tralee road, you follow the signs for Aghadoe. Less than three miles will bring you to one of Killarney's most breathtaking panoramas. The village, the lakes, the mountains beyond can all be seen from this prime vantage point. Some have said that if you have only one moment to spend in Killarney, it should be here. And you wonder if people weren't saying the same thing centuries ago.

    Legend: In pagan times, Aghadoe was said to be the place where lovers met because it was the birthplace of all beauty. Only those who worshipped the gods and goddesses of pure love could survive here. St. Patrick reportedly marveled at Aghadoe and gave it his Christian blessing before drowning the last Irish serpent in Black Lough. There are tales that whoever falls in love here will be blessed for a lifetime. Well—certainly they'll never forget the view.

    On Aghadoe Hill are the ruins of a 17th-century round tower and a church, the first inroads of a Christianity said to have been jealous of the original signs of a pagan 'beauty' in Ireland.

From here, move on to the shores of Lower Lake and *Ross Castle*, which is another well-preserved ruin. Dating from the 14th century, it is believed to be the one-time residence of the O'Donoghue family. Lord Muskerry's Royalist forces defended it against the savagely Puritanical General Ludlow during the Cromwellian Wars. But floating weaponry, brought overland from Kinsale and mounted on barges in the lake, forced the Muskerry garrison to surrender.

    Nearby are traces of ancient copper mines (now sealed off, but reminiscent of Western American ghost-town mineshafts) which date from pagan times. Just across the water is *Governor's Rock*, a horticultural preserve.

    ★ From Ross Castle (or whichever tour you take) follow the clearly marked roads back to Killarney.

    ★ Prepare to travel the 68 miles to Limerick. Depending on where you stay overnight, it's then 16 more miles to Shannon or 16 miles to *Dromoland Castle* (which is definitely suggested). Consider making this countrified yet stately European-style castle your area headquarters.

Kerry's Optional Travels

* An extended Gap of Dunloe tour, picking up where the one outlined in the basic itinerary left off, begins at *Lord Brandon's Cottage* near the shore of Upper Lake. This boat tour of the lakes of Killarney combines with the jaunting car ride through the Gap to make a full day's outing. And well worth it if you can afford the time.

As you begin the boat tour through Upper Lake, you will pass *Eagle Island* (the birds no longer flock there) and *Arbutus Island,* which is overrun with the beautiful evergreen arbutus shrub for which Killarney is famous. Next is *MacCarthy More Island,* known for its majestic Lebanon Cedar trees.

You leave the Upper Lake through an extremely narrow passage called *Coleman's Eye* that leads to a strait known as the *Long Range.* Wooded mountains line the banks of this beautiful river, including Eagle's Nest Mountain, another former haunt of the eagles. Here you are still likely to see deer and wild mountain goats. The boatman will often blow a bugle so passengers can hear the evocative echo. After this point the trip can become a little scary, for it is here that you shoot the river's rapids to emerge under the Old Wier Bridge. But the river then divides and becomes calm at the Meeting of the Waters. Ahead is *Dinis Island,* with its rare sub-tropical foliage, after which the boat moves out over Middle Lake. On its north side are the *Colleen Bawn Caves,* which were hollowed out of the limestone deposits over the years by the lapping of the lake's waters.

After the boat passes under Bricken Bridge, you have entered the largest of the Killarney lakes, Lough Leane or Lower Lake. A few miles along the western shore, you will see *O'Sullivan's Cascade,* a set of three waterfalls that drop 75 feet. There is a grotto beneath a projecting precipice that affords the visitor a thrilling view of the falls. Behind it are some fine forests, and a mile in front is the lake island of *Innisfallen.* Here are the remains of an abbey built in the seventh century by St. Finian the Leper and expanded in the 13th century when it became an Augustinian priory. At the abbey, the famous *Annals of Innisfallen* (a detailed account of world and Irish history) was written between A.D. 950 and 1320. Although the manuscript is now in England at the Bodleian Library, Oxford, a facsimile edition of this historic document has been published by the Dublin Institute of Advanced Studies.

The boat ends its tour at Ross Castle (described above). From here the jaunting cars take visitors back to Killarney.

★ Another tour often ignored by American tourists but noteworthy for its beauty is that of the *Dingle Peninsula*. Some say the Ring of Kerry does not compare with it; certainly Dingle is less frantically explored by the tourist trade. Film producer David Lean was so taken with the peninsula that he made it the setting for his beautiful film *Ryan's Daughter*. It will be given special coverage as an option after the Killarney section.

KILLARNEY'S HISTORY

In fact, Killarney has a less dramatic history than many other places on this itinerary. For historical excitement, the closest site is that of the Killarney Lakes, where Cromwell's armies once mounted a siege. But Killarney itself is just a small old country town that leapt into prominence as a tourist attraction about a hundred years ago as a result of its location and scenery. The amazing thing is that it has kept its taste and dignity, along with its Old-World look, after all these years of galloping tourism.

Three major lakes compose Killarney's lake district. The largest, the Lower Lake, covers over 5000 acres and contains 35 islands. The 680-acre Middle or Muckross Lake with its four islands is connected by a tiny strait to the 430-acre Upper Lake, which has eight islands. At one point the lakes and Muckross Peninsula were owned by the Bourne and Vincent families of California. Fortunately for Ireland, they turned the 11,500-acre estate over to the Irish Government in 1932 for the creation of the Bourne-Vincent National Park.

The Killarney area does have a fascinating geological history, and the effects of the Ice Age are apparent in many places. Ice-shaven boulders and deep caves and hollows testify to the severity of glacial activity here. The neighboring mountains are comprised of red sandstone, and volcanic rocks may be found in the area south of Lough Guitane, which is four miles south of Killarney.

LODGINGS

★ *The Aghadoe Heights Hotel,* two and a half miles from Killarney on Aghadoe Hill (31766), is a modern, rather plain little place with 55 rooms, all with bath, and spectacular views of the Lakes of Killarney. Moderate.

★ *The Arbutus,* College Street (31037), is a small, unpretentious hotel that once served as a shelter for monks. It has 32 rooms, 24 with bath, and the staff is very pleasant. Inexpensive.

★ *The Castlerosse Hotel,* Kenmare Estate (31144), is a luxury motel with a magnificent view of the lakes and mountains. There are 40 rooms, all with bath and phone, plus a swimming pool and an adjacent championship golf course. Located a short distance outside Killarney. Moderate.

★ *The Dunloe Castle,* Beaufort, six miles from Killarney near the Gap of Dunloe (32118), is *not* an old castle, or any kind of castle for that matter. It's a fine modern hotel complete with indoor pool and saunas. There are 140 rooms, all with bath and phone. Moderately expensive.

★ *The Europe Hotel,* Fossa, a few miles outside Killarney (31900), is an immaculate and luxurious Grade-A hotel overlooking the sweep of Lower Lake. Excellent views from the restaurant and the residents' lounge. There are 168 rooms, all with bath and phone, and a health center and saunas for the fitness-minded. Expensive.

* *The Great Southern Hotel,* the Railway Station (31262), is a rambling old Victorian hotel which depended in the old days on the trains bringing visitors who played croquet on its well-groomed lawns. Times may have changed, but the Great Southern hasn't. This is by no means to say that the place is dilapidated, but through all its renovations it has kept the feeling of its heritage. Many of its 180 rooms are still traditional in style, although all now have bath and phone. Generations of Americans have stayed here with satisfaction, including Caroline Kennedy and former President Nixon's wife, Pat, who is remembered as expressing real pleasure in the area.

* *The International Hotel,* College Street (28125), is a no-frills, centrally located hotel with 96 rooms, all with bath and phone. Inexpensive.

* *The Three Lakes,* Kenmare Place (31479), offers small, comfortable rooms—70 of them, all with bath—in the town center. Moderate.

* *Tullig House,* Beaufort, nine miles from Killarney (44183). A charming farmhouse hideaway where the romantic is indulged in every respect: peaceful riverside strolls, pleasant fishing, bouts at quaint local pubs, chats with the colorful Kerry folk—worth the entire journey to Ireland. It's a delightful but totally basic place off the beaten track, where you can feed the chickens or milk the cows if you're so inclined. Mrs. Joy runs one of the neatest houses in the county, and her unpretentious dining room isn't bad: hearty breakfasts and solid dinners of traditional Irish fare at very modest prices. She can also tell you some wonderful stories of the old days. Wine license. Very inexpensive, especially considering all you get. (If you have any trouble finding Tullig House, don't hesitate to ask around Beaufort; almost anyone in the area can tell you how to get there.)

RESTAURANTS

* *The Aghadoe Heights Hotel,* two and a half miles from Killarney on Aghadoe Hill (31766), is an intimate rooftop restaurant overlooking the lakes and mountains—a spectacular view. The French and international cuisine is sometimes excellent and always good. Open 1 to 2:30. D—7 to 9:30. AE, Visa, Master. Expensive.

* *The Deenach Grill,* College Street (31656). Hearty Irish meals, with especially good chicken and Irish stew. Also seafood, steaks, hamburgers, and snacks. Open noon to 11 P.M. Full license. AE, Visa, Master, Diners. Inexpensive.

* *The Cara Restaurant,* Old Town Hall, Main Street (31765), is a basic self-service restaurant serving good carvery roasts and snacks. Open 10 A.M. to 11 P.M. Wine license. Visa, Master, Diners. Inexpensive.

* *The Failte Hotel,* College Street (31893), offers such dishes as fresh Lobster Newburg and a variety of meats. It isn't the Ritz, but it's all right. Open L—12:30 to 2:30. D—8:30 to 10:30. Moderate.

* *Foley's Seafood and Steak Restaurant,* High Street (31217), is an intriguing bar-restaurant combination that serves food in both areas. The dining room has a special charm reminiscent of the Victorian boarding house, with its flocked wallpaper, fluted amber wall lamps, velvet chairs, and dark wood furniture. The bar is a bit more rustic. One of the fine touches here is the

elderly gentleman at the old upright piano playing surprisingly memorable turn-of-the-century ballads like 'Love's Old Sweet Song.' Beside him burns a lovely pine fire, and benches are at hand for lounging and listening with your drink. This place is definitely not for the trendy young set (although one youthful American couple confided that they found the music 'very new and sensuous'!) Seafoods and steaks are specialties, and the lobster salad, seafood platter, Dover sole and T-bone are all good choices. Breakfast and snacks served all day. Open 10 A.M. to 11:30 P.M. AE, Master, Visa, Diners. Inexpensive to moderate.

* *The Great Southern Hotel,* Railway Station (31262), has a Victorian dining room and a smaller Malton Room. The high ceilings and elegant decor recall its 19th-century heritage. Good French cuisine. Open 6:30 to 10:30 P.M. AE, Diners, Carte Blanche. Expensive.

* *Gaby's,* High Street (32519), is one of Ireland's best seafood restaurants. It rates a 10 on a 10-point scale by any standards. The fresh shellfish platter is so enormous it takes up an entire table and has to be elevated on a platform so there's room to eat with your guests (hopefully, they won't order the same thing, or some of you may end up dining on the ceiling). Oysters, prawns, shrimp, lobster, and crab adorn this dish in quantity. Also highly touted are the smoked salmon platter, lobster salad, oysters, lobster in creme cognac, and black sole in cream. Lobster bisque is an excellent appetizer and the house sherry, Romanti, is highly recommended. The less expensive wines are trustworthy here; you don't have to spend a fortune on a fine complement to a deserving meal. Attractive and unusual Mediterranean decor. L—12:30 to 2:30. D—6 to 10 P.M. Closed for lunch Sunday and Monday. Moderate (but so good it should be expensive). Note that reservations are not accepted, so arrive early or you'll have a long wait at this popular spot. But don't miss it.

* *The International Hotel Dining Room,* College Street (28125), offers moderately good Irish fare. The Brewery Grill here features snacks and grills— nothing great, but all right. Open 10 A.M. to 11:30 P.M. AE, Visa, Master, Diners. Inexpensive.

* *The Laurels,* Main Street (32771), is a sing-song pub that serves very fine Irish fare (see Pubs). You could try the cockle and mussel chowder, followed by such down-to-earth entrees as Irish stew, corned beef and cabbage, shepherd's pie, Atlantic seafood salad, or Irish sole. A Tudor atmosphere, with its beamed ceilings and pine tables. Open 10:30 to 11:30 P.M. Inexpensive. Note that the *Coffee Shop* next door is part of the same establishment and offers a similar menu. Self-service, it's open from 9 A.M. to 8 P.M. Closed Sundays. Inexpensive.

* *The Three Lakes Hotel Restaurant,* Kenmare Place (31479), is another good Irish food place with all the traditional dishes. Simple, plain, comfortable. Open all day. Closed November to March. There's also the Brewery Grill here with snacks and grills. Prices range from inexpensive to moderate. Open 10 A.M. to 11:30 P.M. AE, Visa, Master, Diners.

* *Sheila's Restaurant,* High Street, offers everything from snacks to modest dinners like grilled minute steak, pan-fried trout, cold ham salad, and prawns. The appetizer of homemade smoked mackerel salad is tasty. A simple place, open from 10 A.M. to 11 P.M. Inexpensive.

* *The Stella Restaurant,* Main Street (31846), is a very basic spot offering Irish snacks, luncheons, and beef grills. Not thrilling, diners say, but certainly

acceptable. And it's almost never closed—10 A.M. to 1 A.M. Wine license. Visa, Master, Diners. Inexpensive.

* *The Whaler Seafood Restaurant and Bar,* College Square (31816), is an intimate cafe-like seafood spot with candlelight, flagstone fireplace and floor, marble bar, and sugan chairs. The salmon and fresh clam chowder are especially good; Gaelic steak and veal dishes also available. Open noon to 11 P.M. Closed November to March. Full license. AE, Visa, Master, Diners. Moderate.

PUBS

* *Foley's,* High Street, is a wonderfully old and engaging pub—a cross between Victoriana and rustic Irish. Enjoyable early-1900s ballads played on a tinkly upright piano, and there's a warming fire to heighten your pleasure. Foley's also serves good food. (See Restaurants.)

* *The Laurels,* Main Street, is the in pub in Killarney—and it is pleasant. One of the liveliest pub sing-songs in the country takes place here at night. The place is clean, old and very Tudor-looking with its beams and glistening white paint. And note the fine collection of antique bottles in the window. The Laurels also serves good Irish foods (see Restaurants). Note: Be prepared for crowds. It's sometimes difficult at night to struggle into the place, let alone reach the bar to order a drink.

* *The Whaler Bar,* College Square, is done, not surprisingly, with a nautical motif. It's a quiet, intimate place—more for couples. A pleasant drink here is the sherry served from a keg. The fine dining facility on the premises is described under Restaurants.

* *Crock of Gold,* High Street, is another singing pub. It's not nearly as nice as The Laurels, but truly dedicated Irish singers blast away here.

* *O'Sullivan's Beaufort Bar,* in Beaufort near Tullig House, has an accordionist who plays Irish jigs in season.

SPECIAL EVENTS

* The Killarney Bach Festival, held in early July, attracts the country's classical music lovers and performers.

SHOPS

* Threads and Clay at the Old Granary, College Street. Pottery, crafts, handweaving, scarfs, stoles, rugs, placemats, throws.

* McAuliffe's, High Street. Linens, lace, crafts, sheepskins.

* J. O'Leary, High Street. A scruffy store—but there are finds of small silver items and antique dishes.

* Hilliard's, Main Street. Irish glass and souvenirs.

* Inisfallen Gift Shop, High Street. Crystal, jewelry, crafts, Irish books, lace.

* Serendipity, College Street. Irish craft work, pottery, jewelry, knitwear, glass, silks, tweeds, woven rugs.

* The Artist Gallery, Plunkett Street. Fine unusual old Celtic prints—framed. Also updated versions of these prints and original Irish landscape paintings.

* D. O'Neill, Plunkett Street. Fishing tackle and souvenirs.

* White Heather, Plunkett Street. Fresh flowers plus pottery, knits, jewelry, and pewter.

* Antiques Etc., College Street. Lovely Irish crochet work here along with

Limerick lace. The shop also has rare first-period Belleek china, antique furniture, porcelain, silver tableware, books, jewelry, chess sets, watches, paintings, candleholders, mirrors.

* Leather Workshop, College Street. Irish-crafted leatherwear.

* Kerry Glass Seconds Shop, College Street. Unusual smoke-colored heavy ornamental glass items.

* The Celtic Shop, College Street. Knitwear, Belleek, crystal, jewelry.

Roots: Ferriter; O'Donoghue; O'Rahilly or O'Reilly (the Memorial of the Four Kerry Poets); O'Sullivan (Dunloe Castle); Kearney (Kate Kearney's Cottage); Brandon (Lord Brandon's Cottage); O'Donoghue (Ross Castle). Some other prominent names include: O'Downey, McGillicuddy, Cahill, McCarthy.

Literature: The Kerry poets—Pierce Ferriter, Geoffrey O'Donoghue, Egan O'Rahilly and Owen Roe O'Sullivan (see itinerary, Memorial); Victorian novelist Gerald Griffen (used the Colleen Bawn Caves in his murder story *The Collegians,* which was adapted into both the Dion Boucicault play *The Colleen Bawn* and a Benedict opera, *The Lily of Killarney;* Alfred, Lord Tennyson (eulogized the splendor of Ross Castle in his poem 'The Princess'); William Makepeace Thackeray (loved and wrote about the Lakes of Killarney).

AN OPTIONAL TRIP TO THE DINGLE PENINSULA

Dingle Harbour

This new wild paradise to wake for me
—John Millington Synge

This tour can be done in half a day, but can easily extend to a full day if you stop to enjoy the beautiful scenery and the quaint villages, and perhaps have a swim or a picnic. It's also a very pleasant overnight stopping point.

The trip from Killarney around the full circuit of Dingle ending at Tralee is approximately 104 miles. You can shorten it by 30 miles if you exclude western Dingle. If you don't spend the night here, the next stopping point on your itinerary is the Limerick/Shannon area. It's 64 miles from Tralee to Limerick and another 15 to the Shannon region (another 17 if you're going to stay at Dromoland Castle, which is suggested).

* Travel the 14 miles from Killarney to Killorglin (see notes on Killorglin Town in the Ring of Kerry itinerary). Then drive the six miles through Milltown to Castlemaine, site of the castle that guarded the Maine River and was destroyed by the Cromwellians. From here, you will drive the truly scenic 24 miles to Dingle Town. On your right will be the striking Slieve Mish Mountain range and on the left Castlemaine Harbor. Soon you will come to Inch Strand, where you will probably want to stop.

* *Inch Strand* must be one of the world's most spectacular shore-lines. Sweeping out from the mainland four miles into Dingle Bay (which it separates from Castlemaine Harbor), this dazzling white sandbar backed by its towering sandbank hills will live in your memory. There are quite a few tourists swimming in its azure waters at peak season, but in off season the strand is virtually abandoned. A stroll here with the gleaming sea before you, the soft purple mountains of Kerry behind, and the vast expanse of sky above will leave you with the feeling that this is what matters in the world—what life should be all about. Is it any wonder that David Lean chose this setting for many of the scenes in *Ryan's Daughter?* Earlier it was the setting for the film version of Synge's *Playboy of the Western World.*

* Moving on toward Dingle, you will turn inland and come to Annas-caul. This little river fishing village houses the *South Pole Inn,* named in honor of its one-time proprietor Thomas Crean, who accompanied British naval officer Robert Falcon Scott on his exploration of Antarc-tica and the South Pole in the early 1900s. On this fatal journey, Crean found Scott and his companions frozen to death in their tent.

* Three miles southwest of Annascaul are the remains of *Minard Castle,* said to have been built as a stronghold by the Knights of Kerry. It was one of the largest fortresses in the southwest, and much of its destruction can be attributed to Cromwell. Nearby are the remains of a circular stone fort, offering proof that this area was important to the defense of the country even in ancient times.

* Continue on through Lispole to Dingle Town, whose real name is *An Daingean* or the Fortress. Surrounded by hills on three sides, at the northern end of Dingle Harbor, this is the peninsula's major town. It served as the key port of Kerry during the Spanish trading days. The village was so important in the Elizabethan age that the queen had it walled after it was almost destroyed during the Desmond War, an Anglo-Irish confrontation that lasted from 1579 to 1583. Because of those who had remained loyal to the crown (mainly the mer-chants), Elizabeth I granted Dingle its first charter in 1585. This al-lowed it parliamentary seats in Dublin and gave Dingle some control over its own affairs.

During the French Revolution, when Dingle is said to have been a smuggling center, Count James Rice, who owned a house here and was an officer of the Irish Brigade in France, plotted with his colleagues to free Marie Antoinette from prison. She would then be brought by sea to Dingle and offered refuge in the Count's house. But when she discovered she would have to leave the king and her children behind, she refused. The Rice house, called *High House* from its location above the whole city, was on Main and Green Streets; now it has been replaced by a Catholic Presbytery.

* If possible, you should see *St. James Church* (Church of Ireland), built in 1804, which stands on the site of a medieval parish church. The highlight here is the Fitzgeraldine tombstone dating from the early 16th century, which bears a fading carving of the Desmond coat of arms. The Fitzgeralds were the Earls of Desmond and fought the crown bitterly for their territory. There are later inscriptions here too, including one inside the church with the name *John Fitzgerald*, one of the Knights of Kerry who died in the mid-18th century.

* The next stop is *St. Mary's Church* (Roman Catholic) on Green Street hill, which was originally built in 1812. A wealthy townswoman, Clarissa Hussey, who was dissatisfied with its mundane appearance (and her own dull life), literally pelted then Canon O'Sullivan with money for a more inspiring structure. The result was a wonderfully peaceful and serene church whose foundation stone was laid in 1865. Designed by J. J. McCarthy (a brilliant successor to architect Augustus or Alexander Pugin), the church lends its peaceful presence to all of this Old-World town from its position on the steep hillside.

* If you want to stop for lunch, *Doyle's Seafood Bar* on John Street is the suggestion (see Restaurants). For those who wish to stay overnight in this area, the suggestion is the *Scheilig Hotel* just outside Dingle Town (described under Lodgings). You may wish to check in before continuing your tour. Those who are moving on may either cut their journey short by heading east across the Conor pass and proceeding to Tralee (the end of the Dingle ring 30 miles away), or proceed west to see the entire peninsula. This adds an extra 30 miles to the Tralee destination point. The latter option takes you across the spectacular top-of-the-world Conor Pass, which is definitely one of the country's high points in every sense of the word. Bear in mind that it's 64 miles from Tralee to Limerick and another 15 to the Shannon area, your next itinerary stopping point.

* For those doing the westerly Dingle journey, we will proceed from here. (Those not doing it should skip ahead to the next reference to the Conor Pass.) From Dingle, continue to Milltown. Beyond the cemetery and Milltown Bridge is a giant upright stone or gallan called the Milestone. Nearby are two others, the Gates of Glory, and an enormous boulder inscribed with a cup and circle. Their origins are obscure, but one theory has it that they were part of an ancient burial ground, perhaps millennia ago.

* Move on from here to the pleasant little village of *Ventry,* which has its own harbor and lovely beach. Looming behind are the grand slopes of Mount Eagle and Croagh Marhin. The Battle of Ventry Strand is said to have taken place here.

Legend: Here the King of the World—Daire Doon—landed his many ships with plans to take over the country. For over a year he struggled against the forces of the brave Irish Fianna warrior Fionn Mac Cumhaill, or the Finn MacCool, known as the Strongest Man in Ireland, who finally prevailed over the invaders.

* From here the road turns inland for several miles, then meets the sea again at Kilvicadowning. From this point to Slea Head, it traverses the cliffs along the southern slopes of Mount Eagle, affording beautiful seascapes. About four miles out from Ventry, below the road on the left, is *Dunbeg Fort,* which consists of a fortified stone wall jutting out onto a triangular promontory. On the landward side is an extensive system of earthen trenches and defense rings. The remains of an inner building connect with a souterrain, or underground escape passage. The fort, with walls 22 feet thick, is thought to date from the Iron Age and was probably built to defend the ancient settlement of *Fahan,* whose remains include some hundreds of unmortared clochans or beehive huts, plus numerous souterrains, inscribed gallans (upright stones), two sculptured crosses, cave dwellings, and earthen forts. If you wish to see this prehistoric site, watch for the road sign-posted *Beehive Huts.*

* Proceed to Slea Head, from which the views, especially those of the seven Blasket Islands, are spectacular. These islands serve to mark the westernmost point in Europe. Until the early 1950s they were populated by Gaelic-speaking people, as they had been since prehistoric times. When the inhabitants could no longer support themselves, due to poor fishing seasons and other reverses, they were forced to move to the mainland. These islanders were renowned as tellers of folk tales.

It is still possible to visit the Blaskets; there are boats for hire farther down the road at Dunquin. The largest island, or Great Blasket, is about four miles long and three-quarters of a mile wide. Far to the west of these islands the early Celts, like the Spanish Ponce de León, went in search of a land of eternal youth, the legendary island of *Tír na nóg.*

Here in Blasket Sound, during a tumultuous storm, two ships of the Spanish Armada went on the rocks and sank with great loss of life in 1558—the *Santa Maria de la Rosa* and the *San Juan de Ragusa.* The discovery of the first ship, located in the 1960s, served as a reminder that the waters around this area can be very dangerous and should be explored with caution.

This western part of Dingle is one of the few remaining strongholds of the Irish language and is called accordingly *Corca Dhuibhne Gaeltacht.* Only a few areas have refused to be robbed of this beautiful heritage by the speed and the economy of modern times. Here Gaelic is the chosen and most-spoken language. Many Irish parents send their children to this and other *Gaeltachts* every summer in the hope of keeping the language alive through study and use.

* From Slea Head the road moves inland to *Dunquin,* with its lovely sandy coves and rocky cliffs. The slope of Croagh Marhin above Dunquin was the site of the movie town of Kirarry, built especially for the film *Ryan's Daughter.* But look for it no more: it had to be completely demolished, in accordance with Irish law, which demands that the locale be left just as it had been.

* The road from Dunquin passes *Clogher Head,* from which you can see, across the small bay, Sybil Point and a strangely attractive rock formation called the Three Sisters. From this the highest point on your journey, you can also see, on a clear day, the Dunquin cliffs, the Blasket Islands, and to the east Smerwick Harbor and Mount Brandon. A good pair of binoculars will give you a look at the northernmost Blasket, Inishtookert, with its strangely shaped natural outcroppings resembling mammoth shark tails. Though the island is not easily accessible, it was occupied by early Christian hermits. The ruins of their small church, St. Brendan's Oratory, still remain, along with their cemetery and beehive huts. A few brave families seeking seclusion occupied these huts in the early 19th century. Today Inishtookert's lighthouse keepers are the only (and lonely) residents of the Blaskets—except for the bewildering array of seabirds.

* Moving inland from Clogher Head soon brings you to Ballyferriter, which has an interesting weaving and crafts shop, *Siopa an Chnoic.* This part of Dingle, called the Smerwick Peninsula, was the scene of heavy trading at nearby Ferriter's Cove between Ireland and the Continent. About two miles northwest of the village, just above the Cove, are the remains of *Ferriter's Castle,* a 15th-century tower-house castle that included a moat. The Ferriter family came to Kerry with the Anglo-Norman invaders in the 13th century, at which time they

acquired the Blasket Islands and much of this part of the mainland. Pierce Ferriter, the famous Gaelic poet and a gallant soldier, was born at the castle. He was one of the last Irish soldiers to hold out against Cromwell during the war years 1642–53, but he was finally captured and hanged. His great dexterity as a warrior turned his exploits into immortality.

Legend: Ferriter's Castle is also called Sybil's Castle, after the woman its owner loved. After their elopement, they lived happily at the castle until Sybil's raging Lynch kinsmen discovered who had stolen her away. They surrounded the castle, but Ferriter conceived the idea of hiding Sybil in a cave underneath it. When the coast was clear and he went to fetch his love, he found that she had drowned in the rising tide. To this day her ghost is said to walk nearby, pining for Ferriter.

⋆ About a mile north of Ballyferriter is Smerwick Harbor, near which a rocky cliff houses the ruins of a 16th-century fortress called *Dún an Oir* or the Fort of Gold. On a bleak November day in 1580, 600 men, including Italians, Spaniards, English, and Irishmen, supported and financed by the Pope, held out here against the Royalist forces in defense of their Catholicism. The English Protestants, led by Lord Grey and including the poet Edmund Spenser and Sir Walter Raleigh, defeated the papal contingent and slaughtered them to a man.

Note that there's a good small hotel here called *Dún an Oir,* which also has pleasant self-service traditional cottages for rent. Moderate prices.

⋆ Slightly off your route, about three-quarters of a mile east of Ballyferriter, is the recently discovered and excavated site of *Reask,* a seventh-century monastery with beehive huts, small church, and crosses.

⋆ From Ballyferriter head for the signposted *Gallarus Oratory,* which is one of the best preserved early Christian churches in the country. Small, rectangular, looking very much from its curvature like an overturned boat, the church is built solely of unmortared stone. Yet after thousands of years, it's still watertight. Set on the side of a hill overlooking the peaceful countryside, it was reputedly built by St. Manchan and his followers as part of a monastic settlement in the 11th century. Its 'eye-of-the-needle' window symbolizes the narrow porthole or door through which the faithful must pass. Nearby is a five-foot gallan or standing stone which is thought to mark the grave of St. Manchan. Historians believe that originally the gallan was a pagan ogham (strange prehistoric writing) stone, which the monks hastily inscribed with crosses to nullify its paganism so that no evil would be visited upon them. Uphill there are some crosses believed to mark a monastic graveyard. The nearby *St. Manchan's Well* is thought to have been a place of annual pilgrimage in its early Christian days. Even now it is visited by people from around the world, partly because the oratory is an architectural wonder, constructed as it was without any mortar or stone-cutting equipment, but also because it is such an early and monumental testament to the belief in Christianity.

* Two miles north of Gallarus are the remains of the 12-century *Kilmalkedar Church,* which even in ruins is a splendid example of the Romanesque influence on early Irish architecture. There's another ogham stone here that recalls similar stones in India, as well as an ancient sundial and crosses carved with the Latin alphabet. This vantage point offers magnificent views of Mount Brandon. St. Brendan is said to have set forth from nearby Brandon Creek to become the true discoverer of America. In pre-Christian times, a legendary character called Bran, son of Febal, reputedly also voyaged from here to a wonderland thought to have been America. So the towering Mount Brandon really shares its name between Bran and Brendan. This mountain was considered sacred in pagan times, and every year at the end of July or in early August, there was a pilgrimage to the summit for the harvest festival of *Lug-or Lugh.* The dual purpose was to celebrate the harvest and to worship the great Celtic god *Lugh,* who was considered a savior. Later, when St. Brendan and Christianity came along, the reverence was transferred to the saint's holy place.

* From Brandon Creek, head in the direction of Dingle Town. About two miles along, you will come to the *Saint's Road.* You can follow this road a short distance, park your car, and climb the three-and-a-half miles to the summit of Mount Brandon for some spectacular views, if you're so inclined. Then back to the main road toward Dingle.

* At Dingle, take the road for the *Conor Pass.* This is not the easiest and safest road to navigate, but it's more than worth the extra care. Once you see the views, you'll agree. The road climbs steeply to its summit of 1500 feet 4½ miles from Dingle. From here, on a clear day, you can see much of the Peninsula (there is a place to park your car). To the south, you'll see all of Dingle Bay and Dingle Town. In the valley below are the Dingle lakes. To the north, your view is of Brandon and Tralee Bays and the sandy peninsula, Rough Point, which separates them.

* After you've recovered from the splendor of this site, continue down to the village of Stradbally. Along the way (once you've reached sea level again), the road parallels some of the magnificent Brandon Bay beaches. At Stradbally, there's an optional detour from your main

route to Tralee. This will bring you to Castlegregory, a tiny town at the base of Rough Point which, as mentioned, separates the bays of Brandon and Tralee. Castlegregory was named for Gregory Hoare, a 16th-century chieftain who built a castle here of which nothing now remains.

Legend: In 1580 Hoare's son, Hugh, occupied the castle and entertained Lord Grey's royal Protestant forces, including poet Edmund Spenser and Sir Walter Raleigh. They were en route to Smerwick Harbor to attack the papal forces who were holding out for Irish Catholicism at Dún an Oir. So opposed to her husband's hosting the enemy was Hugh's wife that she slipped down to the wine cellar and poured away all the wine before the forces had had a single drink. When Hugh learned of her deed, he was so furious that he attacked and in the struggle killed her. The next day, he too was found dead. The raging ghosts of these two are said to haunt the area (especially in foul weather) to this day.

* Continue back on the main road to Tralee. At Camp, you'll come close to the Slieve Mish Mountains again. One of them, Caherconree, is very close to the village, and you can climb its western section. On a triangular plateau over 2000 feet up are the ruins of a stone fort named for the mountain.

Legend: This was once the fort of Curaoi Mac Daire, pagan king of Munster. He had captured the gorgeous Blathnad, the mistress of Cuchulainn, forced her to marry him, and brought her to the fort. Blathnad was so enamored of Cuchulainn that she sent word to him through a fortress friend that when her husband slept she would pour milk into the Finglas, a mountain stream. Cuchulainn, when he saw the milky water, rushed up and slew the king, thus reclaiming his beautiful mistress.

* Continue on from here to *Tralee,* which many people think of as a beach resort. Quite the contrary, it's a bustling trading town (verging on a city) with a population of about 14,000. This is Kerry's chief center, located where the River Lee flows into Tralee Bay. Known throughout the world for its annual Rose of Tralee Festival, held in August, the town has a history linked closely with the Desmond family branch of the Anglo-Norman Fitzgeralds. Their castle stood at Denny Street and The Mall, and the town grew up around it, but all that remains of it today is a section of the wall. Following the Desmond War (1579–83) against the forces of Queen Elizabeth I, the last Des-

mond earl attempted to flee, but too late. He was captured and beheaded, and his head was sent to the gleeful queen, who promptly
flaunted it on London Bridge. At this stage, the castle and the Desmond
properties were turned over to Sir Edward Denny, after whom the
street was named. Later the Kerry poet Pierce Ferriter fought diligently here with his Catholic pro-Ireland troops in the 17th century.
But after six months the garrison surrendered again to the Protestant
English, and this time the buildings were virtually destroyed. The
castle was rebuilt again in 1653, only to be razed again during the
horrendous wars of William of Orange.

* In Tralee, you might like to see the old *Dominican Church* on
Princes Quay, built on the ruins of an ancient 13th-century church
and designed by the legendary Alexander Pugin. There are many
stained-glass windows here, along with a priory of magnificent sculptured stone gallans or pillars from the ancient church. Nearby are
many examples of fine old Georgian houses.

* A short mile east of Tralee is *Rathass Church*, a national monument, which houses an ogham stone inscribed with the earliest and
strangest form of Irish script.

* You may want to shop, eat, or stay in Tralee, although this is
not part of the suggested itinerary. If so, see relevant entries below.

* From here, make the 64-mile drive to Limerick, stopping briefly
for a look at the tidiest town in Ireland (as voted by the Irish Tourist
Board): Adare or *Ath Dara* (the Ford of the Oak Tree), with its charming thatched cottages. It is set among forests on the bank of the Mai
River. The Anglo-Normans seized the original town in the name of
Henry II, and it became a Fitzgerald domain (the earls of Kildare)
in the 13th century until its incorporation in the 14th century.

Adare has some extremely interesting historical structures, including:

* The 15th-century Franciscan Friary, in ruins except for the nave,
    choir, south transept, and a tower.
* The 13th-century remains of Trinitarian Abbey, including a sec-
    tion of the choir, the tower, and the nave.
* The 14th-century Augustinian Abbey, which retains its square
    tower, and sections of the choir and nave. In 1822 its cloisters
    were converted into a mausoleum for the Quin family, the
    earls of Dunraven. The Kildare and Desmond arms are over
    the doorway.
* The 13th-century Desmond Castle was built on the grounds of
    an ancient ringed fortress. Its ruins are surrounded by a moat,
    and a large courtyard with two buildings, one of them the
    castle's grand hall, remains. This castle was acquired by the

Gallarus Oratory

Fitzgerald family, earls of Kildare, in 1227. In the 15th century a spiteful Turlough O'Brien burned much of it, but the undaunted Fitzgeralds soon restored it to its former grandeur. Although Cromwell ordered the castle to be demolished in the 1600s, the estate remained Fitzgerald property until the following century, when the early ancestors of the present Earl of Dunraven purchased it.

Roots: Desmond, Fitzgerald, O'Brien (Desmond Castle).

* From here, make the 10-mile drive to Limerick, thence another 15 miles to Shannon.

DINGLE TOWN LODGINGS

* *Scheilig Hotel,* west of the village (Dingle 104). You might pass this hotel right by because it does look a little too modern, almost out of place in this rustic part of the country. But go in, and you'll find it very congenial. The place is done up with all the Irish crafts imaginable, from the rugs to the curtains. Even the overstuffed sofas and chairs are native, and covered—of course—with Irish tweed. There are turf fires to boot, and a lovely little crafts shop. Other facilities include a heated pool and a tennis court. There are 80 rooms, all with bath. See Restaurants for dining facility. But the real treat here is the panoramic view of Dingle Bay. If you saw the final romantic scenes of *The French Lieutenant's Woman,* you have the idea. Even though the film was shot in England, this setting is very similar. Hotel is closed from early October to mid-March, Moderate.

DINGLE TOWN RESTAURANTS

★ *An Cafe Lieartha,* Dykegate Street, is a novel twist for Ireland. It's a book and record store that's also a cozy little cafe, where you can lunch while you contemplate the country's literati. The menu includes mixed ham and cheese salad, corned beef, smoked mackerel salad, sandwiches, and cakes. Open 10 A.M. to 9 P.M. Inexpensive.

★ *The Armada,* Strand Street (Dingle 255), is a pleasant seafood restaurant near the pier that converts at night to candlelight. Homemade fish chowders, shellfish specials, fresh Dingle cod, and seafood curries are among the large selection. Open L—12:30 to 2:30. D—6 to 9. Closed Monday except during July and August. Wine license. Visa, Master. Inexpensive to moderate.

★ *Cois Farraige,* Strand Street, is a simple little Irish-type diner serving sandwiches and omelettes. Open 12:30 P.M. to 8 P.M. Inexpensive.

★ *Cuchulainn's Cookhouse,* The Mall, is another fast-food place, this one with a woody masculine decor. Available are sirloin and minute steaks, Irish ham, good hamburgers. Specialties are vegetarian salad and curries. Open 12:30 P.M. to 10:30 P.M. Visa, Master. Inexpensive. (*Note:* At this writing there is some talk of this place being sold or offered in a lottery.)

★ *Doyle's Seafood Bar,* John Street (Dingle 144), is the town's best-known restaurant. It seems that people from all over the world have made their way here. Americans remember it with great fondness and direct their friends to it. Doyle's is very intimate (brick walls and wainscoting, pine tables with sugan chairs) and seats only 34. Since there are no reservations, go early or you may end up standing in line for ages. Some of the foods that everyone raves about include: the tuna pâté, cockles and mussels, smoked haddock, brown trout, baked salmon *en papillote,* monkfish, crab claws and lobster, to name a few. Open 12:30 to 9 P.M. Closed Sundays. Full license. AE, Diners, Visa, Master. Moderate.

★ *Eirinagreinne,* Main Street, offers very basic hearth foods (homemade soups, cakes, fish grills) in a rustic setting. Open noon to 8 P.M. Inexpensive.

★ *The Forge Restaurant,* Holyground, (so named because the ground was once pocked with holes) (Dingle 19) is a pleasant little place with good fresh seafood and meat dishes on the menu. Open L—12:30 to 2:30. D—6 to 8. Inexpensive to moderate.

★ *The Half Door,* John Street (Dingle 300), is next door to Doyle's and some say an equal counterpart. This equally (if not more) intimate dining place seats 38 and *does* take reservations, so you're assured both of not having to wait and of not seeing those in line voraciously eyeing your table as you eat. Everyone seems to love the crab quiche as an appetizer, and entrees include trout in oatmeal, garlic mussels, seatrout, salmon, scallops, or the wonderful seafood au gratin mixture of crab, lobster, and prawns in a delicate cheese, cream, and wine sauce. There are good desserts too—if you can manage them. Open L—12:30 to 2:15. D—6 to 9. Closed Tuesday. Full license. AE, Diners, Visa, Master. Moderate.

★ *Riordan's Seafood Restaurant,* Bridge Street (Dingle 249), is a very tidy little seafood cafe with antique bottles filling the window. Prawns, lobster, crawfish, oysters, crab, fill the menu. Open 12:30 to 10 P.M. Wine license. AE, Visa, Master. Moderate.

* *The Scheilig Hotel,* west of the village (Dingle 104), has a restaurant overlooking the magnificent sweep of Dingle Bay. Fresh fish dishes are the best here; some find the smoked seafood platters a bit overwhelming. Open L—1 to 2:15. D—7 to 9. Moderate.

* *Whelan's,* Main Street (Dingle 41), is another of Dingle's good seafood restaurants, offering seafood pancakes, rainbow trout, lobster and crab salads. Along with these are good Irish stews and Gaelic steaks. Americans also love the homemade soups and the shepherd's pie. The decor is pleasant too—stone walls and tiled floors, dark wood tables. Wine license. Open L—12:30 to 2:15. D—7 to 9. Diners. Moderate.

DINGLE TOWN PUBS

* *O'Flaherty's Pub,* Bridge Street, is an engaging old traditional-music pub in a very rustic, down-to-earth setting.

Literature: John Millington Synge wrote poignantly of western Dingle and the Blaskets. He reportedly collected much of the material for his *Playboy of the Western World* in these areas, although the film version is set in Co. Mayo.

Edmund Spenser loved Ireland, but apparently despised Irish Catholics. Spenser was secretary to the infamous Lord Grey—the Elizabethan captain who defied the Catholics and their religion at the fortress called *Dún an Oir.* He took the fortress and slaughtered all 600 men of the papal force. Spenser, along with Sir Walter Raleigh—himself a poet—stood by and made no attempt to stop this slaughter. Spenser's presence did not go unnoticed; he became so hated that members of the Catholic contingency rushed his Cork homestead castle and burned it to the ground, scattering his cattle. One of his children died in the fire. Spenser fled to England, where he died a year later of starvation. A manuscript came to light later in which Spenser defended Lord Grey and the royalist position.

The Blasket Islands writers include Peig Sayers (*Peig*), Maurice O'Sullivan (*Twenty Years A-Growing*), and Thomas O'Crioffan (*The Islander*).

Sports

Swimming places range from vast strands to small, secluded coves. Real runners say the thrill of running here surpasses that of virtually any other place. The scenery makes uphill slogging almost a pleasure, and the high is unique. There are golf courses galore; also pools, tennis, horse and greyhound racing.

Roots: Scott (the South Pole Inn); Rice (Marie Antoinette and High House); the Fitzgeralds (St. James Church); McCarthy, Hussey, O'Sullivan (St. Mary's Church); Ferriter (Ferriter's Castle); O'Flaherty (O'Flaherty's Pub). Others of note: Browne, O'Connor, Murphy, O'Shea, Lynch, and Clifford.

TRALEE RESTAURANTS

* *Ballyseede Castle,* three miles east of Tralee on the N21 (21959), has a variety of good foods and puts on a medieval banquet, complete with entertain-

ment, in the summertime. Full license. Open for breakfast 8–10. Reopens from noon to 9:30 P.M. AE, Diners, Visa, Master. Moderate.

* *Cordon Bleu,* the Square (21596), is a surprisingly intimate restaurant for such a bustling town. In addition to the veal cordon bleu, you'll find a variety of locally caught seafoods and even spaghetti. Quite acceptable. Open 6:30 to 11:30 P.M. Closed Sundays. Wine license. Diners, Master, Visa.

* *Kirby's Brogue Inn,* Rock Street (21226), is an oversized pub offering good lunches in an old-time atmosphere. Traditional farming equipment forms part of the decor. There's also a coffee shop and, upstairs, a modern restaurant. The downstairs quarters are open from 10 A.M. to 10 P.M.—inexpensive. The upstairs—6 P.M. to 11 P.M.—moderate. Full license. Visa, Master.

* *The Mount Brandon Hotel,* Princess Street (21311), has a pleasant enough coffee shop offering a range from snacks to full meals (inexpensive to moderate). The more elegant and expensive dining room is a bit snobbish, unless you're dressed to the nines, but the food is good. Open noon to 9:45 P.M. AE, Visa, Master.

* *The Oyster Tavern,* four miles west of Tralee at Spa (36102), is a pub well versed in seafoods. All the fresh fish is caught locally. Many rave about the oysters here, but the grilled salmon steak and the sautéed crab in garlic butter are also very good. Open for food 1 to 2:30 P.M. and 7 to 10:30 P.M. Full license. Moderate.

TRALEE PUBS

* *Kirby's Brogue Inn,* Rock Street, is a pleasant Old-World pub described under Restaurants.

* *The Oyster Tavern,* four miles west of Tralee at Spa, is a well-known old watering hole also described under Restaurants.

TRALEE AREA ENTERTAINMENT/ANNUAL EVENTS

* *Siamsa Tire,* the National Folk Theater of Ireland, Godfrey Place (23055), is a program based on Ireland's heritage of music, folklore, and dance—the heart of which is the Irish language. From mid-June to the end of June on Monday and Thursday. July and August on Monday, Tuesday, Thursday, and Friday. Sept. 1 through Sept. 9 on Monday and Thursday. Curtain time 8:30 P.M.

* *Teach Siamsa* is the rural version of *Siamsa Tire.* This theater workshop is held in Finuge (three miles from Listowel off the main Tralee-Listowel road; Listowel is 17 miles from Tralee). Wednesdays during July and August. Curtain at 9 P.M. Another workshop is at Carraig (six miles from Dingle Town between Muirioch and Feothanach; Dingle is 31 miles from Tralee). Fridays during July and August. Curtain at 9 P.M.

* The Rose of Tralee Festival is a six-day celebration with races, concerts, traditional music sessions, games, and general merrymaking. The whole shebang is capped with the crowning of 'the most beautiful girl in all the world'—the Rose of Tralee. Held each year at the end of August/early part of September.

* Listowel Writers' Week. Seventeen miles from Tralee, in Listowel, is an annual working convention (also a lot of playing) attended by writers the first week in July. The fiction workshops cover everything from poetry to short stories, novels to playwriting.

X. SHANNON

Knappogue Castle Banquet

Lovely and fruitful is this land to which we have come . . .

—from the Celtic, 14th century

YOUR PERSONALIZED SHANNONSIDE ITINERARY

Day One

★ Arrive in the Shannon area mid- to late afternoon and check into your lodging. The strong suggestion is *Dromoland Castle* in New-market-on-Fergus, which is 17 miles from Limerick and close to Shannon Airport. Other suitable hotels are also listed under Lodgings.

★ Plan on attending the nine o'clock medieval banquet complete with entertainment at either *Knappogue* (preferred) or *Bunratty* castles, both nearby. Another possibility is the Shannon *Ceili,* a kind of Irish barn dance with food and wine, at Bunratty Folk Park next to the castle. Yet another alternative (sans entertainment as such) is *Durty Nelly's,* a larger-than-life Irish pub dating from the early 1600s. If you want to stay put, Dromoland has fine dining facilities (see Restaurants for details on all these).

★ If you arrive early enough, you could consider some sightseeing. Possibilities include:

(1) A tour of one of the castles. Nearby *Knappogue,* built in 1467, was for centuries the home of the McNamara family, who built 42 such edifices in their extensive domains. Cromwell confiscated the castle for a time, but it returned to the McNamaras once monarchy was reestablished. In the early 1800s it was sold to the Scott family, from whom it passed successively to the Butlers and the Quinns. In 1966 it was purchased by Mark Edwin Andrews of Houston, Texas, a former Assistant Secretary of the U.S. Navy. With the assistance of the Irish Government, he embarked on an extensive restoration program, which included refurnishing the banquet and entry halls and the reception rooms. The building now has elements of the Georgian and Regency periods in addition to its original Norman design. It's open from 9:30 A.M. to 5 P.M. daily, and in the evenings for the banquets. Knappogue is three miles from the village of Quin.

Near here is *Craggaunowen Castle,* a 16th-century structure that has been restored; its ground floor houses portions of the Hunt collection of medieval art. The balance of the collection is at the NIHE College at Plassey, on the Dublin Road in Limerick. Craggaunowen Castle's grounds contain a reconstructed *crannog* (an island built on an inland body of water as an easily defended dwelling place) and a ringed fort. Within the latter are reconstructions of farmers' houses from the fourth century, showing just how much can be done by human labor unassisted by machinery. There's also a souterrain (underground passage which could be used for food storage or escape at need). Open daily from 9:30 A.M. to 5:30 P.M.

Bunratty Castle stands on what was once an island on the northern bank of the Ratty River, where it meets the Shannon. It was built in 1460 on the site of three previous castles, a vital spot that overlooked one of Ireland's major shipping ports in those days. The road by the castle was once an impassable marsh. Originally it was a MacNamara abode and fortress, but in the 1500s the Kings of Thomond—the O'Briens—took it over. During Elizabeth I's reign, the castle thrived and glittered for the aristocracy. This is when the walls and ceilings were ornamented with resplendent stuccowork, elegant furnishings were installed, and magnificent gardens were cultivated. It is thought that William Penn, founder of Pennsylvania, lived in this castle as an infant. In 1954 Lord Gort purchased Bunratty and, with the assistance of the Irish Tourist Board, restored it to its authentic 15th-century state. Today the castle exhibits one of the finest collections of 15th- to 17th-century art, furnishings, and accoutrements in northern Europe. From the great banquet hall, to the captain's quarters, to the kitchen and the solar rooms, the castle is fascinating. Note that even if you are planning to attend an evening banquet at Knappogue or Bunratty, it is best to tour the castles during daytime hours, as you don't have the time in the evening.

Another feature of this area is the *Bunratty Folk Park* just behind Bunratty Castle. Here you will see the rural heritage of Ireland—basketmaking, cooking, breadmaking, candlemaking, agricultural workings, thatching, farming, and housing. It's a valuable insight into history. You should also visit *Bunratty Cottage,* a replica of the early slate-roofed country home which offers a wide range of beautiful handmade Irish goods (see Shops).

(2) If you have a good deal of time before the evening, you could visit the majestic *Cliffs of Moher* (32 miles from Dromoland). Rising 700 feet above the sea and extending five miles along the coast, these cliffs are one of Ireland's most popular sights. At the northern end is the *O'Brien Tower,* built by wealthy landowner Cornelius O'Brien in 1835 as a place from which to observe the beauty of the area. From here, you can see clear to the Aran Islands off Galway and the purple mountains of Connemara.

(3) The Burren or *Boirinn,* a stony area, rises from the background of the Cliffs and spreads out to form northern Clare. This strange, lunar landscape is composed mainly of limestone. While you certainly shouldn't attempt to explore it all (a total of 200 square miles), a

Cliffs of Moher

sample of it will provide you with megalithic tombs, stone forts, caverns and castles, craggy moon-like rocks, and the strangest flora in the country. Many historians feel that this area is the most typical of prehistoric Ireland.

Note: Exploring both the Cliffs of Moher and the Burren caves requires *extreme Caution:* people have slipped to their deaths from the cliffs. And Burren Caves, easily entered, seem then to be inescapable. Take special care.

(4) *Lough Gur,* 10 miles south of Limerick town, is one of the country's most historic sites. The shores of this small horseshoe-shaped lake are dotted with prehistoric pagan monuments. Here you'll see dolmens, stone circles, ruined fortresses, prehistoric graves, *crannogs* (man-made islands), pottery, weapons, and skeletons, along with ruins of the Desmond castles.

(5) *Glenstal Abbey,* a castellated 19th-century mansion, is nine miles east of Limerick City in Muroe. Once the family home of the Barringtons, it was converted into a college by the Benedictine order in 1927. Its stately Romanesque features are of particular interest.

(6) *Limerick City,* 17 miles from Dromoland, is covered in a later optional tour.

Day Two

* Breakfast at Dromoland or other lodging and check out. Travel to Shannon for your departure to America or Europe. That is, unless (hopefully) you're staying on to explore the Galway, Mayo, and Donegal regions as outlined in subsequent itineraries.

SHANNON AREA LODGINGS

* *Dromoland Castle,* Newmarket-on-Fergus (71144), is a rural Irish castle— a kind of country version of the dramatic *Ashford Castle,* also in County Mayo. But Ashford is much larger and more regal than the woody, rustic Dromoland. Built in the 16th century as an O'Brien family fortress, Dromoland has 1500 acres of green lawns and deep forests, as well as a small fishing lake. The property was purchased by Bernard McDonough, a West Virginia businessman, in the 1960s. He refurbished the castle with antique furniture and art, including portraits of the O'Briens, and turned it into a hotel. Also on the grounds is a nine-hole golf course, a tennis court, and a croquet lawn. Horseback riding and salmon fishing are available nearby. The area is excellent for running, cycling, and game hunting. Dromoland has 67 rooms, all with bath and telephone. You'll enjoy the cozy bar whose tall windows overlook the grounds and the high-ceilinged, wood-and-damask dining room with its chandelier. At early-morning breakfasts you're quite likely to see the giant Irish hares—big as wolfhounds—frolicking on the lawns. Note: Dromoland is closed from November 1 to April 1. Expensive.

Dromoland Castle

* *Jury's Hotel,* Ennis Road (55266), is a fine choice for a modern hotel in the area. It's on the outskirts of Limerick (within easy walking distance) and modeled on the lines of the other Jury's Hotels in the country. There are 96 rooms, all with bath. Good dining (see Restaurants).

* *The Limerick Inn,* Ennis Road (51544), is a very good modern hotel with 133 rooms, all with bath. Moderate to expensive.

* *The Old Ground,* Ennis (15 miles from the Shannon area) (21127), is an old hotel that was once the abode of the O'Gorman Mahon family. Its cozy, public rooms, furnished with rustic antiques, are a strong part of its appeal, along with the Old-World restaurant. There are 63 rooms, all with bath. It's a little far from the Shannon area if you're planning to attend one of the castle banquets there, but it's very pleasant. Moderate.

* *The Shannon Shamrock Hotel* (Fitzpatrick's), Bunratty, next to Bunratty Castle (61177), is a very modern and comfortable Irish hotel with 100 rooms, all with bath. It offers fireplace sitting rooms, stately dining rooms, a pool, a sauna, and tennis and squash courts. Altogether very pleasant, and close to the castle and the airport. Moderate.

SHANNON AREA RESTAURANTS

* *Chef's Cold Buffet* at the Piano Bar of Jury's Hotel, Ennis Road, on the fringe of Limerick City (47266). Excellent carvery luncheons, snacks, and dinners at Jury's bar. Besides meat dishes and salads, there are also seafoods. Good choices. Open noon to 12:30 P.M. AE, Diners, Visa, Master. Inexpensive.

* *The Coffee Dock* of Jury's Hotel, Ennis Road, on the fringe of Limerick City (47266). Offers everything from fast foods to full meals. All good and hearty, just as they are in the other Jury's hotels around the country. Open 7 A.M. to 11 P.M. Full license. AE, Diners, Visa, Master. Inexpensive to moderate.

* *The Copper Room* of Jury's Hotel, Ennis Road, on the fringe of Limerick City (47266). Limerick's only intimate, elegant dining room serving Old-World—particularly classical French—specialties. One of western Ireland's most-reserved places. Open 7:30 P.M. to 11 P.M. AE, Diners, Visa, Master. Expensive.

* *Dromoland Castle,* Newmarket-on-Fergus (71144), has a stately dining room that's the height of country elegance. The food is good too—a mixture of Irish and Continental dishes, both seafood and meat. The roast turkey and ham with sausage dressing were especially good, as was the thinly sliced rare beef in a Madeira sauce. Grilled salmon steak, scampi, and lamb were other good choices. There's often live music in the bar after dinner. The buffet breakfast here includes fresh fruits, juice, homemade breads, croissants, and preserves along with the full traditional Irish breakfast. They'll even broil a fish, if that's what you want. Open B—7:30 to 10. L—1 to 2. D—7 to 9. Full license. AE, Diners, Master, Visa. Expensive.

* *Bunratty Castle,* Bunratty (61788—Shannon Castle Tours), holds medieval banquets with entertainment twice each evening (6 and 9) year round. Here you're ushered up the stone staircase to the great hall and given the customary mead to sip while you have a look at some of the castle's wonderful antiques and art. A traditional program of music and entertainment accompanies the dinner of rather-too-basic Irish food. Be forewarned that this place is popular—reserve early. You might want to do this as soon as you arrive in Ireland, and that applies to the other castle banquets as well. Major credit cards. Moderate.

★ *Durty Nelly's Pub,* Bunratty (74072), is reportedly one of Ireland's most popular pubs. The crowds who throng it at all hours would seem to confirm this. Dating from the early 1600s, it's thatched outside and dimly lit inside. The crowds have made no impression on the original stone walls, the wooden settees and benches, and the turf fires. This pub is very much as it was when the castle's guards used to hustle in for refreshment. The fact that much of its clientele is Irish shows that it's authentic and not just a tourist stop. Upstairs there's a quieter rustic bar, and next to it is The Oyster, where you can get everything from a full Irish meal to sandwiches and snacks. Many choose Durty Nelly's for their evening out in Shannon, starting with the meal and staying on for drinks. There are also frequent impromptu sing-songs here.

★ *Knappogue Castle,* Quin, northeast of Sixmilebridge and 10 miles from Shannon Airport (61788—Shannon Castle Tours). Like Bunratty, Knappogue serves mead before ushering you into a vast dining hall for several hours of banqueting and entertainment. But Knappogue seems a little more spontaneous and less forced about it all. Most people prefer the food here, which is of the hearty Irish type and plentiful as well. Although some of the entertainment verges on the frivolous, there are meaty chunks of Irish history tossed in as well. (Word has it that some of the sillier aspects of the program are about to be pruned.) Beautiful harp music is a welcome feature. Banquets at 6 or 9 daily. Major credit cards. Moderate.

★ *The Limerick Inn,* Ennis Road between Limerick and Bunratty (51544), subdues its modern style with an elegant candlelit restaurant serving very acceptable meals from French haute cuisine to Irish basic. Worth a try. This Bunratty Room is open from 6 to 10 P.M. AE, Diners, Visa, Master. Moderate.

★ *The Shannon Shamrock Hotel,* Bunratty (61177), has one of the area's finer, more sophisticated restaurants. It's a great place if you're stuck—or waiting—to head off to America. If you don't want the castle-type places (especially on your last night in Ireland), you might prefer the more conventional facilities here. Open 12:30 to 11 P.M. AE, Diners, Visa, Master.

★ *The Old Ground,* O'Connell Street (21127), is a classic Old-World dining room that holds out in the midst of modern turmoil. It's worth the try that many satisfied patrons have given it: the selection of French and Irish food is excellent. Open L—12:30 to 2:30. D—7 to 9. Grill area open later. AE, Diners, Visa, Masters. Moderate to expensive.

★ *The Shannon Ceili,* Bunratty, near Bunratty Castle and Folk Village. A rural version of what you get at either of the Shannon Castles: a sherry reception, a hearty Irish meal, and a couple of hours of entertainment. At this reconstructed medieval barn, which resembles a fisherman's warehouse, you sit on benches at long pine tables to be plied with Irish stew, boiled potatoes, and soda bread. This is accompanied by jugs of red wine and followed by fresh apple pie with cream and Irish tea. With the country-style entertainment (tin whistles, flutes, fiddles, spoons, and accordions), the whole event comes across as an enjoyable Irish version of an American barn dance. Open nightly. One sitting at 5:45, the other at 9:00.

PUBS

★ *Durty Nelly's Pub,* Bunratty, is one of the country's most popular watering holes (see Restaurants).

SHOPS

* *Shannon Airport Duty-Free Shop* was once the greatest shopping deal in the Western world (from the late forties when it opened right into the seventies). People traveling back to America from Europe would go out of their way to stop over at Shannon. Everything from expensive perfume and liquor to watches, cameras, binoculars, radios, crystal, and apparel was tax-free. Of course, it wasn't all duty-free when you reached America, but people came up with marvelously inventive ways of sneaking the goods in anyway; this was, of course, part of the fun. But times have changed. While the Shannon shop is now an enormous department store (too big to cover in the short Aer Lingus stopover time allotted for flights from Dublin to America), the prices no longer seem so appealing. This probably has a lot to do with the vast and growing number of discount stores in America, rather than with changes at the Shannon shop itself. But this said, the shop is still very worthwhile. It has a composite of nearly all the Irish crafts, along with Irish books, foods, and liquor. So if you haven't had the opportunity to shop in Ireland, this is ideal. Note that you can bring Irish meats (sausages, bacon, etc.) back to America with you (a privilege given to no other country). If a raw-recruit customs inspector tells you it's not so, ask to speak to the chief inspector who will immediately approve it.

The Shannon Duty-Free Shop is open daily, but can be visited *only* when you're about to leave the country.

* *The Bunratty Cottage,* Bunratty (opposite the Castle) is a 100-year-old restored country home converted into a two-story shop. Emphasizing the fashions of owner-designer Vonnie Reynolds, the shop also carries Donegal tweed apparel, Aran sweaters, Pringle cashmeres, Irish linen, Donald Davies womenswear, and a large collection of Waterford crystal, Belleek, and Wedgwood china. The shop will mail your purchases anywhere in the world. Open daily from 9 A.M. to 6 P.M. except during the fall and winter months; then open 10 A.M. to 5 P.M.

Roots: McNamara; Scott; Butler; Quinn (Knappogue Castle); O'Brien; Penn (Bunratty Castle); O'Gorman Mahon (the Old Ground Hotel, Ennis).

Book Two

THE OPTIONAL TOURS FROM LIMERICK CITY TO THE HIGH REACHES OF DONEGAL

Mayo Seascape

XI. LIMERICK CITY

O'Connell Street, Limerick

Better to know the world that's gone past
The true beauty is there.
                              —from the Celtic, 12th century

YOUR PERSONALIZED LIMERICK ITINERARY

This tour comprises only a couple of hours, unless you plan on extensive shopping, dining, or other activities. Note that Limerick is one of Ireland's oldest cities and one of the few in the Irish Republic that gives an impression of dinginess (comparable to such Northern Ireland cities as Derry). Towns like Wexford and Kilkenny gleam by comparison, but this is not to say that Limerick is lacking in fine restaurants, hotels, and shops.

* Start at *Thomond Bridge,* which was built in 1840 from the designs of Irish architect James Pain. It replaced a 13th-century bridge erected during the reign of King John. The drawbridge, guard house, and gate are still intact.

* Here at the western end of the bridge is the *Limerick Treaty Stone,* marking the city's allegiance to William of Orange after the Williamite Wars.

* *King John's Castle* at the eastern end of the bridge is a superb example of medieval architecture, erected, like Thomond Bridge itself, in the 13th century. Its imposing towers and curtain walls have survived the years. During the 18th century British military barracks were installed, along with still-standing castle yard houses. All in all, it offers a representative picture of the Irish past.

* Proceeding to Nicholas and Bridge Streets, you'll come to *St. Mary's Cathedral,* founded in the late 12th century as a residence by Donal Mor O'Brien, one of the last kings of Ireland. He reportedly deeded it to the Irish Church, and it is atypical of the country's churches in its Romanesque doorways, pilasters, and palatial halls.

* Moving down Mary's Street, you'll come to *Ball's Bridge,* from which you'll see the old *Limerick Walls,* a defense against marauding medieval armies. By the 18th century they had become a nuisance that prevented the city's expansion. Finally the city fathers acted on their discontent and the walls came tumbling down. Fortunately for historians and later generations, a few sections escaped oblivion.

* Moving down Lock Quay and Clare Street, you'll come to Lelia Street and another section of the Limerick Walls. More ruins may be seen at the nearby *St. John's Hospital* Green, including two fascinating ancient gateways within the grounds.

* Nearby at Cathedral Place is *St. John's Cathedral,* a 19th-century Gothic structure with a magnificent 280-foot tower and beautiful marble carvings of the Madonna by Benzoni. Adjacent *St. John's Square*

was a fashionable address in the mid-18th century, when western landed gentry established their townhouses here. From this point you may want to find a dining place or glean the shops.

Roots: O'Brien (St. Mary's Cathedral).

LIMERICK'S HISTORY

Limerick is the third largest city in the Irish Republic. Located on the River Shannon, sixteen miles from Shannon Airport, it is one of the country's main port and passenger-arrival cities. Limerick is known worldwide for its cured bacon and ham and for its traditional Limerick lace.

The first signs of settlement here date from the ninth century. The Danes who were marauding the countryside established a base near the river. For over a century, this colony was under frequent attack by the Irish, until Brian Boru plundered the town and sent the settlers fleeing. In the latter part of the twelfth century, the Normans took the town and held it until the O'Brien family gained control. In 1210, when King John visited Limerick, he immediately ordered the construction of a castle and a bridge to span the Shannon.

The security of the city was so much enhanced by additional walls over the years that the British crown considered it a suitable place to convene its parliaments. But as secure as it seemed, Confederate forces took control in 1642. In 1651 the Cromwellians, under Ireton, laid siege to Limerick, and for six months the citizens resisted. They would have continued to resist if some of the garrison soldiers hadn't betrayed them to the Cromwellians.

After defeat at the Battle of the Boyne in 1690, the Irish soldiers retreated to Limerick, pursued by William of Orange and his large forces. The Orangemen prepared for a siege, anxiously awaiting the arrival of their heavier artillery. But the great Irish leader Patrick Sarsfield intercepted and stopped the artillery train at Ballyneety. After three futile attempts to overpower the city, William gave up and stormed away in a rage—one that he didn't forget. A year later, he dispatched an army to Limerick under General Ginkel. After several months of futile siege, the aggressor entered into negotiations that would culminate in the Treaty of Limerick of 1691. Under its terms, the Irish garrison marched out with full honors. Eleven thousand of them later joined the standard of Louis of France, but that was only the beginning of the exodus. During the next half-century about half a million Irishmen went off to France and Spain to become soldiers. The Treaty of Limerick itself was never ratified, because the Protestant parliament refused to comply with the stipulation for religious tolerance.

LIMERICK LODGINGS

* *Clifton House,* Ennis Road in Limerick's suburbs (26996), is a small, congenial guesthouse hotel with open fires, gardens, and terraces. Twenty-three comfortable rooms (18 with bath). Inexpensive.

* *Jury's Hotel* (55266) and *Limerick Inn* (51544), both on Ennis Road, are described under Shannon Lodgings.

* *Limerick Ryan,* Ennis Road (45922), is one of the modern Ryan chain hotels with 184 rooms, all with bath. Moderate.

* *Woodfield House,* Ennis Road (53022), is a cozy, intimate little hotel with

25 rooms (18 with bath), a pleasant dining room, pub, and open-fire lounge. Inexpensive.

RESTAURANTS

* *Jury's Hotel* restaurants (the Coffee Dock and the Copper Room), Ennis Road (55266), are described under Shannon Restaurants.

* *The Limerick Inn,* Ennis Road (51544), whose Bunratty Room is described under Shannon Restaurants, also has the Clare Room, open from 7:30 A.M. to 11 P.M. for everything from tasty snacks to complete meals. Inexpensive to moderate. AE, Diners, Visa, Master. Note that the Inn also has a dinner cabaret on Wednesday, Friday, and Saturday nights at 8:30. Moderate.

* *The Limerick Ryan,* Ennis Road (53922), also has two restaurants: a dining room open from 6 to 9:30 P.M. offering acceptable Continental and Irish cuisine at moderate prices, and a grill room open from 12:30 to 11:30 P.M. for good snacks to full meals (inexpensive to moderate). AE, Diners, Carte Blanche, Master, Visa.

* *Lydon's Galleon Room* and downstairs *Bistro,* O'Connell Street (48358), offer very acceptable food and wines (inexpensive); the Spanish-style Galleon emphasizes hearty Irish fare, and the French-style Bistro highlights simple French and Italian dishes. Galleon open 11 A.M. to 11:30 P.M. except Sunday when it doesn't open until 5 P.M. Bistro open noon to midnight, but closed Sunday.

* *Miller's Bistro and Wine Bar,* Lower Cecil Street (41166), is a brand-new Limerick delight specializing in remarkably good seafood and wine at equally remarkable low prices. Pleasant pine-paneled decor. Lunch, noon to 3; dinner 6 to midnight.

* *Ted's Brazen Head Grill,* O'Connell Street (47412), is a cushiony restaurant/pub with booths, dim lighting, air-conditioning, and fine snacks, meat, and seafood. Open 10:30 A.M. to 11:30 P.M. Inexpensive to moderate.

PUBS

* *The Glory Hole Pub,* O'Connell Street in the Royal George Hotel, is a woody, candlelit spot offering Irish traditional music and ballads Tuesday through Friday nights.

* *The Lucky Lamp,* Ellen Street, is an ancient attraction that was once the greatest wine shop in the area; now a dark paneled pub with barrel seats and good food ranging from shepherd's and steak and kidney pie to hearty sandwiches, accompanied by great traditional singing at night.

* *Joe Malone's Pub,* off O'Connell Street and Market Ward, is another old haunt with barrels on bare floors to serve as seats and the threat of a singsong impending at any time of day.

* *The Olde Tom,* Thomas Street, is a bar/restaurant with reasonable food and traditional music at lunch from 12:30 to 2:30. More music on Monday, Wednesday, and Friday nights.

ENTERTAINMENT

* Belltable Arts Centre, O'Connell Street (49866), does a mixed bag of evening entertainment ranging from plays to ballads and 'crack' (good talk) to Yeats remembered.

* *Seisiún* at King John's Castle, eastern end of Thomond Bridge (47522), offers a fine display of the Irish traditional music heritage, including song and dance, on Tuesday and Thursday nights.

SPORTS

This area is a treasure trove for the sports-minded:

* *Fishing.* If salmon is your goal, you'll find them in the tidal parts of the Shannon, while the Mulcair River and its tributaries are good for trout and grilse. Please note that daily or weekly permits are required for salmon and trout fishing on the Shannon, Newport, and Mulcair Rivers. Be sure to get one from the Electricity Supply Board (ESB) Showroom on O'Connell Street in Limerick to avoid a fine. The Bunratty River, which also has trout, salmon, and grilse, does not require a permit.

If your sport is game angling or coarse angling, this area is also for you. Detailed maps of the favored haunts are available from the Irish Tourist Board office at 62 O'Connell Street in Limerick.

* *Hunting.* There is plenty of hunting from November through March in this area, but not of the kind that involves scouring the woodlands and country-side on foot in search of bear or deer. 'The hunt' in Ireland, as in Great Britain, is that of the group on horseback in pursuit of foxes or hares. If it's done on foot with dogs, the sport is called beagling. Visitors are generally welcomed, but there are fees involved. If you're interested, the Irish Tourist Board office on O'Connell Street has all the details.

* *Riding and cycling.* There are several stables in the area for horseback riders, and bicycles may be rented from a number of downtown Limerick shops.

* *Golfing.* There are two 18-hole golf courses and several pitch-and-putt courses within a few miles of the city.

* *Running.* Very flat surfaces compared to much of the country: site of the annual Limerick Marathon.

* *Other sports.* The area also offers tennis and squash courts, greyhound racing, horse racing, swimming, rowing, Gaelic football, and hurling.

SHOPS

* Irwin Bros., Patrick Street—antique jewelry
* Irish Handcrafts Shop, O'Connell Street—all handcrafts
* Once Upon a Time, Ellen Street off Patrick Street—small items, antiques
* Cottage Industries Craft Shop, Ellen Street—Irish handcrafts
* The Ellen Street Market, down a cobblestone lane off Ellen Street—a good deal of junk here, but mixed in you might find a number of small treasures, especially antique dishes and silver
* Todd's, O'Connell Street—Limerick's best, with its Waterford crystal and Aran knitwear
* Colleen Bawn, Upper O'Connell Street—Irish crafts
* Goodwin's, Lower Cecil Street—Irish glass and china
* O'Mahony's, O'Connell Street—wonderful selection of books of Irish interest.

Literature: Kate O'Brien wrote poignantly about dismal Limerick (then rushed off to exciting London to recover herself).

Special attraction: The Granary Tavern (47266) Wonderful candlelight banquet nights carrying you back to the 18th c. 8 P.M. nightly, except Sun. Moderate. Overstuffed sandwiches during regular pub hours. Inexpensive. Full license. AE., Master, Visa.

XII. GALWAY, THE ARAN ISLANDS, AND CONNEMARA

Galway mirror

The harp of the wood plays melody,
its music brings perfect peace.
> —from the Celtic, ninth century

YOUR PERSONALIZED GALWAY ITINERARY

This delightful tour of Galway City, the Aran Islands, and Connemara could take weeks or months, or it can be done in a few hurried
days. In either case, it is unforgettable, in the way that Dingle is
unforgettable for its richness or Donegal for its ruggedness. Galway
is a spectacular blend of the two, which you could spend years enjoying:
one of Ireland's most luminous places.

It is recommended that you drive up from Limerick in the morning
so as to have the afternoon for sightseeing, shopping, and a pub or
two in Galway City.

★ Drive the 65 miles from Limerick to Galway on the N18, which
passes through the village of Gort. About a mile outside the village
is the turn for *Coole Park,* the once grand estate of Lady Gregory,
the famous Irish playwright. With William Butler Yeats and others,
she was a founder of the Abbey Theatre. Her mansion was a meeting
place for such literary lights as Sean O'Casey, George Bernard Shaw,
and John Millington Synge, some of whom, including Yeats, wrote
at Coole Park. In fact, Yeats lived there for a number of years to
recover from a period of ill health. While the house has been destroyed,
the fine beech tree where these notable writers carved their initials
still remains, as does the wooded glen along the lake that made its
way into many Yeats poems.

★ About a mile farther down the Galway road, take the signposted
road for *Thoor Ballylee.* The square 16th-century castle keep there
was erected by the de Burgo family and later purchased, restored,
and named by William Butler Yeats. Here he spent many summers
writing his poetry in the years between 1917 and 1929. You will find
a book shop here and a place to have tea.

★ Continue on to Ardahan, where you may wish to break off left
of the Galway road through Owenbristy to Kinvara, site of the 15th-
century Irish castle of *Dunguaire.* It overlooks the sea and has medieval banquets comparable to those of Knappogue and Bunratty (some
say even better). Richard Martyn, who was the Mayor of Galway,
occupied the castle in 1642, and the Martyns stayed on until the 1900s.
It was purchased in 1924 by Lady Gregory, Oliver St. John Gogarty,
and other Irish writers.

★ Moving on, you'll come to the tiny village of Kilcolgan which is
known throughout Ireland for an engaging little thatched-roof pub/
restaurant called *Moran's of the Weir.* This itinerary should bring

you here around lunch time. But be forewarned that there's only a tiny sign indicating the left turnoff for Moran's after you pass through Kilcolgan village; if you blink, you'll miss it.

Moran's, on the shores of Galway Bay, is also referred to as Moran's Oyster Cottage for the delicacies served (in season) with its delicious homemade brown bread and a creamy glass or pint of Guinness. But there's far more: fresh salmon, smoked salmon, crab claws, prawns, summer salads, and seafood cocktails. You can go all the way and have a full meal, or just sip the seafood soup or sample the crab legs. Facilities include the casual dining room, the bar, or an old-fashioned snug. The woman who carries on the family tradition is extremely pleasant. Open 10:30 A.M. to 11:30 P.M. daily. In winter, open on Sunday from 5 to 10 P.M. only. Inexpensive.

* North from here on the Galway road, you'll come to Clarinbridge. If you haven't had lunch, or are parched for a drink, you might like to check out *Paddy Burke's*. It's a dusky old-time pub that offers especially good food, snacks to full meals—homemade vegetable soup, Clarinbridge chowder, roast pork, chicken, beef, or ham, and salads. Open 12:30 to 10:30 P.M. Moderate.

* Proceed from here to Galway for an afternoon of sightseeing, shopping, and pubbing. You may wish to check into your overnight lodging before you begin. Two suggestions: the *Great Southern Hotel* at Eyre Square, in the heart of Galway, or slightly more secluded, the *Ardilaun House Hotel* on Taylor's Hill, a delightfully quiet and comfortable place with charming sitting rooms and a garden restaurant. Both are expensive. More moderate accommodations are also listed under Lodgings.

* Begin your tour at *Eyre Square,* named for an old merchant family here. The *Padraic O'Conaire Monument,* sculpted by Albert Powers, honors one of the most prolific Gaelic writers of the 20th century. *The Browne Doorway* of carved stone, circa 1627, is a relic of the prosperous trading days and shows the strong Spanish influence on Galway's architecture and on the affluent families of the times. This massive portal was once the entrance to the Browne mansion, home of another prosperous merchant family whose peers included Lynches, Joyces, and Frenches.

* At the north end of the Square is a memorial to a Galway patriot of the 1916 Rising, *Liam Mellowes.* The entire square is landscaped as a memorial garden to the late President John F. Kennedy, who once spoke here to the citizens of Galway.

* Follow William Street (which becomes Shop Street) to Lombard on the right. Here near Market Street is the *Church of St. Nicholas,* established by the Normans in 1320. Columbus is said to have prayed

in this church, with its unusual triple nave, before setting sail for America, accompanied by Galwayman Rice de Culvy as a member of his crew. Near the church is the *Old Jail*, built in 1624. Carved in the black marble wall are a skull and crossbones, with the inscription: *This memorial of stern and unbending justice to the chief magistrate of the City, James Lynch Fitzstephen, elected mayor A.D. 1490, who condemned and executed his own guilty son, Walter, on this spot.* The Gothic door and window have withstood the rigors of time.

   ★ At the corner of Shop Street is *Lynch's Castle,* one of Ireland's finest examples of a castellated mansion within a town. It was established in 1320 as the abode of the Lynch family, who gave the town many of its mayors. It has now become a bank, but the building retains its original style.

   ★ From here move along Bridge Street across *O'Brien's Bridge,* then down Dominick Street to Claddagh Quay. *The Claddagh* is probably Ireland's oldest fishing village. When Galway was in Norman hands, the native Irish lived and fought here for their culture and language in the face of many Anglo restrictions. Modern buildings now replace the attractive thatched cottages that once housed over 8000 people. You may wish to purchase a Claddagh ring while you're in Ireland; it's formed by two hands clasping a heart, the symbol of the proud Claddagh Village, and has become a traditional wedding ring.

   Crossing the *Claddagh Bridge,* you'll come to the *Spanish Arch,* built into the old town wall in the late 16th century to help protect offloading Spanish merchantmen against thievery. Extending from the Arch is the *Spanish Parade,* once a favored haunt of the foreign traders and their families. Attached to the arch today is the *Galway Museum,* home of the city's relics. You can climb to the top and view the once densely populated Claddagh across the River Corrib.

   ★ Some other sights of possible interest run a short distance northeast of the town (any distance in Galway City is reasonably short). At the *Salmon Weir Bridge,* on early spring and summer days, you can watch the salmon leap upstream on their way to spawn.

   ★ Opposite the bridge is the Catholic Cathedral of *St. Nicholas and Our Lady Assumed into Heaven.* This looming modern edifice retains the feeling of Renaissance architecture, although it was completed in 1965. The facade is of Connemara marble and limestone and the building is nearly 300 feet long and over 150 feet wide (you can't miss it).

   ★ Proceeding down University Road, you'll reach *University College,* a magnificent example of Tudor-Gothic architecture founded in 1845. It is located outside the city near the River Corrib, and its library houses the minutes of the Galway Corporation from 1485 to 1818,

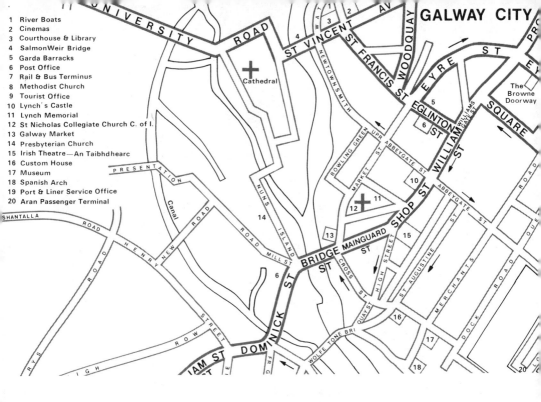

1 River Boats
2 Cinemas
3 Courthouse & Library
4 SalmonWeir Bridge
5 Garda Barracks
6 Post Office
7 Rail & Bus Terminus
8 Methodist Church
9 Tourist Office
10 Lynch's Castle
11 Lynch Memorial
12 St Nicholas Collegiate Church C. of I.
13 Galway Market
14 Presbyterian Church
15 Irish Theatre—An Taibhdhearc
16 Custom House
17 Museum
18 Spanish Arch
19 Port & Liner Service Office
20 Aran Passenger Terminal

plus a map of the city from 1640 and many rare books. The college is one of the country's leading Gaelic centers.

* Nearby on St. Francis Street is the *Franciscan Abbey,* constructed in the mid-17th century on the site of a friary built in the 13th century by the Burke family.

* From here, you may wish to return to the center of Galway to spend the rest of the afternoon exploring its bustling streets and lanes. (Listings follow.)

* Dinner suggestions are the rooftop Claddagh Room of the Great Southern or the dining room of the Ardilaun Hotel. For descriptions of these and others, see Restaurants. After dinner, one of Ireland's most interesting pubs—*Seagan Ua Neachtain*—is at Quay and Cross Streets. It's the real thing: basic, but cozy and well-lived-in after more than a hundred years. Spontaneous traditional music and storytelling often. Sometimes only Irish spoken.

* Although there are theater ventures here, you'll probably want to turn in early so as to catch the Aran Islands steamer next morning (they leave early).

GALWAY'S HISTORY

A fort city was erected here in 1124 by the original Connachtmen—mainly the O'Flaherty and O'Halloran clans. But in 1232 Richard de Burgh (Burke) took the city and made Galway a thriving Anglo-Norman colony. Its settlers comprised the Fourteen Tribes of Galway, including Brownes, Blakes, Kirwans, Lynches, Morrisses, Skerrets, Deans, Bodkins, Martins, and Athys.

These settlers long segregated themselves from the native Irish. In 1396 Richard II granted Galway its first charter in an attempt to compel the loyalty of all its inhabitants, but as late as 1518 a city by-law stated that 'Neither O nor Mac shall strutte ne swagger thro' the streets of Galway.' However, the native clans still raided the city so frequently and successfully that the settlers placed an inscription over the west gate: *From the fury of the O'Flahertys, good Lord deliver us.*

In 1651 the city surrendered to a siege by parliamentary forces under Sir Charles Coote. Forty years later it was forced to yield again, this time to the Williamite troops led by General von Ginkel.

For centuries Galway traded exclusively with Spain, whose influence on the community was very strong, especially in terms of architecture and dress. After Galway burned to the ground in 1473, the rebuilding included the Spanish influence still evident in parts of the city. And to this day some of the off-coast islanders occasionally wear the vivid red-flannel skirt of Spanish derivation. You may see it if you visit the Aran Islands.

GALWAY LODGINGS

* *Anno Santo Hotel* on Threadneedle Road, outside Galway in Salthill, a popular seaside area (22110). A quiet little hotel that offers 17 rooms (8 with bath). It's cozy and tasteful, has lovely lawns, and is near a golf course and tennis courts. Inexpensive to moderate.

* *The Ardilaun House Hotel* at Taylor's Hill (21433) was once a stately mansion. Expanded now, it has 73 rooms, all with bath. Located among sheltering trees, shrubs, and gardens in the town's finest residential section, it's as quiet as a country hotel. Especially pleasant are the sitting rooms with their grand fireplaces, the dining room with huge windows overlooking the lawn and gardens, and the fine bar. Expensive.

* *The Corrib Great Southern Hotel,* Dublin Road outside Galway (65281), is the modern sister hotel of the Victorian Great Southern in Eyre Square. It's a posh place with 115 rooms, all with bath and private phone, plus a duplex suite, an indoor heated pool, and saunas. Expensive.

* *The Great Southern Hotel,* Eyre Square in the heart of Galway (64041), is Galway's finest hotel. Built in Victorian times, it now has a modern wing and a total of 125 rooms, all with bath, private phone, and television. (If you want one of the old, high-ceilinged rooms, be sure to ask when you reserve.) Rooftop (indoor) pool and sauna, fine restaurant, and comfortable bar. Expensive.

* *The Skeffington Arms,* Eyre Square (63173), is also an old hotel, but much smaller and more intimate with 21 rooms (13 with bath). A simple, genial place. Visa and Master only. Moderate.

RESTAURANTS

* *The Ardilaun House Hotel* at Taylor's Hill (21433) has a very pleasant, intimate dining room overlooking secluded gardens. It serves a wide variety of meat and seafoods, from escaloped veal in white wine and cream sauce to sole Florentine. The pâté maison is good, the fresh seafood chowder excellent. Entrees include the Coquille St. Jacques (scallops tossed in vermouth butter), crepe aux crevettes (thin pancakes filled with prawns and glazed with

cheese), and the house specialty, rack of lamb: all excellent. Open for breakfast 8 to 10. L—1 to 2:30. D—6:30 to 9:30. AE, Diners, Visa, Master. Moderate to expensive.

* *The Cellar Grill,* Williamgate Street (65727), is just around the corner from the youth-oriented Cellar Bar. The Grill attracts all age groups with tasty fare including hamburgers, country pâté, grilled sea trout, fried chicken, and sirloin. Bright atmosphere with an almost American-colonial feeling. Open 10 A.M. to 9 P.M.; Sundays, 12:30 to 9 P.M. Full license. Inexpensive to moderate.

* *The Claddagh Room* of the Great Southern Hotel, Eyre Square (64041), is a stately rooftop restaurant serving Galway Bay's catch of the day—excellent seafood. But this is not to slight the outstanding meat dishes, especially the Gaelic steak, flamed at the table in whiskey, cream, and brandy. Crabmeat salad and poached salmon are unerring choices here too. Open breakfast 7:30 to 10. L—1 to 2:30. D—7 to 11. AE, Diners, Visa, Master. Expensive, but well worth it.

* *Lydonhouse Restaurant,* Shop Street (64051), is a Galway institution like Bewley's in Dublin. It has its own bakery and a menu ranging from hamburgers to sirloins and seafood, quiche to omelettes and Irish stew. The food is good, and there's a wine license. The old restaurant is Tudor in style and contains many trappings of historic Galway—Spanish carved stone windows with wrought-iron stripping from a local residence, circa 1350; a map of Galway from 1651; marriage stones from the 1600s (carved limestone slabs cut when the marriage date was set to join the families' coats of arms). Open 11:30 A.M. to 11 P.M. daily. Sunday open noon to 9:30 P.M. Wine license. Inexpensive.

* *The Old Railway Restaurant* in the Great Southern Hotel, Eyre Square (64041), offers everything from fine snacks to grills and good three-course meals. Open 7:30 A.M. to 11 P.M. AE, Diners, Visa, Master. Inexpensive to moderate.

* *The Skeffington Arms Hotel,* Eyre Square (63173/4/5), is noted for its excellent steaks and seafood. Open breakfast 8 to 10. L—1 to 2:30. D—6 to 9. Bar food served throughout the day. Visa, Master. Moderate.

PUBS

* *The Cellar Bar* behind the Cellar Grill on Eglington Street is smoky and crowded at almost any hour. It's definitely a hangout for youth from all countries. Inexpensive food includes steak and kidney pie, beef, and chicken curries. Frequent evening jazz and blues sessions.

* *Freeney's,* High Street, is a good old talk pub/fishing-gear shop.

* *The King's Head,* High Street. Dark and woody, with a fireplace, this cozy haunt offers traditional music nightly during the summer season—from 9 P.M. Monday–Saturday, from 8 P.M. on Sunday. The surprisingly inexpensive fare ranges from sandwiches to roast beef, lasagne, and salmon steaks.

* *The Lion's Tower,* Eglington Street, is one of Galway's finest (and neatest). It's an old-style woody pub/lounge with comfortable velvet seats and trestle tables. This is a great place to sample oysters and stout during the September Oyster Festival. Morning and afternoon coffee available; lunch from noon to 3, evening specials from 6 on. Sandwiches are served all day. The pub specializes in seafoods and smoked salmon; in season, offers fresh salmon, sea trout, oysters, and prawns. Steak and chicken dishes are also well prepared. Inexpensive to moderate.

* *The Railway Bar and Lounge* in the Great Southern Hotel, Eyre Square

(near the railway station), may be Galway's answer (though not as fancy) to Dublin's Saddle Bar in the old Shelbourne Hotel. The international set alights here often.

* *Seagan Ua Neachtain,* Quay and Cross Streets, is the real thing in Irish pubs: old, smoky, and dim (you expect the gas lights to go on at any second). You may arrive to a lively spontaneous music session of an evening, or to the lonely, plaintive sound of a tin whistle on a rainy afternoon. There's nothing forced or stagy here; it's all natural and from the heart. You can drift from one group to another to hear fascinating stories of the old days— although some may be told in Irish. Warning: Don't go if you're hungry. There are a few strange items posing as sandwiches, but they are best ignored. This is not the place to eat, just a great grass-roots Irish pub. Enjoy.

* *The Yacht,* Francis Street near Eyre Square, serves up good shepherd's pie and Irish stew along with an old-time atmosphere. Inexpensive.

SHOPS

* The Treasure Chest, Eglington Street, is Galway's best all-around shop for Irish crafts. Certainly it's the place to go if you're pressed for time: Irish apparel for all age groups, including fisherman and Blarney knitwear, plus crystal, pottery, china, linens, souveniers, post cards, and much more.

* Moon's, Eglington Street, is Galway's department store. Irish apparel, sweaters, and pottery often interest American visitors, and there's usually an attractive sale during July.

* Taffee's, William Street, is undeniably a dowdy-looking store, but worth a visit even if you aren't planning to buy a sweater from its vast selection of strikingly handsome Irish knitwear (at low prices). But be prepared—you could easily mistake the shop for a kennel. Literally dozens of cheerful dogs bustle about the place and burst from the doors, greeting shoppers with such exuberance that the footpath becomes impassable. But who cares? It's a circus in itself, and one of Galway's memorable little moments (unless you hate dogs).

* White Gold (the Porcelain Shop), Mainguard Street, offers Irish Dresden, crystal, Belleek china, hand-painted porcelain.

* L. O'Donnellan's Craft Shop, Quay Street, has traditional Irish and local Galway handcrafts, knitwear, tweeds, Irish crochet, Carrickmacross lace, Claddagh door knockers, sheepskin slippers.

* Frank McDonagh's, Eyre Square, offers Irish knitwear, mohair throws, shawls, linens, tweeds, tablecloths, placemats, Irish dolls, souveniers.

* Royal Tara Factory Shop, Tara Hall, is a showroom for fine Irish bone china located in one of the grand old houses of Galway. Open Monday–Friday 9 A.M. to 6 P.M.; Saturday 10 A.M. to 6 P.M.; Sunday 2 to 6 P.M.

* Cobwebs, Quay Lane, has fine small antique items including jewelry and porcelain.

* Archway Antiques, just off Eyre Square, offers furniture and a wide variety of other items.

* Crock of Gold, Middle Street, is a newly opened antique shop.

* Antiquarian Books, Cross Street, offers a good selection of books of Irish interest and others, plus well-framed old maps of the country and the area.

* Kenny's Bookshop, High Street, offers wonderful Irish prints and books along with a fine selection of Irish landscape paintings.

* O'Gorman Books, Shop Street, has a very attractive array of contemporary Irish books and travel guides.
* The Peddler, High Street, sells riding equipment.
* Arch Tack Rooms, Quay Lane, specializes in fishing equipment attractively displayed.
* Glynn's, Shop Street, has a fine assortment of Connemara marble items, crystal, Irish jewelry including Claddagh rings, handcrafts, and souveniers.
* Faller's, Williamsgate Street, has Irish jewelry, crystal, china, and linen.
* Dillon's, Shop Street, Irish jewelry and Claddagh rings.
* K & W Giftware, Eglington Street, for Irish crafts and crystal.

ENTERTAINMENT/ANNUAL EVENTS

* *Taibhdheare na Gaillimhe,* Middle Street, is the Irish-speaking theater founded in 1928, which does regular productions of plays in Irish plus evenings of traditional music, song, and dance.
* Druid Lane Theatre, Chapel Lane, was founded in 1965 and does evening performances with particular emphasis on Anglo-Irish plays like those of Synge and O'Casey.
* The Galway Oyster Festival in September, when you indulge yourself in plentiful oysters savored with creamy glasses of stout.
* The Galway Horse Show at the end of June; then again at the beginning of July.
* The Galway Races (horseracing) held at the end of July/beginning of August, then again in September.
* The Claddagh Festival held the first week in August to celebrate the traditional fishing village and its folk tales.
* The Galway Bay International Sea Angling Festival, held in September.

SPORTS

* Water sports—the area is famous for swimming, boating, sailing, fishing, and deep-sea diving.
* Golfing is provided for in neighboring Salthill where there is an 18-hole course.
* Riding—you can rent horses just four miles away in Claregalway.

Roots: O'Conaire or O'Connor (the Padraic O'Conaire monument in Eyre Square); Browne (the Browne Doorway, now in Eyre Square); Lynch (Lynch's Castle in Shop Street); O'Brien (O'Brien's Bridge). Other important Galway family names include Joyce, French, Burke, Morris, Darcy, Blake, Martin, Kelly, O'Toole, O'Flaherty, Murphy, Conneely, and King.

Literature: Padraic O'Conaire (a prolific Gaelic writer honored by the monument in Eyre Square); Charlotte Brontë (borrowed the surname of her heroine Jane Eyre from a prominent Galway family during a visit to Ireland); James Joyce (was very attached to Galway, where Nora Barnacle, who bore him two children, was born in a cottage at 8 Bowling Green).

ARAN

Aerial View of Aran

Golden chariots across the plain of the sea
rising with the tide to the sun . . .
                              —from the Celtic, 7th-8th century

Oh, these islands have their way of telling ye that ye belong, that your years should be lived out here. Ah, I'll tell ye that life's too short to pass it anywhere else.

—Bridget Johnston-Hernon
Kilmurvey House
Inishmore

The Aran Islands are three limestone reaches or reef tops looming above the waves 30 miles out in the stormy North Atlantic. For centuries this craggy landscape has been home for many Irish-speaking fishermen and their families. Before that, the sheer cliffs served as fortresses for brave prehistoric warriors who held out against fleets of invaders. These rugged lands born of the sea, lands that in many ways time seems to have forgotten, offer rewards beyond the merely picturesque or scenic. You will need at least a full day for the adventure to Aran, but it would be well worth your while to stay longer if you can.

YOUR PERSONALIZED ARAN ISLANDS ITINERARY

★ If you're sailing to Aran (you can also fly), be sure to check on which boat is operating the day before and the time and dock of departure. The Aran steamers usually leave very early, and they leave *promptly;* even if you're running for the dock, you may be left behind. This is a question of time and tide waiting for no man. Tidal changes are swift here, and the docking systems on Aran are marginal; close timing is required to beat the tide back to Galway.

There are two steamers, the *Galway Bay* and the *Naomh Eanna.* The former is more sophisticated (which isn't saying much) in that it transports only people. The latter—you guessed it—takes animals too. No, it's not Noah's Ark, but it often looks like it, as cattle are lifted by winch from the pier into the well. But neither craft is a luxury liner; once aboard you're moving into the past. Since you may as well go all the way into it, the *Naomh Eanna* is worth a try. It often calls offshore at the two smaller Arans, Inishere and Inishman, and curraghs (canoe-like vessels) row out to collect passengers, supplies, and livestock. (The docks here don't accept steamers.) On a stormy day it's a melee, as people and cattle are lowered into the curraghs for transport to the smaller islands.

Should the *Naomh Eanna* not be sailing, the *Galway Bay* will also provide an authentic sense of the past: it's only a little less basic. But with either boat, you must be prepared—these waters can be treacherously stormy. Have your sealegs together, or take a motion-sickness tablet before you leave. For those interested in prehistory, this journey is a must.

Both boats are C.I.E. transports: Phone 68906/63081/62141/62347. Both serve tea, coffee, sandwiches, and drinks (full licenses).

★ If you decide to fly instead of chancing rough seas or spending the several hours each way required by the boat trip, Aer Arann has frequent twenty-minute flights at reasonable fares. The planes are tiny, but the flight is smooth and the pilots are experienced. The Galway phone numbers are 65119/65110/62595. You can split your trip between boat and plane. Plane takes credit cards at Galway *only.*

★ The choice of islands should fall on the largest, Inishmore, if your time is limited. While the two smaller islands remain less in touch with today's world, a factor that may enhance their appeal, they are correspondingly more difficult to reach. Only the *Naomh Eanna* visits them, and it doesn't sail every day. Even when it does, you must transfer to a curragh for the final leg of the trip, and this is not for the faint-hearted in a rough sea. The Aer Arann flights touch down here only a few times a day. And while all three islands have many historic sites, Inishmore seems to have the greatest number.

* Assuming you plan to spend the day at Inishmore, you can either return via the boat or the plane that same night, or stay overnight or longer. Some people stay several weeks: it's a wonderful way to get away from the modern world. On longer stays you may want to check with the local fishermen about taking a trawler to the other islands. For details on accommodations, see Lodgings. The suggestion is the *Johnston-Hernon Kilmurvey House* at Kilmurvey.

* The Aran boat docks at Kilronan, where you can either rent a bicycle or hire a jaunting car to tour the island. The jaunting car usually brings passengers up the hill from Kilronan Harbor and Village to head west for Kilmurvey Strand and Village, which is about halfway across the six-and-a-half mile island. From here you may walk (it's a strenuous hike) up to the cliffs and the site of the ancient stone fort *Dun Aengus*. The fort is named for the legendary chief of the prehistoric *Fir Bolg*, a tall, dark Mediterranean people said to be the original settlers of Aran. This is one of the finest forts in Western Europe, covering some 11 acres and commanding a point 300 feet above the sea. Comprised of three semi-circular enclosures of massive dry-masonry, hand-cut stone walls, the fort is believed to have been circular when built. The speculation is that the missing half fell away into the sea. Looking out at the vast indigo Atlantic, you will be tempted to move closer to view the crashing breakers: be careful. It is not advisable to look over the edge at close quarters unless you lie down first. Looking east from these cliffs, you will have a splendid panorama of Galway Bay and the Connemara coastline. The banks are alive with the beautiful Aran wildflowers. Be sure to stop on the outer side of the middle wall and note the dramatic *chevaux-de-frise* of treacherously sharp stone slabs set at irregular angles to prevent attacks from marauding tribes.

Near the rendezvous with the jaunting car, you can see *Teampall MacDuach,* a tiny pre-Romanesque stone church with a holy well and a carved stone cross. The fine medieval arch and the chancel are part of subsequent Romanesque extensions.

Also near Kilmurvey township are *Dun Oghil* (another impressive prehistoric fort) and, slightly to the north, a small prehistoric beehive-type dwelling.

* If you do stay overnight at Kilmurvey House as suggested, spend some time on Kilmurvey Strand, with its unparalleled views of the sea and Connemara and the majestic purple Twelve Bens mountain

range. This island offers some of Ireland's most spectacular scenery, and you may wish to spend (or plan) a fortnight here.

★ If you have time, Killeany, on the eastern end of Inishmore, has the remains of St. Enda's monastery on *Trá Nor*, the Big Strand. Enda was reputedly pushed into the religious life by her sister, who became a devout nun at Leinster in eastern Ireland. Apparently, Enda was less well-suited to the spiritual life.

Legend: St. Enda's place in hagiography is as dubious as that of St. Kevin, who reportedly killed a woman who fell passionately in love with him because he rejected carnal love as evil. In Enda's case, jealousy superseded sanctity when St. Colmcille intruded upon her Aran Island territory. The tales say that he begged her for land for a hermitage, but she refused in the belief that he would take precedence on the islands and her reputation would be eclipsed. When he didn't get his plot of land, Colmcille cursed the islands, depriving them of their alleged powers to generate perpetual youth and rendering the soil barren and the cows dry forever.

You could spend months on the Arans, exploring both history and natural beauty: they are unforgettable.

ARAN LODGINGS

★ The *Johnston-Hernon Kilmurvey House*, Kilmurvey Strand (61218), is unquestionably the best place to stay. This imposing grey-stone manor house (the only one on Aran) looks almost as intimidating as Miss Havisham's in Dickens's *Great Expectations*. But once inside, that impression yields to the presence of Bridget Johnston-Hernon herself, who has more tales to tell than the sea has waves, as they say here. Bridget has seen the best and the worst of human nature, as guests from almost every country have passed through her iron gateway over the years. Her recollections range from the heartbreaking to the comic, including visitors who bring full evening dress to the islands and those who refuse to pay their bill because it sprinkled during their visit. She can tell you about the old days when they burned kelp on the strand while the men drank poteen and told ancient tales, and about the times when the winds were so fierce she thought the house would come down. Transplanted from Galway, she was widowed by Mr. Johnston and later married an island kinsman, Sonny Hernon. Bridget's life has not been easy, but it exemplifies the experience of struggle and survival on these wind-swept islands in the middle of the harsh Atlantic. You won't forget this place, or Bridget. She serves good basic Irish food too. There are only 10 rooms, none with private bath. Inexpensive.

If you have trouble getting reservations at Kilmurvey House, there are several other (though less desirable) places to stay including:

    Bay View, Kilmurvey, with 10 rooms, one with bath. Wine license. Inexpensive.

Mrs. Conneely's *Beach View House*, Oatquarter, Kilronan (61156). Six rooms, no private baths. Inexpensive.

Mrs. Dirrane's *Gilbert House*, Oatquarter (61146). Six rooms, no private baths. Inexpensive.

Mrs. Beatty's *Radharc na Mara*, Kilronan (61115). Four rooms, no private baths, folk museum attached. Inexpensive.

RESTAURANTS

* *An Cuan* (The Bay), about three miles from where the boat docks at Kilronan Harbor, is on Kilmurvey Strand and is undoubtedly the finest restaurant on Aran. This converted fishing shack/warehouse overlooks a gentle little beach. Proprietor Brian Elliott and his wife, Mary Ann, just starting out, have whitewashed the walls, beamed the ceiling and hung it with gas lamps, and installed rectangular bench tables. The basic seafood—caught just an arm's length away—is superb. The turkey, chicken, and ham are also good, but you do yourself a disservice if you don't try the excellent salmon, mackerel, or shellfish.

If you're staying in the Kilmurvey area (suggestions above), you may want to have your main meal at night, in which case you can visit *An Cuan* for a light lunch while you're on the beach. At this writing, Elliott is still waiting for his wine license, but an off-license (liquor store) in Galway, such as Richardson's on Eyre Square, can provide you with a good bottle of Pouilly Fuisse or a comparable wine to bring with you just in case. Sink it into the cold sand of Kilmurvey Strand while you're sunbathing (the sea is calm here, so it won't be sucked out to sea). Or Brian Eliott will chill it for you. But don't miss this special place that blends old and new so successfully. Open L— 12:30 to 2. D—6 to 9. Snacks all day. Inexpensive.

* *An Tsean Cleibh*, Kilronan Harbor, is a sprightly place with indoor and outdoor seating catering to the youth trade. Primarily a chatty little coffee shop that serves adequate meals. Inexpensive.

* *Dun Aonghasa*, near Kilronan Harbor on the main road (61208), has a lovely seaside atmosphere with its light pine tables, white walls, and fireplace. With its harbor view, this should be the best place on Inishmore, but it isn't. The seafood dishes struggle to be great but they don't approach it. (The proprietors say they're working on it.) Disappointing scampi, trout, and salmon, considering the location. Breakfast, snacks, tea, and coffee also served. Open 10 A.M. to 11 P.M. daily. No wine license. Inexpensive, although it could be moderate if the food were better.

* *Petrel's Restaurant*, Kilronan Harbor, is a kind little cafe for those leaving the rigors of the Aran steamers. Wildflowers and sea grasses, fish nets, lobster pots, and oil lamps enhance the atmosphere. Its offerings are more snacks than meals: crabmeat salads, pollock chowder, mackerel pâté, tuna salad, and chili, but this is a good place. Lunch and dinner hours. Wine license. Inexpensive.

PUBS

* *The American Bar*, Kilronan Harbor, is rustic, old, and faintly disreputable looking and offers wonderful pints of stout. Why it's called 'American' remains something of a mystery, unless in honor of its many visitors from our shores. There is a brisk business in signature T-shirts. Altogether a good watering spot.

* *Sean O'Craig's,* near Kilmurvey Strand is another rough-hewn place dimly lit by gaslight, where locals hold forth with old Gaelic songs well into the night.

* *Brigid Ui Dalaig,* up the hill from Kilronan Harbor on the main road, is an authentic small old pub—whitewashed walls, a fireplace, and plenty of chat. Enter through the back door, left-hand side of the street.

SHOPS

* *Carraig Dun* (Rocky Fort), Kilronan Harbor. Irish crafts, sweaters, hand-knits.

* *Catherine Mullen's,* up the hill from Kilronan Harbor on the main road. A pleasant little shop offering such local crafts as a silver replica of the fortress *Dun Aengus* set in stone, ornaments, sweaters, seashells, Aran maps and books.

* *An Pauc* (Small Boat), on a signposted road off the main road just above the Mullen's shop. Irish craft items, sweaters, and books in an old-cottage setting.

Roots: O'Brien (O'Brien's Castle, Inishere), O'Flaherty, Faherty, Hernon, Conneely, O'Craig, Dirrane, McDonagh, Connolly.

Literature: Liam O'Flaherty, Thomas O'Flaherty (short stories with Aran Islands settings); John Millington Synge (the brilliant one-act play *Riders to the Sea* and the winning profile *The Aran Islanders*); Pat Mullen (author of *The Man of Aran,* source of the fine film made by Robert Flaherty).

Legend: Many romantics speculate that Aran is part of the lost continent of Atlantis, which sank into the sea in ancient times. Others say that Aran is really Avalon, the legendary earthly paradise of the Celts, where such heroes as King Arthur were transported at their deaths. A few have maintained that ancient Aran was the land of perpetual youth, and that its secret is still hidden somewhere on the islands or in those portions of them which sank into the sea. More plausible is the belief that the islands were once populated by the Fir Bolgs, the first settlers, who built such forts as Dun Aengus, beehive huts, and pagan places of worship that evolved into Christian churches. This theory has supporting evidence still dramatically on view.

SPORTS

* Sea angling from the cliffs, the shore, currachs, or deep-sea fishing boats for which you can arrange at Kilronan.

* Swimming is best at Kilmurvey; although the water is usually cold, it's crystal clear and invigorating.

* Hiking, walking, running (there's a 10-Kilometer race in July) are all excellent and offer a background of magnificent scenery.

* Botanic exploration of the wide variety of unusual plants growing here.

* Cliff climbing is an unusual activity here, but the cliffs around Dun Aengus offer an excellent opportunity. (Be careful.)

* Deep-sea diving could be arranged with boatmen at Kilmurvey.

Inishmore Cliffs

ENTERTAINMENT

* Dancing—Traditional *ceili* dances are held twice a week in St. Ronan's Hall, Kilronan.

* Ballad Sessions—The islanders hold forth during the summer and early fall seasons in many of the island pubs.

CONNEMARA

Connemara Afternoon

I have not heard of music ever such as your frame makes . . .
                              —Gofraidh Fionn O Dalaigh, 14th century

YOUR PERSONALIZED CONNEMARA ITINERARY

* Connemara is so attractive that you could spend days here. The majestic Twelve Bens mountains and the rugged Maamturk range compete with the unspoiled seascapes and lakes for your appreciation. This is another of the country's remaining *Gaeltachts,* where Irish is widely spoken. It has very little industry or farming.

* The Connemara region has several suggested hotels, as described under Lodgings: the *Cashel House Hotel* in Cashel, *Ballynahinch Castle* in Ballynahinch, the *Abbeyglen* in Clifden, the *Renvyle House* in Renvyle, and *Sweeney's Oughterard House* and *Currarevagh House* in Oughterard. You may wish to choose one from Lodgings if you're staying overnight, so that you can follow the route that brings you to it. All have very good dining rooms.

* *Cashel* is 41 miles due west of Galway and is reached by taking the coastal road out through Salthill, Barna, and Spiddle to Inverin, where the Connemara marble is processed. (Barna has a fine though expensive Breton Seafood restaurant, *Ty-ar-mor,* with delicious seafood pancakes. Phone 65031) *Cashla* or Costelloe, to give it its other names, is near the dramatic stony section of Ireland called Carraroe.

* *Clifden* is about 24 miles from Cashel on the road hugging the sea. At Roundstone, you'll see a magnificent beach called Dog Bay's Strand, with Urrisbeg Mountain behind the town. At close to 1000 feet, it is excellent for climbing and as a vantage point for the sea and the lake-splashed country to the north. From here you go up the coastline to Ballyconneely, then along Mannin Bay, on whose shores is a coral strand with the colors of the rainbow—and then some—among the smooth sea rocks. Moving from here to Clifden, you will pass the area where Alcock and Brown landed after the first trans-Atlantic flight in 1919, commemorated by a monument about half a mile from the main road. Clifden itself is the region's main village, an attractive little town set out by the sea with mountains in the background. Its resources are described below so that you can spend a little time here.

* Should you wish to visit the isolated promontory of Renvyle, which seems way out at the world's end, it can be reached by leaving Clifden on the scenic Sky Road, a nine-mile stretch that climbs around the promontory. This is one of Connemara's highlights, if not its major attraction. The sweeping seascapes are so compelling that you must be careful driving the rather treacherous roadway. There is a parking

area about halfway up where you can stop. (If you're an experienced runner or hiker, this is your road.) At Gleggan, a fishing village, you may take the mail boat to Inishbofin Island where there are ruins of the seventh-century monastery founded by St. Colman and the remnants of a Cromwellian castle.

Roots: This sea-lashed island was once the property of the O'Flaherty family.

Legend: The would-be pirate queen of the Irish seas, Grace O'Malley (or Grainne Ui Mhaile*), damned the reign of Queen Elizabeth and vowed to thwart her in every way she could. But Grace's bold departure with her war vessels was soon followed by an inglorious retreat to Inishbofin.*

★ Go on to Letterfrack, where you'll find the turnoff for Renvyle. But don't speed away without seeing one of the finest craft shops in Ireland or anywhere else: *Connemara Handcrafts.* A mile out of town, it has a superlative array of Irish craft goods. Also in Letterfrack is the interesting *Connemara West Centre* crafts shop. Both have very good tea rooms, but the former has excellent homemade snacks to offer. AE, Diners, Visa, Master. Inexpensive.

★ From Letterfrack, drive the lonely few miles to Renvyle.

Roots: O'Flaherty, Joyce, and Blake are all families involved with this area or property-owners here at various times.

Legend: The fiery Grace O'Malley is said to have wanted Renvyle for her own. (Some recall that what she really desired was the dashing scion of one of its ruling families.) But her land-based romantic efforts were no more successful than her attempt to become the scourge of the local seas.

★ The peaceful little Oughterard area in the well-watered region around Lough Corrib is 32 miles east of Clifden beyond Ballynahinch Lake. This is another strong O'Flaherty territory and the site of Ballynahinch Castle, now a hotel. The town of Recess brings you into the shadow of the Twelve Bens. Going on to *Maam Cross,* you'll see *Peacocke's Maam Cross Craft Shop,* a fine large store offering Irish crafts, knitwear, clothing, souveniers, and books. This quiet crossroads also offers *Peacocke's Restaurant,* whose tables are laden with wildflowers. Good fresh seafood and beef by a grand turf fire. The bar/lounge offers fine salmon mousse, seafood salads, homemade pâtés, and sandwiches.

Open 12:30 to 10:30 P.M. (Sundays to 9:15 P.M.) Closed October through March. Full license. AE, Visa, Master. Moderate.

★ Go on to *Oughterard,* which can also be reached direct from Galway; the distance is only 17 miles. On the way you'll pass through Moycullen, where you can purchase hand-carved marble products at the *Connemara Marble Shop.* Also a bit off the main Moycullen thoroughfare is a rustic crystal maker. He does hand-cut crystal that some insist is cheaper and finer than the Waterford. This place is worth seeking out. Moycullen boasts a fine seafood restaurant called *The Sliver Teal* (85109) with great French seafood cuisine, especially lobster. There's excellent game in season with superlative sauces. Intimate atmosphere and moderate to expensive prices. Open 10:30 A.M. to 11:30 P.M. Explanation: Some people like to eat early. AE. Moderate to expensive.

Oughterard offers *Keogh's* for fine crystal and china and *Egan's* for hand knits (all age groups), Irish sheepskin runs, stoles, scarves, hand-embroidered linens, and local marble products.

★ The suggested stop after the Connemara area is an overnight at the famous *Ashford Castle* just inside County Mayo at Cong. If you're traveling from Oughterard, it's about 30 miles. Go northwest from Oughterard to Maam Cross, then due north to Maam, where Keane's, a fine old Tudor bar, is located. From here, go east to Connemara, skirting Joyce's Country (not, as many think, a reference to the writer).

Roots: The Joyce reference here is to a clan that came from Wales to settle in this kindred terrain during the 13th century. The first Joyce settler is believed to have been Thomas de Jorse, whose descendants still live in this region between Connemara and County Mayo, which touches on Loughs Corrib and Mask. The Joyce River area affords sweeping views of the Maamturk and Partry ranges. From here, go north to Cong and Ashford Castle.

★ If you're coming from Clifden to Cong—a distance of about 45 miles—you will be near some of the same territory as that described above. From Clifden, travel to Letterfrack, as outlined in the Connemara Itinerary. On the way to Leenane is Kylemore Pass, which brings you to the majestic *Kylemore Abbey.* This was one of the last castellated mansions to be built in Ireland. Constructed by a wealthy English merchant around the time of America's Civil War, the vast estate, mirrored in one of Kylemore's three peaceful lakes, is now a girl's school run by a Benedictine order. There's a craft shop here selling pottery, and an inexpensive tearoom as well, both run by the nuns.

Crossing along the top of the Maamturk Mountains, Lough Fee is to the left as you descend toward Killary Harbor, the only Scandinavian-type fjord in all of Ireland and a beautiful sight. Here at *Leenane* you'll have access to *Killary Shop,* an attractive Irish craft store with a rustic restaurant extension serving everything from good snacks to four-course meals. Try the homemade pâté. Open all day. Wine license. AE, Diners, Visa, Master. Inexpensive. Also in Leenane is *Mweelrea Craft Shop,* which features Irish pottery and sweaters and has an inexpensive tearoom of its own. From Leenane, follow the shores of Lough Mask to Cong.

Kylemore Abbey

CONNEMARA LODGINGS AND RESTAURANTS

Reserve well in advance so you won't be disappointed, because these places are extremely popular. (Note that lodgings are described here as they come up in the Itinerary, rather than in their usual alphabetical order. Since these accommodations also have the best restaurants, they have been included in the Lodgings section instead of forming a separate Restaurant heading.)

* *Cashel House Hotel,* Cashel (Clifden 252) is a wonderful 19th-century country house (some say unequivocally the best in Ireland) poised at the headland overlooking Cashel Bay. William Makepeace Thackeray once lingered here over his work. Much later, French statesman Charles de Gaulle and Madame de Gaulle were so taken with Cashel that they spent a fortnight here. The hundreds of years between these two visits made no change in Cashel's tranquility and seclusion. Its natural beauty offers both aesthetic pleasure and activity: sea sports and horseback riding adjacent to the 50 acres of floral gardens compete as attractions with the woodlands, where trees from around the world flourish. Indoors there are open turf fires and 23 rooms, 21 with private bath. Moderate to expensive.

Cashel's dining room has been widely praised under the long-time direction of Dermot and Kay McEvilly. It offers excellent Continental fare and traditional Irish specialties, both meat and seafood. L—12:20 to 2. D—7:30 to 8:30. Visa, Master. Expensive—but worth it.

* *Ballynahinch Castle,* Ballynahinch (Clifden 135), built in the late 16th century by the Normans, became an O'Flaherty fortress. In the 18th century, the Martin clan flattered English royalty so successfully that they were rewarded with lands all over Connemara, including Ballynahinch. The enraged O'Flahertys, now dispossessed, were accomplished duelists, but no more so than the Martins; despite all the feuding that ensued, the property remained in Martin hands. This eccentric family went on courting the throne and were soon being treated like royalty themselves. One of them, dubbed 'Humanity Dick,' had a rare impulse to do something constructive and formed the Society for the Prevention of Cruelty to Animals. Thackeray wrote about this enigmatic man, whom he found a fascinating character study.

The Martins prospered until the potato famine (1845–47), when they lost their home and many of their Connemara lands. The castle faded from prominence until the Roaring Twenties. Then it was purchased by the Maharajah Jam Sahib of Nawanagan—reportedly a lover of Isadora Duncan and better known as Ranjit Singh, the famous cricketer—who lavished money on it and turned it into a *Great Gatsby* kind of place. It was converted into a hotel in 1945.

Today it is a disarmingly peaceful spot amid mountains, woods, and hills streaked with lonely rivulets and a fine anglers' river. While it lacks the overall appeal of Cashel House, Ballynahinch is still well worthwhile. There are 20 rooms, all with bath.

The food is basic (often the residents' catch of the day) but good. Snacks and tea are available. Open L—1:30 to 2:30. D—7 to 9. Full license. AE, Master, Visa. Moderate to expensive.

Roots: O'Flaherty, Martin.

* *The Abbeyglen Hotel,* Sky Road, Clifden (Clifden 33). This hotel is an astonishingly successful mixture of the old and the new. The main entryway section of the building, which houses its excellent dining room, was an orphanage a century ago. Two rooms without bath remain in the old section, while 42 with bath encompass the new (a little too modern) wing. The hotel overlooks its own outdoor pool and the village with the mountains behind. (Visa and

Master only.) Proprietor Paul Hughes is a very genial host. But the biggest single attraction at the Abbeyglen is the food.

Paul Hughes is a chef who sets out to please—and he delivers. While this part of Ireland now abounds in good dining places the Abbeyglen goes overboard. For starters, there's a wonderful salad called Melina filled with fresh shrimp, walnuts, celery, apples, melon, and that *rara avis*, fresh lettuce, and dashed with a sprightly (not too sweet or sour) dressing. It makes you long for more. The eloquent hot quiche is a rarity in Ireland (cold quiche isn't), and this one is full of surprises, including fresh tomatoes, chunks of fresh lobster, and solid, mellow crust. The mushroom soup is the real thing, complete with chunky fresh mushrooms and cream. The scalding onion soup is so well made that it rivals that of New York's *Brasserie* in its heyday.

As an entree try the lamb, which will be served rare on request. And it's *not* mutton (as in many places). Skip the mint sauce; it spoils the magnificent flavor. The poached salmon with hollandaise is superb. Unfortunately, the vegetables need a little more work: not bad—but not great.

For dessert the fresh lemon mousse is a must; even people who loathe desserts will love it. The only *caveat* is the chicken cordon bleu: adequate, but disappointing here where the best is available.

Breakfasts include the hearty Irish variety or an excellent brunch including fresh fruits and juices, croissants, and newly milled Irish butter. The attractive bar often has traditional music at night. Open 8:30 A.M. to 9 P.M. Visa, Master. Moderate to slightly expensive.

* *Rosleague Manor,* Letterfrack (Moyard 7). This is an old Georgian manor house on Bearnaderg Bay. It glows with turf fires, fine Irish paintings, and antiques. Seven miles north of Clifden, its scenic settings includes mountains, lakes, rivers, and the nearby sea. The Manor has 16 rooms, 14 with bath, and is near the 5000-acre Connemara National Park.

The dining room offers beef and seafood dishes with a Spanish touch. The salmon, sea trout, turbot, and monkfish are especially good. Full license. Open D—8 to 9:30 P.M. (earlier for snacks and tea). Visa, Master. Inexpensive to moderate.

* *Renvyle House,* Renvyle (Renvyle 3/18). This bleak area seems to be at the end of the world and is actually one of the farthest points in Ireland—still real frontier territory. The hotel seems unchanged since it was first built a century and a half ago, but during the civil war in 1923, when Renvyle was the vacation home of writer/surgeon Oliver St. John Gogarty, it was almost burned to the ground by the I.R.A. (Instead of supporting their free-all-Ireland campaign, Gogarty compromised in favor of the northern Ireland partition.) He was so deeply attached to Renvyle that he painstakingly reconstructed it as it had been and extended it for lodgers, as he could no longer support its costs.

And an engaging place it is, with its cozy lounges, turf fires, rustic Irish bar, solarium, and the house's old library. The furnishings are those of the traditional Irish manor. An appropriate ode to Renvyle House is mounted on one of the walls: *A house to dream of the past in, of rollicking Irish hunting parties, surprise visits and lavish hospitality and joviality, of rattling good stories told over the turf fire in the capacious dining room, of ghosts upstairs, of fascinating Irish Dianas with infathomable grey eyes changeable in colour like the Connemara streams, of knightly squires and sprightly crimes.*

Filmmaker John Houston's second wife, the fascinating Leslie Black, said of Renvyle that you must not visit, you must stay, and take a share in the long nights of 'crack' (telling the old tales), 'because that's what Renvyle is.' There are 69 rooms (63 with bath), old and new. But if you're there for quiet romance, be sure to request a room that's not over the bar/lounge—because people really *do* stay up all night talking, roaring, and singing.

Legend: We've come a long way with no word of ghosts, but an occasional group holds séances here. It is said that poet William Butler Yeats and his bride recalled spirits here on their honeymoon and that Yeats's ghost itself now haunts the halls.

This is to say nothing of the drama of the sea's meeting with the lake at Renvyle, the mountains behind it, and the lonely stretches of rocky land. The mysterious, almost ethereal quality of this other-worldly spot is nearly scary in its effect. It brings you into touch with the deeper nature of life, and if you linger, you'll leave much more of a sage. Visa, Master. Moderate.

The food in the rustic dining room is especially good, most visitors agree: basic and satisfying. Some suggestions: Irish Beef Bourguignonne, fresh Killary salmon, poached lemon sole. L—12:30 to 2:30. D—7:30 to 8:45. Visa, Master. Moderate.

Literature: Yeats and Gogarty (who became the model for Buck Mulligan in Joyce's *Ulysses*).

* *Sweeney's Oughterard House,* Oughterard (82207), is a lovely ivy-hung Georgian country house opposite the Owenriff River with its plentiful salmon. Sweeney's gives you the rare feeling that you're a guest in someone's home rather than in a hotel, from the time you arrive and are greeted by old dog Shane, who will camp at your feet while you have tea in one of the period lounges. Unpretentious charm characterizes the country-gentleman bar, the cozy dining room, the bay windows overlooking the well-kept lawns, and the flowering gardens. There are 21 rooms, 19 with bath. Be sure to ask for one of the older rooms, rather than one in the newer extensions—they are much more interesting and livable. Visa, Master only. And it is expensive.

The dining room at Sweeney's is one of the most popular in the Galway-Oughterard area. Even if you're staying here, you must reserve in advance or you'll be relegated to bar food (though this isn't the worst of fates). The smoked salmon on brown bread is superlative, not to mention the homemade fruit cake and scones served with fresh blackberry jam, the homemade pies, and the deliciously thick fresh-vegetable soup. The major evening meals include excellent meat and seafood dishes. This place is special for dining, with its atmosphere of easy, gracious country living. Be sure to try the salmon in season. Open for bar lunch noon–3, D—7:30 to 9. Visa, Master. Moderate to expensive.

* *Currarevagh House,* Oughterard (82313), is a fine example of a 19th-century landed-gentry homestead. Its peaceful setting is a hundred yards from Lough Corrib and has acres of private woodlands. The Hodgson family has always owned it. Old furniture and paintings, seemingly from every period in the house's lifetime, ornament the fifteen rooms with 11 baths (rooms with

turf fires should be requested in advance). Currarevagh is very popular during
the late-spring fishing season. Open April to October. No credit cards. Moderate
to expensive.

The old-fashioned dining room offers hearty fare: roasts, seafood, homemade
soups, local fresh vegetables, homemade cakes and ice cream. Full license.
Dinner at 8, but notify in advance if you want a reservation—even if you're
staying at Currarevagh. No credit cards. Afternoon tea. Moderate.

★ *The Connemara Gateway Inn,* Oughterard outskirts, (82328) was once a
very modern motel-looking lodging. But not any more. The whole place has
been completely stripped and refurbished to resemble a fine old country inn.
This its owner feels is so important because it allows it to become a handsome
part of the wonderfully rustic countryside. Inside, all native Irish materials
and crafts are used, including furniture, pottery and artwork. Memorabilia
stresses Irish farm implements. There's a library, along with a heated pool
and a tennis court. The 48 rooms are all with bath. Visa, Master, Carte
Blanche.

The restaurant serves typical Irish-fare meals and overlooks the garden
and pool. Full license. Open breakfast 8 to 10. L—12:30 to 2:30 (Sun. only)
D—7 to 9. Again Visa, Master, Carte Blanche only. Moderate.

CLIFDEN RESTAURANTS

★ *Abbeyglen Hotel* (see Lodgings).

★ *Atlantic Coast Hotel,* Market Street (Clifden 19). Good and reasonable
Irish fare. Open 8:30 A.M. to 9 P.M. Closed October-April. AE, Master, Visa.
Inexpensive.

★ *Billy's Vintage Car Bar,* Main Street, claims via window sign that its
'fast foods are furious.' Soups, salads, and snacks are offered all day in a
cafe atmosphere—furious or otherwise. Inexpensive.

★ *Connemara Delicatessan,* Main Street, is an all-day coffee shop that specializes in fresh fish and smoked salmon dishes. Upstairs, there's an exhibition
of contemporary Irish paintings. Inexpensive food.

★ *O'Grady's Restaurant,* Market Street (Clifden 263/110). This snug little
candlelit place looks as if it's been transported bodily from Greenwich Village
or Little Italy. It specializes in fresh fish—salmon, monkfish, and turbot are
good—grills. Open noon to 10. AE, Visa, Master. Wine license. Moderate to
expensive.

★ *Marconi Tavern and Grill,* Main Street (Clifden 193), specializes in seafood
dishes such as baked mussels in garlic butter, mussel salad, grilled salmon
steak. Open daily till 10. Inexpensive to moderate.

CLIFDEN PUBS

★ *Griffin's Bar and Lounge,* Main Street. Drift into the back room here, if
you want to hear some good, down-to-earth traditional music—often to the
accompaniment of an accordion. It's also relatively quiet.

★ *The Celtic Hotel,* Market Hill. There's traditional music in the lounge
here too, but this spot verges on rowdy.

★ *The D'Arcy Inn,* Main Street, is a small Tudor-style bar, a young people's
gathering place for talk and song. The restaurant attached offers some good

foods at inexpensive to moderate prices. Unlike most Irish youthful spots, this one (and its patrons) are well kept.

* *E. J. King's,* Castle House, is another young people's place with traditional music and a small cafe.

* *The Atlantic Coast Hotel,* Market Street. The basement bar/lounge here is dark and dingy, but it offers the most beautiful and wistful traditional Irish music to the accompaniment of piano and accordion. All age groups frequent this place.

CLIFDEN SHOPS:

* Gerald Stanley & Sons, Market Street. Irish crafts, knitwear, tweeds.
* Atlantic Craft Shop, Market Street. Small native craft items.
* The Silver Shop, Main Street. Irish silver crafts and jewelry. Also tweeds.
* The Celtic Crafts, Main Street, specializes in marble items. Also has a stock of Belleek china, Irish books, tweeds, leathers, and other crafts.
* Millar's Connemara Tweed Shop, Main Street, has a large array of fine Irish tweeds and knitwear along with an excellent collection of Irish pottery, woodworking, glass, and oil paints.
* Tara Jewellers, Main Street, has a good collection of Claddagh rings and Belleek.

CLIFDEN SPORTS:

* All water sports.
* Fishing, sea and still water.
* Riding
* Golfing at the 18-hole links eight miles away at Allbrack.
* Running: The experienced runner will find the nine-mile, largely uphill road here a uniquely rewarding experience, but this course is not for the occasional runner (or hiker).
* Mountain climbing at many of the nearby peaks.

XIII. MAYO

Mayo Hills

A man travels the world over
in search of what he needs
and returns to find it.

—George Moore

Going west on a journey
by the light of my heart.

—Anthony Raftery
the Blind Poet of Ireland

Ashford

YOUR PERSONALIZED COUNTY MAYO ITINERARY

★ Arrive mid-afternoon at your suggested lodging, *Ashford Castle*, Cong (22644), which is expensive, but well worth it. You'll feel you've stepped into the pages of a book like Evelyn Waugh's *Brideshead Revisited* when you pass the gatehouse and enter the massive iron gates to the thousands of acres comprising the estate. A leisurely curving road finally brings you in view of the castle, which is an imposing sight. A composite structure with every flourish known to castellated architecture, Ashford is something straight from a fairy tale. (But if you have any qualms about splurging, bypass Ashford and go on to other County Mayo itinerary points.)

Legend: The original structure (still part of Ashford) was built in the early 13th century by the de Burgo family, part of the Norman invasion team. For years the de Burgos feuded with the O'Connors for supremacy in this area, only to be superseded by the Oranmore and Browne families. During the 18th century Sir Geoffrey Browne constructed a French-style chateau designed to connect and integrate with the older castle. In the mid-19th century, the estate was sold to Sir Benjamin Guinness, who expanded it to its present 26,000 acres, built the road, reclaimed the land and installed a drainage system, and planted thousands of trees. It was he who added two major extensions to the Browne section of the castle. His son, Lord Ardilaun, later designed the gardens and laid out over 20 miles of attractive walkways. Still dissatisfied, he decided that the castle needed a more baronial air, even at the estimated cost of two million pounds. So in 1884, with a crew to rival that of a Cecil B. DeMille production, he undertook to have the stonework cut just as the ancient Egyptians did it (is there any other way?). Some 31 years later, with only the western portion of the refurbishment completed, Lord Ardilaun died. Many feel that his work at Ashford was inspired; it is certainly dramatic.

The estate was controlled by the Iveagh Trust for the Guinness family until it was sold to Noel Huggard, who started transforming it into a hotel at the beginning of World War II. The present owner, John Mulcahy, picked up where Lord Ardilaun had left off and completed the restoration at a cost of millions of pounds.

* From this scenic view of the structure, which looms over Ireland's second-largest lake, Lough Corrib, cross the bridge and enter the castle to be delighted by the lavish elegance of its appointments. From the massive carved oak doorway onward, the sense of grandeur is enhanced by suits of armor, oil paintings (hundreds of them), plush carpeting, enormous fireplaces, a grand sweeping staircase, carved wainscoting and ceilings, and priceless antique furniture.

The castle is so vast that you literally do get lost in it. Numerous lounges overlooking the grounds are staffed by solicitous attendants eager to ply you with tea or sherry; you almost anticipate Lady Marchmain's arrival to preside over the scene.

Ashford has 79 elegant bedrooms, including six executive suites that include bedroom, large sitting room, bath, and cocktail bar. All bedrooms have bath and phone, and a view of either the lake or the river. The hotel is closed from January through March. Very expensive.

SPORTS AT ASHFORD
* Golfing (nine-hole course on the grounds)
* Tennis
* Running
* Hunting (pheasant, snipe, duck, and woodcock in season)
* Fishing and/or boating (Arrange for a boatman to take you out on Lough Corrib which has hundreds of islands. The fishing's good, and Ashford will pack you a picnic lunch.)

DINING AT ASHFORD

Perhaps influenced by the glitter of old Waterford chandeliers overhanging Doric columns, some claim that Ashford offers the finest dining experience in Ireland. Well, the food is very good, but it's not the best in the land, in view of the challenge now offered by the many excellent new restaurants. The crabmeat appetizers are highly recommended and the pâté is good. The chilled avocado soup is enjoyable, but the carrot soup is too sweet and creamy. Beautiful roast beef— tender and rare; the roast rack of lamb is almost as good. Poached filet of sea trout in a delicate sorrel sauce and the fresh salmon are both praiseworthy. The wine list can be either extremely expensive or reasonable, depending upon your choice, and the inexpensive wines are good. If strawberry mousse is on the menu, go for it.

An unwelcome negative must be added about the dining room staff here (of whom Lady Marchmain would not have approved). It is reasonable to expect in such an elegant place that the waiters should not ask for your room number for charging purposes at the start of every course, but they do. Not only should they be instructed beforehand as to whom they are serving (especially residents), but there should be no thought of *settling up* until your departure. The intrusion seriously detracts from the atmosphere that the hotel tries to maintain.

Fortunately, the service elsewhere at Ashford gets high marks. The attractive young women at the reception desk seem to anticipate your questions, and their interest goes beyond mere formal courtesy. When a sudden thunderstorm blew up during this writer's visit, they were concerned about two children who had gone out to explore the grounds on their own. They hastily dispatched attendants to collect the boys and phoned the parents' room to let them know. Where else would you get this kind of attention? The boatmen, too, are extremely pleasant and often tell tales of their experiences on Lough Corrib.

Legend: On the banks of the Cong River near the castle is a cave called the Pigeon Hole, *once the haunt of wild birds. Inside is a wide deep stream running through on an unknown course, and the only sound is that of underground waters. As the story goes, an Irish maiden once fell deeply in love with a wiry young* Fir Bolg *(allegedly the country's first settlers, from the Mediterranean). But she had another admirer who seethed at their affair. In a fit of passion, the rejected suitor killed the* Fir Bolg *and rowed his body out onto Lough Corrib, where he threw it overboard. When the body drifted ashore and the maid discovered the tragedy, she vanished, never to be seen again. But soon afterward, in the cave where the lovers had kept their passionate rendezvous, a beautiful white trout began to appear and reappear. Rumor had it that this was the spirit of the bereaved girl, which finally disappeared for good. But to this day, in the deeper confines of the cave, an eerie white light creeps out over the waters. Its source is still thought by some to be her spirit, lighting the way through eternity for her lover's return.*

Closer to our own time, and rather more verifiable, is the appearance at Ashford of John Ford and the cast of his excellent 1952 film *The Quiet Man*, which was filmed at Ashford and environs. Maureen O'Hara and the other cast and crew members stayed at the castle during the filming.

ASHFORD AREA SITES

* Inchagoill Island, one of Lough Corrib's largest, houses the ruins of two ornate stonework churches, one of which is attributed to St.

Patrick around the year 500. Nearby a stone obelisk with one of the oldest Christian inscriptions in Europe is said to mark the burial ground of his nephew, the Navigator.

* Augustinian Abbey ruins dating from the early 12th century are upstream on the Cong River about half a mile from Ashford. They occupy the site of what is believed to be the seventh-century hermitage of St. Fechin. Roderick O'Connor, the last High King of Ireland, in a losing fight with the Norman de Burgos, died here alone and deserted of a broken heart.

* The Cross of Cong is now in the National Museum, but its history remains. This processional cross is considered one of the wonders of religious art. Made of oak plated with copper and ornamented with gold-fringed designs, it was fashioned in County Roscommon for a cathedral in Tuam, Co. Galway, by order of Turlough O'Connor. The cross came to Cong with his son Roderick, last High King of Ireland, who had an abiding reverence and affection for it.

* The Plain of Southern Moytura, which lies between Cong and Neale, is one of Ireland's prehistoric battlefields. Here the legendary Tuatha de Danaan and his followers scored their first victory over the early Mediterranean settlers, the *Fir Bolg*, many of whom fled to the Aran Islands. Megalithic monuments bear witness to the region's history.

* Ballintubber Abbey in Ballintubber, 17 miles north of Cong just off the main Castlebar road to the right, is three and a half miles outside Partry. This is the only known church in the English-speaking world where Mass has been celebrated daily for almost 770 years, despite Henry the VIII's attempts to suppress the Abbey and an attack by Cromwell which left it roofless. Ballintubber was founded in 1216 by Cathal O'Connor, the King of Connacht, on the site of a fifth-century church established by St. Patrick. It is perhaps one of the most beautiful and peaceful of all rural churches. Walking through its early-Gothic main entrance, you're struck by the gleaming whitewashed walls, the rustic beamed ceilings, the flagstone floors, and the simple wooden benches. The nave is lit by eight pointed windows. Over the altar are three stained-glass Norman windows, crowned by a fourth, all framed with double dog-tooth moulding. The ancient monks' quarters extend to the right of the church.

Literature: George Moore, novelist, playwright, and poet, was born near Ballintubber at Moore Hall—now in ruins—on the shore of Lough Cara. His ashes lie beneath a cairn on the lake's Castle Island.

Roots: O'Connor (Ashford Castle and the Augustinian Abbey, Cong); Browne, Guinness (Ashford); Moore (the ruins of Moore Hall, Lough Cara).

* *Note:* The next major stopping point on your personalized itinerary is Sligo town, which is 67 miles from Cong. But you may wish to consider some of the other County Mayo possibilities first, as below. If not, proceed from Cong to Ballinrobe and Claremorris, then on to Knock, the scene of several religious apparitions, according to 19th-century accounts. The little Knock shrine church is visited each year by many pilgrims. The next town is Kilkelly; from here continue to Charlestown, Curry, and Tubbercurry, then to Collooney and Sligo.

Literature: Anthony Raftery, the Blind Poet of County Mayo. A few miles north of Knock—off the main Sligo route—is the village of Kiltimagh where Raftery was born in 1780. His folk poetry can be heard in the area pubs on summer evenings.

OTHER COUNTY MAYO SITES

* From Cong, travel the 30 miles to Westport by following the road that hugs Lough Mask through Clonbur and up to Trean, Tourmakeady, Killavally, and finally Westport.

* Westport or *Cathair na Mart* (Stone Fort of the Beeves or Oxen) is one of Ireland's most beguiling towns, tucked away in the arm of Clew Bay. The main street or Mall drifts along both banks of the River Carrowbeg in a leisurely fashion, connected by quaint stone bridges and lined with lime trees. But the main reason for visiting here is *Westport House.*

* One and a half miles west of the village on the T-39, Westport House is a magnificent Georgian mansion owned by the Marquess of Sligo (a direct descendant of the Pirate Queen of Connaught, Grace O'Malley). It occupies the site of the old O'Malley castle and was built in 1731 and furnished with the best that Georgian artists and craftsmen could provide, especially Irish silver, paintings, crystal, and furniture. Visit the downstairs drawing rooms with their grand fireplaces and chandeliers, then take the sweeping marble staircase to the bedrooms. (The owners ask that visitors refrain from wearing stiletto heels, as they ruin the flooring.) Numerous shops here deal in antiques, second-hand and antique furniture, glass and fashionwear, second-hand books, wine, and information on heraldry. There's also a tea room, which was the main kitchen in the old days, featuring the delicious homemade Irish *barm brack* cake. The house is open from 10:30 A.M. to 6 P.M. June through August. Also open April, September, and the first five days in October from 2 to 6 P.M.

If you're here for the evening, Westport House has recently opened an elegant dining room (phone 171) offering both Continental and regional dishes. Open 7 to 10:30 P.M. Closed Sundays. Reservations required, wine license. Visa, Master. Expensive.

Additional reasons for visiting Westport include a children's zoo and Grace O'Malley's former dungeons, which have been turned into a mock-scary place to visit. On the grounds: horse and pony riding, horse-drawn caravans, boats, bikes, and holiday homes for rent.

If you wish to stay in this area, a brief listing of Lodgings and Restaurants follows. Westport is an ideal headquarters from which to visit more distant parts of Mayo.

* Drive the 12 miles to Louisburgh. On the way you'll pass the small village of Murrisk, which rests under Ireland's holy mountain, 2500-foot *Croagh Patrick*. Here St. Patrick is said to have spent the 40 days of Lent in 441 fasting and praying for Ireland and its people. To this day there is a national pilgrimage to its peak each year on Garland Sunday, the last Sunday of July, when Mass is celebrated in a modern oratory at the summit. Near the chapel is an ancient ruin, now a pile or rocks, called *Leaba Phadraigh* or Patrick's Bed.

Legend: Here St. Patrick is said to have rung the bell that signaled the flight of the snakes and other reptiles from the land.

* At Murrisk is *Murrisk Abbey*, founded in the 14th century by the O'Malleys for the Augustinian friars. Be sure to have a look, if you stop, at its magnificent east window before you go on to the pleasant little fishing village of Louisburgh, which has many good beaches.

* From Louisburgh, a road to the west leads to Roonah Quay, where you can take a day-trip boat to *Clare Island* just off the coast. It's about 4000 acres in extent, with a population of only 350. There's a Grade-A hotel on this quiet island called Bay View (moderate) and good beaches.

Legend: Grace O'Malley, the Irish pirate queen, touched base on Clare Island. Its eastern coast has one of her former 16th-century castles, now a Coast Guard station. Grace was the daughter of Owen O'Malley, who was hailed as chief of the western islands, a title that she promptly appropriated upon his death. When she married MacWilliam Oughter, a powerful landed proprietor, she dismissed his retainers and staffed his castles with her own. Then she dismissed MacWilliam himself and confiscated all the properties.

Roots: O'Malley, Oughter.

* Return to Westport and then drive the 31 miles to *Achill Island*. Head due north eight miles to the picturesque seaside village of *New-*

port with its backdrop of mountains. Two miles west of Newport, a road on the left leads to Burrishoole Dominican Abbey. Built in the mid-15th century, its ruins include the central tower and some excellent pointed arches. Several miles farther along the Achill road, another left turn discovers the remnants of yet another O'Malley castle. From here, proceed to the seaside town of Mulrany, from which it is 12 miles to Achill.

Roots: O'Donnell, Newport House (see Lodgings).

★ Achill is Ireland's largest off-coast island—15 miles long and 12 wide—and is connected to the mainland by a bridge. It has three great mountains, heather-covered hills, and spectacular cliffs. This is another fine holiday center, with excellent swimming, surfing, fishing, golfing, and tennis. The main resort town of Keel has a three-mile beach.

★ Head back to Westport and prepare to drive the 65 miles to Sligo town, the next major stopping point on the itinerary. You should take the route through Castlebar, Swinford, Tubbercurry, and Collooney into Sligo.

COUNTY MAYO LODGINGS

★ *Breaffy House Hotel,* two and a half miles from Castlebar on the Claremorris road (22033), is a stately grey-stone mansion surrounded by over 50 acres of forested grounds. It has 41 attractive modern bedrooms, all with bath, radio, and phone. For all its castle-like exterior, the hotel is comfortable and unpretentious, with its old-fashioned bars and lounges with fireplaces. Moderate.

★ *The Great Southern Hotel,* on a hill above the N59, Mulrany's key road (41255), is one of Ireland's grand old railway hotels. The railroad no longer extends into this arm of the country, but the hotel, with its 71 updated rooms (48 with bath), is still a point of departure for Achill Island 12 miles farther west. Moderate.

★ *Newport House,* eight miles north of Westport in Newport (41222), is an impressive Georgian country house that was the long-time home of the landed O'Donnell family. It has 21 stylish rooms (all with bath) and a very good restaurant, described below. Excellent fishing nearby, both fresh and saltwater. Moderate.

★ *The Westport Ryan,* near the Westport quay (333), is a very modern motel-like hotel with 56 rooms (all with bath), part of the Ryan chain. Largely inexpensive to moderate.

COUNTY MAYO RESTAURANTS

★ *Breaffy House,* two and a half miles from Castlebar on the Claremorris road (22022), is a modern dining room in a stately old Georgian mansion serving excellent seafood, good beef and lamb. Open L—1 to 2:30. D—7 to 9. Bar lunch in the Mulberry. Full license. AE, Diners, Visa, Master. Inexpensive.

* *Chalet Swiss,* The Quay, Westport (231), is a special little place opposite the entrance to Westport House. Seafood is the best choice here, and more Irish than Swiss in style, but you can also get Continental dishes. Open 7 P.M. to 10 P.M. in the winter, 5:30 to 10:30 P.M. in the summer. Wine license. Visa, Master, Carte Blanche. Moderate.

* *La Petite France,* Castle Street, Castlebar (22709), is the local attempt at French haute cuisine. While it doesn't quite make it, it's still very good. Open 7:30 to 10 P.M. on Tuesday–Saturday, 7:30 to 9 P.M. on Sunday. Closed Mondays. Wine license. Mostly expensive.

* *Ozzie's Coffee Shop,* the Castlebar Shopping Arcade (22632), is a contemporary quasi-French fast-food spot: homemade pâté, soups, baked goods, and a variety of quiches. Fine if you're just passing through. Open 10 A.M. to 6 P.M. Inexpensive.

* *River Rooms Restaurant,* Bridge Street, Westport (17), is a pleasant modern dining room with an intimate feeling. Stick to the seafood and forget the rest. A good rendezvous for lovers on a budget. Open 10 A.M. to 11 P.M. Wine license. Inexpensive.

* *Westport House,* Restaurant and Tea Room (see Mayo Itinerary).

XIV. SLIGO

Benbulben Mountain

*And I shall have some peace there, for peace comes
dropping slow,
Dropping from the veils of the morning to where the
cricket sings;
There midnight's all a glimmer, and noon a purple
glow,
And evening full of linnet's wings.*

—William Butler Yeats
The Lake Isle of Innisfree

YOUR PERSONALIZED COUNTY SLIGO ITINERARY

You will want most of the day to see the Sligo area. The suggestion is that you arrive near Sligo town from County Mayo late in the afternoon, stay overnight, and take up the 30-mile journey to Rossnowlagh, County Donegal, in the mid-afternoon of the following day. If you are one of the many deep admirers of William Butler Yeats, you may wish to spend several days here visiting the places about which he wrote so movingly, for Sligo is Yeats country.

Day One

★ Travel the approximately 65 miles from your County Mayo departure point to arrive in the Sligo area early in the evening. The suggestion for your overnight stay is *Ballincar House,* approximately two miles from Sligo town on the Rosses Point road, in the heart of Yeats country. Several other possibilities are listed under Lodgings, below. See also Restaurants and Pubs for dining and entertainment options.

Day Two

★ Breakfast at lodging and check out.
★ Plan a morning's stroll of old Sligo, once a small country town and today close to a city in size. Start on *Abbey Street,* where the town's only remaining medieval building is located—Sligo Abbey. Built by Maurice Fitzgerald, it was destroyed by fire in the early 15th century when a candle overturned accidentally, but was immediately rebuilt.

Legend: It is said that here the ancient Celtic kings and nobles were brought to their eternal rest. Tighernan O'Rourke, the king of Breifne, and many noble O'Connors are thought to be buried here.

★ Follow Abbey Street straight to Castle Street, thence to John Street, the site of the 17th-century *St. John's Church* which connects with the *Catholic Cathedral,* a 19th-century Romanesque building.
★ Slightly off the beaten path, but within easy reach, is the *Sligo County Museum* on Stephen Street, not far from the Hyde Bridge. Here you'll find the *Yeats Memorial Museum,* which houses literally everything Yeats wrote, including letters to all the notable literati of his day, and his Nobel prize—a treasure trove for those in love with words. It's also the home of the *Sligo County Library* and *Art*

Museum, where you'll see masterly oils by Yeats's father and brother (whom many feel were equally brilliant painters).

★ At this point, you may wish to visit some of the town's shops or have lunch at *Beezie's Dining Saloon* on O'Connell Street (other suggestions under Restaurants and Pubs).

Legend: From Sligo town, you can head east on the L-16 for a few miles to a hillside on the left where there is an enormous megalithic tomb called Leacht Con Mhic Ruis *(the Stone of Cu, Son of Ross). Cu is believed to have been an ancient Celtic warrior who was slain by his wife's lover. Only one of three original entrances to the inner chamber remains, but these ruins lend credence to the prehistoric tales centered on the site.*

★ This hillside affords a fine view of Lough Gill, which rivals the lakes of Killarney for beauty. On the lake are Cottage Island and Church Island, whose ruined church was reportedly founded by St. Coman in about the sixth century. But for most, the lake's main attraction is the Lake Isle of *Innisfree,* memorialized in the Yeats poem that many consider one of the finest ever written. The island is nearest the southeastern shore.

★ Proceed along the lake until you reach the N17 heading back to Sligo. You will pass Glencar Lake, which Yeats fans will also want to explore. This is the region woven into the memorable poem 'A Stolen Child': *Come away, O human child, to the waters and the wild.*

★ Now travel back to Sligo town and then westward to the Rosses Point road. Rosses Point, only some five miles from Sligo, has a fine seafront restaurant called *The Moorings* (see Restaurants).

★ After lunch the Rosses Point strand offers another Yeatsian landscape worth viewing.

★ Go back to N15, the Bundoran road, and proceed to Drumcliffe. Here is the churchyard where Yeat's body was brought back from France to be buried. In the background is the imposing Benbulben, a familiar and well-loved sight to the poet.

★ A road diverging to the left leads to the famous *Lissadell House,* birthplace of the poetess Eva Gore-Booth and her sister, the Countess Constance Markievicz. The Countess was a passionate partisan of Irish independence who played a major role in the 1916 Easter Rising.

★ Return to N15 and follow it to Bundoran, which is in County Donegal; thence to Ballyshannon. From here, head west to the inviting seaside resort of Rossnowlagh.

SLIGO'S HISTORY

The Sligo area has been important to commerce since ancient times, when all traffic on the western coastal route forded the River Garavogue here. It was plundered by Norse and Viking pirates as early as the ninth century, and in the early 13th century de Burgo invaded the land and bequeathed it to Maurice Fitzgerald and his family. Fitzgerald built a castellated fortress in 1245 and established a Dominican friary. Sligo town was ravaged and partially burned during the Anglo-Irish struggles of medieval times, when the Fitzgeralds feuded with the O'Connors and the O'Donnells for possession of the fortress and its environs. In the mid-1600s Cromwell's armies took the town and established a castle here.

COUNTY SLIGO LODGINGS

★ *Ballincar House,* Rosses Point Road two miles from Sligo town (5361), was an old private homestead now transformed into a 17-room Grade-A hotel on six acres of grounds. While the bedrooms (all with bath) are modern, the dining and public rooms maintain their old-fashioned appeal. In the heart of Yeats country, this is Sligo's finest hotel. Sauna, squash court, and sun bed. AE only. Expensive.

★ *Hotel Innisfree,* Lord Edward Street (2101), is a very quiet Old-World hotel located in central Sligo but surrounded by landscaped gardens. It was once a grand Great Southern Railway hotel, now, disappointingly, not nearly so grand, but adequate, and less expensive. Forty-five rooms, 40 with bath. The lounges have turf fireplaces. Moderate.

★ *The Silver Swan,* Hyde Bridge (3231/2), is a well-established Grade-A hotel overlooking the Garavogue River in the center of Sligo. It has 24 rooms, 16 with bath. Moderate.

★ *The Yeats Country Ryan Hotel,* Rosses Point (77211), is a big modernized place near the shores of the Atlantic. There are 79 rooms, all with bath, making this the area's largest hotel. Often very busy. Tennis court on grounds and adjacent to an 18-hole golf course. Inexpensive to moderate.

COUNTY SLIGO RESTAURANTS

★ *Ballincar House,* Rosses Point Road two miles from Sligo town (5361), offers very good seafood, especially lobster and salmon. The dining room of this former country estate turned hotel overlooks the gardens. L—1 to 2:30. D—6:30 to 9. Breakfast served to lodgers. Full license. AE. Moderate to expensive.

★ *Beezie's Dining Saloon,* O'Connell Street (3031), started life in the early 1900s with a classic mahogany bar, marble counters, and stained-glass partitions. Fortunately, these features of the old pub have been retained and are echoed in the later restaurant extension. The food is hearty—boiled ham, shepherd's pie, mixed grills, chicken—and plentiful. A colorful place that blends the best of old and new. (Men only, note the old-time marble urinal: they don't make them like that anymore!) Open noon to 11.

★ *The Bonne Chere* Restaurant, High Street (2014). This is a spacious beamed-ceiling dining room lit by oil lamps. Good poultry and steak dishes (especially steak). Open for breakfast at 9 A.M., closes 10:30 P.M. Full license. AE, Visa, Master. Inexpensive.

★ *The Coffee Bean,* the Mall (5936), is a good place for snack-type meals ranging from fresh salads to homemade pizzas, grills, and hamburgers. Informal barrel tables, stool seating. Freshly ground coffee and fresh pastries. Open 8:30 A.M. to 8 P.M. Wine license. Closed Sundays and bank holidays.

* *The Knockmuldowney Restaurant,* Ballisodare, five miles from Sligo town and just off Main Street past O'Gara's Garage (71270). This converted old stone schoolhouse, complete with fireplace, offers excellent meat and seafood dishes. Open 7:30 to 11 P.M. Wine license. AE, Visa, Master. Moderate.

* *MacArthur's Coffee Pot,* High Street off Castle Street. A small place with snack-type foods. Open all day. Inexpensive.

* *The Moorings,* Rosses Point, five miles from Sligo town (77112). A fine little restaurant right on the seafront, open for seafood light lunches from 12:30 to 2. Dinners 7 to 10. Closed Sundays. Diners, Visa, Master. Moderate to expensive.

* *The Ritz Cafe,* O'Connell Street (2219). If you want the best value in town in a basic meal, this no-frills old chestnut is for you. Popular with the locals and so busy you'd think they were giving away the food (which is almost the case). Full meals including soup, entree of meat or seafood with vegetables, dessert, and coffee are rock-bottom priced. Roast chicken and rib of beef especially good. Hamburgers, mixed grill, or fish and chips are also available. L—12:30 to 3. Snacks and tea till 7 P.M. D—7 to 9. Inexpensive.

* *The Silver Swan Hotel,* Hyde Bridge (3231/2). The dining room here overlooks a waterfall and features good seafood dishes. Open L—12:45 to 2:45. D—5:30 to 9:30. AE, Visa, Master. Moderate.

COUNTY SLIGO PUBS

* *Tommie Regan's Pub,* High Street, is the pubgoer's choice, visually one of Ireland's finest. Old framed mirrors, antique lamps, mahogany snugs, and upholstered stools complement the antique bar fixtures. A memorable place that's too hard to leave; good talk here.

* *The House of Wines,* O'Connell Street. This place combines an old spirit shop dating from 1870 in the front with a slightly newer bar/lounge in back offering sandwiches and snacks.

* *M. Gilmartin,* Castle Street. Another traditional spot featuring snugs, an ancient bar, and good talk above all. Shouldn't be missed.

* *Curran's White Star,* Grattan Street. Snugs, traditional music nightly.

* *Ellen's Pub,* Maugherow, several miles from Sligo, is a fascinating old spot that goes back to the 17th century. Traditional music sessions nightly.

* *Yeats Tavern,* Drumcliffe. Very plain, but good traditional music nightly in summer season.

SLIGO TOWN SHOPS

* C & M Enterprises, Old Market Street. Antique items, furniture, prints, vases.

* Sligo Crafts, Market Yard off High Street. Irish earthenware crafts made on the premises, including pitchers, wine jugs, plates and other dishware, lamps.

* Wehrly Bros., O'Connell Street. Irish jewelry and glass.

* Mullaney Bros., O'Connell Street. Beautiful Irish apparel for both men and women, including tweeds and cashmeres.

* P. F. Dooney & Son, O'Connell Street. Fine Irish knitwear for men, beautiful smoky-colored sweaters.

★ Castle Crafts, in a lane off Castle Street. The owner makes his own craft items, including pottery, paintings, and framed prints.

★ Keohane's, Castle Street. Books of Irish interest.

★ Joy's Craft Centre, Castle Street. Irish woven baskets, pottery, glass, patchwork pictures, sheepskin rugs, hand-made gifts.

ENTERTAINMENT/ANNUAL EVENTS

★ The Hawk's Well Theatre, Temple Street, under the Tourist Board offices (61526/61518), is a venue for traditional music and Yeats memorabilia, along with plays and films by other Irish artists.

★ Ellen's Pub, Maugherow (see County Sligo Pubs).

★ The Yeats Summer School, during two weeks in mid-August, draws admirers of the poet from around the world to its seminars led by prominent Irish lecturers. This is one of the most popular summer literary courses ever, and with good reason—it's great. Request applications if you're interested, and reply months in advance through Kathleen Moran, The Yeats Society, Douglas Hyde Bridge, Sligo. (Phone 071-2693) Lodging reservations must also be made far in advance of the date.

COUNTY SLIGO SPORTS

★ Mountain climbing on dramatic Benbulben.

★ Sea sports (swimming, fishing, yachting, sailing, deep-sea diving, etc.)

★ Running and bicycling

★ Golfing at the 18-hole Rosses Point course.

Literature: The whole area belongs to William Butler Yeats (1856–1939), who captured it in his immortal poems: Lough Gill, Innisfree, Benbulben, Rosses Point, Lissadel, Glencar, and beyond.

Roots: Yeats; Booth and Gore-Booth (Yeatsian connections); also O'Connor, O'Donnell, Kelly, Connolly, Conway, Gilmartin, and Gallagher, among others.

Legend: On Bulben's slopes a legendary Celtic lover, Dermot, seduced the daughter of the Finn MacCool and carried her up to a whitened crevice where they continued their passionate lovemaking. In such a rage was Finn that he took his chance to savage Dermot to death, which cost him his daughter's life. Wandering disconsolate on the mountain, she collapsed and died of a broken heart.

XV. DONEGAL

Mountain Stream

That was a lovely glen with a lovely green gushing stream

—from the Celtic, 12th century

A MAJOR NOTE ABOUT COUNTY DONEGAL

While Donegal is not the largest county in Ireland (Cork is), it seems larger than the state of Texas. This ruggedly beautiful county has narrow, winding, often switchback roads that lead around and up craggy mountains, through hidden valleys and along jagged coastlines. The miles—while weaving through constantly enthralling scenery— take longer to drive here than they do in any other part of the country. So you will want to consider this before making your plans.

Donegal is part of the province of Ulster, which includes Northern Ireland, *but* it is still part of the Irish Republic and not Northern Ireland. The county's connection with the rest of the Republic is a narrow little four-mile strip leading from Ballyshannon to Belleek in Northern Ireland. This gives Donegal an almost insular feeling. It's as if it were a separate country. And since so much of the county is not developed, it's like a frontierland.

Covered here is one relatively long tour, which can be trimmed somewhat for timing purposes. Then there is a far briefer tour that touches upon the very southern portions of the county. *Note:* Both tours suggest that when you're leaving Donegal you travel through Northern Ireland down to Dublin for your departure from Ireland via Dublin Airport. The reason is that it's far, far faster than traveling all the way back down through the Republic to Shannon. The roads through Northern Ireland are excellent, and the miles fly by. They are also safe for tourists—if you're worried about the Northern Ireland troubles. You may occasionally see a tank with British soldiers, but other than that, you'll see only peaceful rolling green countryside— if you follow this itinerary. And it is better to travel during daylight hours.

Some lodgings are stressed in the personalized itinerary, but because time stays in Donegal can vary so greatly, further references have been relegated to an extensive listing of lodgings after the itinerary, so that you can work the stays into your timetable.

YOUR PERSONALIZED DONEGAL ITINERARY

The Longer (Recommended) County Donegal Tour—Including Short Cuts

* Drive the 32 miles from Sligo to Rossnowlagh in County Donegal. On the way, you will pass through the oversized seaside resort town of Bundoran and the hilly village of Ballyshannon. Moving northward, you will come to a left hand turn for Rossnowlagh. You should plan it so as to arrive early or mid-afternoon.

* Rossnowlagh is a sleepy little resort area with two miles of sandy beach. The suggestion is that you stay overnight here in one of Ireland's nicest modern hotels—*The Sand House*. See Lodgings and Restaurants for details.

* You might like to spend your afternoon hours before dining at the Sand House strolling on the beach. Other options include good swimming, surfing (the hotel supplies the boards), pony trekking, canoeing, fishing (game and coarse), tennis. Adjoining the hotel is a nine-hole golf course, and there's an 18-hole course five miles away. You may want to stay on here longer.

* Afterward, you might like to drift directly from the beach, barefoot and all, into the Surf Lounge at the hotel, which is right off the beach. It's doubtful that there's any other pub in Ireland so wisely attuned to the beach. It has an almost Hawaiian feeling. If you're more formally inclined, there's a lovely pub lounge in the main part of the hotel.

* Dine at the hotel. Have after-dinner drinks there or stroll the evening beach. Turn in early.

* Breakfast at your lodging. Check out.

* Travel back to the main road and drive the 11 miles to *Donegal town* (from the Celtic for Fortress of the Foreigners—probably so named because of the country's invasion by the Vikings during the 10th century). The town is laid out around a diamond-shaped area, as opposed to a town square. The Diamond here is not unlike other such town centers in the north of Ireland and was the product of British town planners after the demise of the O'Donnell family, who ruled County Donegal for nearly four centuries. Around the Donegal Diamond are many pleasant shops, described under their own heading.

In the early 16th century, Viking Castle in Donegal town was replaced by *Donegal Castle*. Built by Red Hugh O'Donnell, it became the main fortress of his family. The ruins remain on Bridge Street by the River Eske and the stately stone bridge that spans the river. They are open to the public. Just across the road is the *Church of*

Ireland, which was erected in 1828 and updated with a chancel and vestry in 1890.

Down quayside near the Tourist Board office, you'll see *The Anchor,* fifteen feet wide and weighing a ton and a half. It was shorn from one of Napoleon's boats and recovered from the sea at Doorin Rock near Mountcharles, Co. Donegal. This is a monumental reminder of the time when Napoleon sent a fleet to Ireland to thwart the British in an Irish uprising. The British stopped the frigates point blank and sent them speeding back to France.

(The question remains: What would have happened had the Napoleonic sailors succeeded—and eventually the French had conquered Ireland? Imagine a French Belfast today, with quiet little cafe-like pubs on the winding streets.)

A little farther along is the *Franciscan Friary,* built by the O'Donnell family in the 1400s. The British colonists sacked it upon the family's downfall. Monks from this friary compiled one of Ireland's most important sources of early national history, religion, and genealogy—a book called *The Annals of the Four Masters.* A red granite obelisk 25 feet high stands in the Diamond to honor these men.

* From Donegal town, drive the 17 miles on the N56 to *Killybegs.* This town is one of Ireland's major fishing ports. The arrival of a fishing fleet heralded by hundreds of sea gulls is an impressive sight.

* Heading west, it's eight miles to the restful little village of Kilcar, which is considered the center of the Doengal handwoven tweed industry. Many other cottage industries are represented in this area, including knitting and embroidery.

* It's three miles from here to the village of Carrick. This is the cut-off point for a climb up the Slieve League Mountain (1972 feet) and beyond to Teelin village, which leads to Carrigan Head and the cliffs of Bunglass. Here at *One Man's Pass,* the precipice is more than 1800 feet above the sea.

* As you move from Carrick to *Glencolumbkille,* a distance of 10-miles, you will enter the Owenwee Valley where you climb 600 feet before descending into the glen. Glencolumbkille, or *Gleann Cholaim Cille*—the Glen of (Saint) Columcille—is one of the most remote and beautiful areas (especially for seascapes) in the country. This lonely valley, which runs back between the hills from Glen Bay, is where the saint came during the sixth century to build a monastic retreat and prayer haven. Later he founded a famous monastery in Iona in the Hebrides. Of all the Irish saints and anchorites, Columcille is believed to have been the one most enamored of solitude.

Legend: Among the many stories about the saint is one that relates how he saved the poets of the land from banishment. In the sixth century, with the dawn of Christianity, the church was opposed to writers, whose stories often concerned pagan gods and customs. At the Convention of Druim Cett in 575, Saint Columcille—himself a notable writer—achieved a compromise between the church and the poets: the church would allow the writers their work if they treated mythology as history, thus humanizing the pagan gods. This saint was one of the early and leading scribes (manuscript copiers), credited by many with the development of scribal art. His work was held as an example by those who would later inscribe the Book of Kells.

There are frequent pilgrimages to Glencolumbkille. One of the most popular is held on June 9, which is the saint's day. Pilgrims cover a three-mile area, performing their devotions at ancient stone crosses, megaliths and stone habitats or cashels. At the Church of Ireland (Protestant), there is one such cross that is thought to be magical. If you look through one of its openings and then close your eyes, it is said that you can see through the coming years and into eternity.

* While you're at Glencolumbkille, you will want to visit the *Folk Village,* which consists of four cottages reproduced to represent different periods of Irish life, including furniture and utensils from those periods. Here you will find a handcraft shop where you can make purchases. Adjacent to the village are a group of thatched cottages which you can rent for a few days, if you'd like to see what it's like to live in one.

Back in the Sixties, when this village was rapidly becoming a ghost town due to emigration, a very enterprising local priest, Father McDyer, formed a cooperative of the remaining citizens; this made work available and not only halted the emigration but attracted new people from other parts of the country. The cooperative developed cottage crafts and inspired the development of tourism by building vacation cottages.

* While in this area, you might like to walk to Glen Head, a sheer cliff that rises some 700 feet from the sea and is slightly north of Glen Bay. You might also wish to take a drive nine miles to the south to Malinmore, which offers both dramatic cliff scenery and a fine beach.

* From Glencolumbkille, go northeast toward *Ardara,* which is 16 miles away. As you do, you will climb through the spectacular Glengesh Pass almost 900 feet before you drop down (usually along with the winds) into the windy but lovely little village of Ardara, where

the Owentocher River flows into nearby Loughros More Bay. If you have time, you'll want to stop and stroll about to sample the local color in the shops, hotel, and pubs. Here in this antique town, renowned for its tweedmaking and tweed shops, time seems to have stopped many years ago.

While here, you might like to explore the nearby Maghera sea caves; but check to see that the tide's well out before such an expedition, or you may find yourself up to your ears in deep trouble.

Legend: In days of yore, poteen makers brought their kegs here to the sea caves to secretly trade their illegal brew. It was common to sample, since quality varied so greatly, and with hooch distilled at over 100 proof, some soon forgot they were in caves—and many a drowning tale was told.

★ From Ardara, drive the 10 miles to the lovely twin fishing villages of *Portnoo* and *Nairn,* also seemingly untouched by the world. Resting at the foot of gently sloping hills, they are located on the southern shores of beautiful Gweebarra Bay. Here you'll find secluded strands and coves that you're likely to share only with a sea bird or two. At Nairn, there's a magnificent wide beach that's two miles long.

★ Opposite Nairn is Iniskeel Island and its ruins of a sixth-century church. You can stroll to the island from the mainland at low tide, but be sure the tide is *very* low when you begin the journey; it does come in with a vengeance.

★ Move along from Nairn strand to *Maas Village,* a distance of four miles. Here you have the opportunity to travel into northern Donegal, or, if your time is short, to head east through Ballybofey and into Northern Ireland on your way back to Dublin Airport. If you opt for this, the distance is 171 miles, and a brief discription of the journey follows. If you wish to proceed into northwestern Donegal, skip over the following and pick up the itinerary with the next reference to Maas Village.

★ Travel from Maas the four miles to *Glenties,* one of Ireland's tidiest towns. Then move on the 26 miles to the twin towns of Ballybofey and Stranorlar. Along the way, you pass by Aghla Mountain (1961 feet) and Lough Finn.

Legend: In days of old, the strong Celtic warrior Fergoman presided over the area. Always looking for sport, he spied a litter of young boars one day and slaughtered them. Unfortunately for him, the wild sow was nearby, and when she discovered her loss she attacked and gored Fergoman. His cries for help were overheard by his sister Finna who was on the same side of the lake as he. But what Finna actually heard was the echo of her brother's voice from across the lake. So she swam frantically to the other side of the lake, only to hear Fergoman's agonizing screams behind her. She crossed and recrossed until she heard the unmistakable note of death in his cries and was so overwhelmed with sorrow that she drowned herself. Her spirit is said to haunt the lake to this day.

★ The road continues on to *Fintown* and follows the Finn River through very lonely country to Cloghan and finally to *Ballybofey/ Stranorlar.* If it's anywhere near meal time, you should consider the wonderful dining room in *Jackson's Hotel* here (see Restaurants). If it's evening, think seriously of staying overnight, because it's a good 130 miles to Dublin from here (see Lodgings).

★ From Ballybofey/Stranolar, drive the 15 miles to *Lifford* where you will enter Northern Ireland and the large town of *Strabane,* County Tyrone, on the banks of the River Mourne.

Roots: O'Donnell (the family had an important castle in Lifford in the 16th century, a fortress that was later destroyed).

★ As you pass through Strabane, or *An Srath Ban* (The Fair River-Meadow), you might like to have a look at *Gray Printer,* a printing press shop. This is the very shop where John Dunlap served his apprenticeship before coming to America to found the first daily newspaper, the *Pennsylvania Packet,* in 1771. James Wilson, who was the grandfather of President Woodrow Wilson, also worked at Gray's before emigrating to America in 1807. His Strabane homestead still stands.

★ Travel the 20 miles from Strabane to *Omagh.* You'll find the road is excellent and swift. Omagh is another large town, where in 1641 Sir Phelim O'Neill demolished a major castle.

★ From Omagh, drive the 15 miles to Ballygawley and then the four miles to Aughnacloy where you will re-enter the Irish Republic. Proceed the 12 miles through Emyvale to Monaghan town.

Roots: MacMahon (Phelim MacMahon founded a Franciscan monastery in Monaghan town in 1462 which was suppressed by the English); also Duffy, McKenna, O'Connolly, Martin, Murphy, Hughes, McCabe, Smith, Quinn, Kelly.

★ Follow along the N2 to Carrickmacross (where you can buy the lovely Carrickmacross lace at the local convent), then on to Ardee and Dublin—a total distance of 75 miles.

⋆ Back to Maas in County Donegal, for those of you who have decided to explore the northern reaches of that county. Move along the extremely twisty road to the Gweebarra Bridge and into Lettermacaward, then on to *Dungloe* (pronounced Dunlow), a distance of 13 miles. This picturesque village has several interesting hotels, described under Lodgings. Each year from the end of July through early August, the Mary From Dungloe International Festival is held here, and the town can become very crowded, worth noting if you're planning to stay here. The festival includes traditional folk entertainment and of course the selection and crowning of a new Mary. But in the end, the town itself is far more interesting than the festival.

⋆ From Dungloe, travel five miles to *Burtonport,* one of Ireland's major fishing ports. More salmon and lobster are landed here than at any other port in Ireland or Britain. Here you can take one of the frequent boats to Arranmore Island. Three miles off the coast, this island is four miles long and almost three miles wide, with a population of nearly 700. This is a fine island with cliffs, strands, lovely heathered stretches, and even a lake where you can catch the delicious rainbow trout.

Legend: When Donegal chieftain Red Hugh O'Donnell fled Ireland for the Continent in 1607, having failed in his nine-year war against the British, he is said to have hidden four enormous pearls on this island. Some say the pearls are still there for the finding; others insist that an Englishman found them shortly after they were hidden and that they have been in London for centuries. Still others, while agreeing that there are such pearls in London, adamantly disclaim that they are the O'Donnell pearls.

⋆ Before you leave the Burtonport area, you might like to drop into the *Aran Bar,* where many of the fishermen drink, or *The Thatch.* The latter is relatively new and on summer evenings provides professional entertainment of the traditional type. But it may be closed during the day if business is slow.

⋆ From here move north past the peaceful Keadue Strand, where in the spring one of the Irish circus companies sets up a very respectable big top. A bit farther along the road toward Annagary and Bunbeg/Gweedore, there's a left-hand turn for *Cruit* (pronounced Keer-itch) *Island.* Large and rocky with some fine beaches, this island is linked to the mainland by a bridge built during penal times. Today the island has been especially attractive to the tourist for the recent development of a rent-an-Irish-thatched-cottage village. While there are many such developments in Ireland today, few if any begin to compare in quality and taste to the village Conor and Mary Ward have set out here. (See under *Donegal Thatched Cottages* in the Lodgings section.) You might like to consider heading here early on in your vacation, if you want a peaceful, out-of-the-way, and ruggedly dramatic locale with fishing and swimming facilities. It should be said that the cottages give you the sense of an old-time Irish homestead without sacrificing modern facilities.

* Next comes *Kincasslagh* village in the midst of craggy hills, with a wonderful narrow old pub with genuine artifacts called *Logue's*. The crack (chat) is very good and in the fine old Donegal vernacular.

* From this area, drive on to *Annagary*, a total of seven miles from Burtonport. There's an inexpensive pub/restaurant here called *Jack's* (see Restaurants). Outside Annagary, there's a signpost to the left for the tiny village of *Rannafast*, which is the heart of the Donegal Gaeltacht. Students come here each summer from all over Ireland to perfect their Irish language skills. This is also one of the few villages in the country without a pub. Back on the main road, it's six miles to Bunbeg in the Gweedore area of Donegal. On the way, you'll see a signpost for the left-hand turn *to Leo's Singing Pub*. It's a dingy, smoky stone box of a place, but traditional songs in both Irish and English can be heard at any hour. Don't go with a friend for an intimate chat, especially not during nighttime hours. A quieter spot is the little shop-pub in *Crolly* village, at which point you'll be making a left turn as you proceed toward *Bunbeg/Gweedore*.

* Soon you will come to another left-hand turn for Bunbeg. Here you have a choice of alternate routes—all of which will meet at Letterkenny for your journey back to Dublin. You can follow the coastal route into Bunbeg (see Lodgings for *Ostann Gweedore*, with its panoramic view of the sea), through Derrybeg, and past one of the county's most spectacular headlands, *Bloody Foreland* (named for the effect of the setting sun). From here you can see Tory Island. Then on to *Gortahork* (see Lodgings for *McFadden's Hotel*) and *Falcarragh*. Falcarragh is the closest stopping point to the 2197-foot Muckish Mountain, if you wish to climb it.

Legend: A mile from Falcarragh at Ballyconnell is MacKinley's Stone, said to be named for the chieftain MacKinley. The story goes that he was beheaded on this rock by a Formorian (sea warrior) called Balor of the Mighty Blows, who ruled Tory Island, off the Irish coast. A red vein spreading to the center of the stone is said to be the crystallized blood of MacKinley.

Off the coastline near Falcarragh are *Inishbofin* and *Tory Islands*. The former is about three miles out and has a population of about 150, while Tory is about nine miles out and has a surprising population of nearly 300—surprising because Tory is located in one of the stormiest parts of the North Atlantic. Sometimes, particularly in the winter, the island can be severed from the rest of the world for weeks at a time. Helicopters often struggle futilely to cross these nine miles with food and medical supplies. But while the population does decline as the years go by, most islanders refuse to leave, claiming that this is their heritage and that they would rather die than live on the mainland. The island is shrouded in legend, from the days of the warrior Balor of the Mighty Blows to more recent times when St. Columcille was said to have established a monastery here. Ruins of these ancient times remain. And you can, if you wish, journey to the island for a day trip from nearby Magheraroarty Pier. You should however be sure that the weather's going to be good or you may have to linger a little longer than you had planned. If so, the population is extremely cordial.

★ Moving out of Falcarragh on the main road to Letterkenny, you'll pass by one of the best craft/antique shops in the country. Located on a hillside, it's called *The Gallery*—and it's a composite of much that is Irish (both old and new), including paintings, of course. Do plan to spend a few minutes here, no matter what your time schedule might be.

★ From Falcarragh on the main road you'll come to *Dunfanaghy* and its turnoff for a thrilling (and possibly chilling) little side trip up and around *Horn Head*. For when you reach the top of the sheer cliffs and begin to curve around them, you see no more ground ahead of you. There's just the vastness of the Atlantic. Suddenly you feel as if you're in a plane flying out over it. And that's the danger: there are those who literally do forget for an instant, they're so taken by the feeling and the overwhelming beauty. But an instant can be fatal here. So be prepared and remain calm. When you've found a place to park, you can walk back and linger over the view that seems to suggest the end of the world, spinning off in a heaven-sent direction. If you're not moved by this scene, you need a longer break from your work-a-day life—to be infused by such beauty. From Dunfanaghy, you move through the beautiful seacoast village of Port-na-Blagh. See Lodgings for the *Shandon Hotel* and the *Port-Na-Blagh*. From here, you move south to *Creeslough,* passing by the *Ards Forest Park* which is open year round and is a lovely peaceful area shaded by ancient trees. There are appealing walks and picnic sites, and a silky white strand at the forest's edge from which the swimming is spectacular. After you pass through Creeslough, there's a turn to the left for a 10-mile side trip to the seacoast resort of Carrigart on Mulroy Bay. (See Lodgings for the *Carrigart Hotel.*) From here you can journey around the scenic Atlantic Drive. On your way to and from Creeslough and the main road to Letterkenny, you will pass *Doe Castle.*

Legend: This well-preserved 15th-century castle was one of the key fortresses of the McSweeney, McSwiney, or in true Irish MacSuibhne *family. This clan had come to Ireland from Scotland. The men were heavily armed foot soldiers known as the gallowglasses and considered mercenaries. They came to fight for the O'Donnell chieftains and thus established them as land owners.*

Roots: McSweeney, more commonly known as Sweeney today (Doe Castle between Creeslough and Carrigart).

Moving on from Creeslough, the main road takes you past Strangraddy Mountain to Kilmacrenan (St. Columcille spent his childhood in this area during the sixth century) and on into Letterkenny. You might be interested in the 17th-century *Church of Ireland* here. The profound Gothic structure across the road, *St. Eunan's Cathedral,* dates from the early 1900s.

This journey through Bunbeg, around the coast, and down into Letterkenny is 51 miles. This is the longest route to Letterkenny, which is the pivotal point for moving into Northern Ireland and the descent to Dublin and its airport.

There are two other routes to Letterkenny: perhaps the best is the one that bypasses the left-hand turnoff for Bunbeg; instead you proceed on the straightforward road due east for about five miles. Here you'll come to a dual signpost which looks like the funniest in all Ireland. (But wait—it's not.) One arrow points in the direction of *Letterkenny 39,* the other in the opposite direction—*Letterkenny 29.* Funny as this seems, it's not a mistake. The longer 39-mile route leads you over very flat, barren inland territory westwardly to Gortahork and picks up on the previously detailed and longer coastal itinerary at this point. This route cuts 12 extremely difficult yet beautiful coastal miles past Bloody Foreland from this itinerary.

The shorter, and for many the most rigorous route, is the *Letterkenny 29* suggestion. But if you're tired of seascapes at this stage, this one might be for you. Known by locals as 'the mountain road,' this strangely beautiful drive carries you through mountain landscapes where the wind sweeps up desolate verdant canyons and makes waves in the reedy waters of mountain tarns, past rushing streams and over flowery boglands. For most of the journey, you will see no farms, no houses, very few other cars—no petrol (gas) stations at all. Here you can feel you're at heaven's gate on a wonderfully sunny day, but be the day misty or ice-laden and you may think of it more as the gates of hell. Even if you're a complacent and expert driver, you must always be prepared for the sudden switch-back curves and some narrow-road cliffside driving. If you're at all apprehensive, don't take this route— unless the day is perfect.

On this route, the skinny road rises sharply above *Dunlewy Lake* and *Village* and the valley of the *Poison Glen* for spectacular views. From this point, you can climb the highest mountain in the county, Errigal (2466 feet)—if you're very skilled that is. From the top, you can see much of the province of Ulster.

Legend: This one has been beaten around the bush; some say that the waters here are naturally poisoned by lethal weeds that reputedly grow in the area. Others say that Poison Glen obtained its name during the penal times when the Catholics held their Masses in secrecy. Afterward, they would drink from the waters. When the British learned of their defiance, they poisoned the waters, thus killing many Catholics.

Farther along on this road, you will traverse the glaciated Derryveagh Mountains and pass the *Glenveagh Estate;* off the main road on Glenveagh Lake is *Glenveagh Castle.* It dates from the late 1800s and is in excellent condition. This mountain road will eventually lead you to the main road to Kilmacrenan and Letterkenny.

Note: There are a number of other magnificent northern areas of Donegal, including the Fanad and Inishowen peninsulas. But since they are distant, most tourists would find it difficult to find the time for them.

The Shorter (Southern) County Donegal Tour

★ This will bring you to Dublin in 145 miles. From Donegal town, you will travel the 15 miles to the twin towns of Ballybofey/Stranorlar, taking the curved road through the majestic Bluestack Mountains and the Barnesmore Gap.

Legend: In days of old, what seems such a peaceful, untouched countryside today breathed terror into the hearts of many a traveler, for this area was the highwayman's paradise. If you passed through the Barnesmore Gap without incident, you truly thanked your lucky stars.

After Ballybofey/Stranorlar, you drive the 15 miles through Lifford to your point of entry into Northern Ireland at Strabane, County Tyrone. Then you move southerly for 20 miles to Omagh, from Omagh to Ballygawley (15 miles), then on to Aughnacloy (four miles).

At Aughnacloy, you re-enter the Irish Republic, then drive 12 miles through Emyvale to Monaghan town. From here, follow the N2 to Carrickmacross, Ardee and on into Dublin—a distance of 75 miles.

Note: For details on the areas from Ballybofey to Dublin, check the longer (previous) itinerary.

LODGINGS

* *The Sand House,* Rossnowlagh (65343). This lovely hotel couldn't be any closer to the rolling Atlantic without being in it. Indeed its name comes from the two-mile sandy carpet just outside its doors. Inside, the hotel somehow

Glenhead

manages to combine a cozy atmosphere and a feeling of gracious stateliness. This is a winning combination that few places can claim. There are many fine things to relate about the Sand House: its restful lounges where turf and log fires always burn, its two exceptional bars (see Pubs), its tasteful dining room (see Restaurants), its immaculate and beautiful bedrooms, abundantly furnished with antiques (owner Mary Britton loves to surround herself and her guests with them). The amenities include tennis, pony-trekking, miniature golf, surfing, wind surfing, and canoeing (equipment available at the hotel). There are two 18-hole championship golf courses five miles away. The Sand House has 40 rooms all with bath. Moderate.

  ★ *The Hyland Central Hotel,* the Diamond, Donegal town. (Donegal 27). A pleasant old hotel with 44 comfortable rooms with bath. There's also a good restaurant and a fine bar, described under Restaurants and Pubs.

  ★ *The National Hotel,* Main Street, Donegal town (Donegal 35). This is a very small old hotel (15 rooms, two with bath) that's filled with antiques and features a lovely dining room and a pleasant bar. (See Restaurants and Pubs.) Inexpensive.

  ★ *The Glenbay Hotel,* 1½ miles southwest of Glencolumbkille at Malinmore and near the Glencolumbkille Folk Museum (Glencolumbkille 3). A pleasant old seaside hotel with 10 rooms, two with bath. No credit cards. Inexpensive.

  ★ *The Nesbitt Arms Hotel,* Main Street, Ardara. (Ardara 51) A big old inn (for a small town) with 30 rooms, none with private bath. Plain, comfortable with cheery service. Inexpensive.

  ★ *Jackson's Hotel,* just off Main Street, Ballybofey (Ballybofey 21) Another well-run old hotel, this one with 39 rooms, all with bath. But the main reason for staying here comes from the kitchen. Fine cuisine. (See Restaurants.) Moderate, but no credit cards.

  ★ *Ostann Na Rosann,* just outside Dungloe on the Burtonport road (Dungloe 91). It's a large (50 rooms, 50 baths) relatively modern, plain hotel. But it's well-run, the service is good, and there's an indoor heated pool. Moderate.

  ★ *Sweeney's Hotel,* Main Street, Dungloe (Dungloe 6). This place is a bit of an oddment. When you first walk into this old white-facade inn, you'll meet the bar—a little drab and plain-looking. Straight ahead, the dining room is even plainer. But give it a chance. This place bubbles with local color. And it truly has a sense of the past—a sort of rough-hewn frontier-town feel about it. Wander upstairs to the Victorian sitting room and look around. If this sort of atmosphere is your cup of tea, you'll soon be hooked. While everything may not be perfection, over the years Sweeney's has gone beyond the bounds of a mere lodging. For all its faults (which may not be faults at all), it has graduated into that legendary land of the institution. A good one at that. Seventeen rooms, 5 with bath. No credit cards. Very inexpensive, but reserve in advance.

  ★ *The Donegal Thatched Cottage Complex,* on Cruit Island, which is connected to the mainland by a simple stone bridge. Near Kincasslagh (phone arrangements should be made through the Sligo exchange—071—either 77197 or 61201). This is a wonderful experience. If you really want to know what it's like to live away from the world in frontier style, this is it. But it's all done with finesse. The painstaking taste level of these cottages enriches them with an infectious rural appeal that is very rare. These ethereal country houses are gleamingly spotless with their high beamed ceilings, cozy lofts, open hearths, old-time flagstone floors, sugán furniture, original and fine oil paintings (nothing has been spared) fashioned just for the cottages. There are fully equipped kitchens (including beautiful china and dishwashers) if you wish to cook. The local *Coop* grocery is only a few miles away in Kincasslagh; it also sells wines. For your fireplaces, there's a communal turf pile at hand. Miles of virtually vacant beautiful beaches here, and the nearby fishing is superb.

Owners Conor and Mary Ward have established a wonderful holiday complex that Americans should consider because it offers such a wonderful picture of Irish country life—presented with taste, dignity, and an attraction that is not so much appealing as compelling. Totally unforgettable. If you love rural Ireland, this place will become addictive. No credit cards. Inexpensive (must reserve in advance). These people cater to people who appreciate the Irish past.

★ *Ostann Gweedore,* off the Main Road, Bunbeg (Bunbeg 85). This is a very modern hotel on a dramatic seascape. There are 30 rooms with 30 baths. The bar/lounge is the finest feature, perched over often turbid waters. Moderate. Note: The owners have a less expensive, more rural hotel called *Seaview* on the Main Road. It's very plain, but there's a good bar and hearty, reasonable home cooking (see Restaurants).

★ *McFadden's Hotel,* Gortahork (35267). It's a lovely country, almost Tudor-like, hotel. Very cordial and cozy. Thirty-five rooms, seven with private bath. No credit cards. Inexpensive.

★ *The Port-Na-Blagh Hotel,* Port-Na-Blagh, main road (36129). This rather modern, very Irish hotel with 58 rooms (29 with bath) overlooks the sea. It's not great, but the view is dramatic. No credit cards. Moderate.

★ *The Carrigart Hotel,* Main Street, Carrigart (53281). This is a lovely hotel, although slightly on the modern side. It's located on the edge of a very beautiful frontier of scenery called the Atlantic Drive, one of the most spectacular drives in Ireland. The hotel has a strong sporting sense—heated pool, sauna, squash court, children's pony-trekking, tennis, croquet, crazy golf, solarium, masseur. Wonderful beaches and swimming. No credit cards. Moderate.

★ *Gallagher's Hotel,* Main Street, Letterkenny (22570). This is a small old-time businessman's hotel which also caters well to tourists. It has 33 rooms with 16 private baths. The place is tidy, clean and very comfortable. Visa, Master only. Moderate.

★ *Rathmullan House,* half a mile from Rathmullan on the Portsalon road (Rathmullan 44). This endless 18th-century mansion is one of Ireland's finest country estates. With its 21 rooms (16 with bath), the atmosphere is established by beguiling libraries, a drawing room, log-burning lounges, a lovely old kitchen, and a cellar bar. AE, Diners only. Moderate.

RESTAURANTS

★ *The Sand House Restaurant* in the Sand House Hotel, Rossnowlagh (65343). This is a very pleasant dining room specializing in tasty fresh fish like sea trout and poached salmon. But there are also fine meat dishes. The emphasis is on local produce. Here the kitchen is so spotless that owner Mary Britton invites her guests in for an inspection. Open L—1 to 2:30. D—7 to 11. AE, Visa, Master. Moderate.

★ *The Central Hotel,* the Diamond, Donegal town (Donegal 27). Good food, both meat and fish, in this homey dining room. Open L—12:30 to 2:30. D—7 to 9:30. AE, Visa, Master. Moderate.

* *The National Hotel,* Main Street, Donegal town (Donegal 35). The food is good here, especially traditional Irish dishes. But the antiques are even better: it's worth a visit. Open L—12:30 to 2:30. D—7 to 11. No credit cards. Inexpensive.

* *The Sail Inn Restaurant,* Main Street, Killybegs (Killybegs 130). This is a pub-type restaurant offering good bar foods as well as larger a la carte meals. Full license. Open for pub foods 9 A.M. to midnight. The bar lunch is from 12:30 to 2:30. A la carte from 6:30 to 10:30 P.M. (The latter is not available on Mondays.) Inexpensive to moderate.

* *The Glenbay Hotel,* 1½ miles southwest of Glencolumbkille at Malinmore (Glencolumbkille 3). Good fresh seafood and meat dishes in this pleasant old inn. Open D—6:30 to 9. No credit cards. Inexpensive.

* *Jackson's Hotel,* just off the main road in Ballybofey (Ballybofey 21). This dining room has excellent food and meticulous service. Certainly it's one of the best in Donegal. Here they know their cuisine, and it's difficult to recommend one dish over another. The salmon is superb, but so are the other selections. Even the pub foods available in Jackson's Bar are good. Open L—1 to 2:30. D—5:30 to 9. No credit cards. Moderate.

* *The Nesbitt Arms Hotel,* Main Street, Ardara (Ardara 51). Good basic Irish cooking is the trademark of this well-known place. L—1 to 2:30. D—6 to 9. AE, Diners. Inexpensive.

* *Ostan Na Rosann,* just outside Dungloe on the Burtonport road (Dungloe 91). This often busy and very popular area restaurant offers vast portions of food at inordinately low prices. The steaks here are superb and carefully done to your specifications. Open L—1 to 2:30. D—6 to 9. AE, Diners. Moderate.

* *Sweeney's Hotel,* Main Street, Dungloe (Dungloe 6). There's good, basic down-to-earth food in the plain dining room of this popular old hotel. Hopefully you'll get Aggie to wait on you. She cares about each customer and takes the time to discuss the menu with you even when the place is packed. Open L—12:30 to 2:30. D—6 to 9. No credit cards. Inexpensive.

* *Seaview,* on the Main Road, Bunbeg (Bunbeg 18). This is another very good basic food place in an older hotel. Open in season L—12:30 to 2:30. D—6 to 8. No credit cards. Inexpensive.

* *Viking House,* on the main road from Burtonport to Annagary near the village of Kincasslagh and the turnoff for Cruit Island (Kincasslagh 3). This is a very good seafood restaurant high on a hill in an old seafarer's house. But you must reserve in advance. Wine license. Open noon to 9:30 P.M. Closed Sundays. Visa, Master. Moderate.

* *McFadden's Hotel,* Gortahork (35267). A very attractive and cozy dining room has been fashioned here with bare wood tables and cushioned antique chairs. The food is very good, especially the seafood. Open L—1 to 2:30. D—5:30 to 8:30. No credit cards. Inexpensive to moderate.

* *The Port Na Blagh Hotel,* Port Na Blagh, main road (36129). Good basic Irish food along with French cuisine available here in a dining room that overlooks the sea. Go for the seafood. Open from 9 A.M. (for breakfast) to 9 P.M. No credit cards. Moderate.

* *Carrigart Hotel,* Main Street, Carrigart (53281). There's an excellent restaurant in this resort hotel. Everything is good, especially the salmon if it's on the menu. Open L—1 to 2:30. D—7 to 9. No credit cards. Moderate.

* *Gallagher's,* Upper Main Street, Letterkenny (22570). Good hearty Irish cooking in this pleasant little dining room. Open L—12:45 to 2:30. D—5:30 to 8:45. Visa, Master. Inexpensive to moderate.

* *The Mews,* Lower Main Street, Letterkenny (21737). Donegal has at last discovered romance with this reconstructed old mews residence. There's candlelight and love songs play softly in the background. The menu is both Irish and Continental, and its good. Full license. Open for dinner only—7 P.M. to 10:30. Closed Sundays, June to September. Closed Sunday and Monday October to May. Visa, Master. Moderate.

* *Rathmullan House,* half a mile from Rathmullan on the Portsalon road (Rathmullan 44). There are two dining rooms in this wonderful 18th-century mansion. The Pavilion serves haute cuisine. Go for the lobster, salmon, or sea trout dishes here. The other dining room is in the old kitchen of the house where charcoal-broiled lunches are served. Full license. Open L—1 to 1:45. D—7 to 9. AE, Diners. Moderate to expensive.

PUBS

* *The Sand House,* Rossnowlagh has two fine pubs. There's a sophisticated one decorated with muted stained glass, dark woods, and rich hammered copper. It's pleasant and comfortable; you could easily spend a couple of hours chatting and relaxing. The hotel's other pub is completely separate from this one. Decorated with fish nets, it's a kind of surfers/swimmers/beachcombers lounge. Stroll in from the beach barefoot if you wish. It's doubtful that you'll find another pub in Ireland comparable to this interesting spa that seems to have migrated from California or Hawaii. Naturally, it's much frequented by the young sporting set, and on weekends there are ballad sings. It's very wise of the hoteliers to cater to different moods with two such distinct and yet equally appealing pubs.

* *The Olde Bar* in the Hyland Central Hotel, the Diamond, Donegal town. A fine old drinking spot with sturdy round wooden tables and captain's chairs, a hutch with blue porcelain, lovely dark oil paintings.

* *The National Bar* in the National Hotel, Main Street, Donegal town. In a hotel chock-full of antiques, this is another fine old watering spot and very comfortable.

* *Biddy O'Barnes,* Barnesmore Gap. A kitchen-cottage pub with brown bread thrown in for free. Very rustic.

* *The Sail Inn,* Main Street, Killybegs. The ground floor is a fisherman's pub. Upstairs is a restaurant/cocktail bar with pub foods.

* *Ostan Na Rosann Bar* in the Rosses Hotel (*Ostan Na Rosann*), on the Burtonport road just outside Dungloe. A large but very common hotel bar/ lounge. What's pleasant is that you can sit by the windows and view the very pleasant old pastel-colored village of Dungloe nuzzling the sea. There's weekend musical entertainment here year round and nightly during the summer season.

* *Sweeney's Bar* in Sweeney's Hotel, Main Street, Dungloe. A tiny little bar in this very old hotel which is always pleasantly attended. Very plain, but wander around, perhaps take your drink upstairs to the lovely old sitting room. This place has a strange way of growing on you. You'll remember. (See Lodgings and Restaurants.)

* *The Aran Bar,* Burtonport. A rustic old fisherman's pub.

★ *The Thatch,* Burtonport. A newer Donegal pub, but clean and pleasant. May or may not be open during the day—depending on the demand.

★ *Logue's,* Kincasslagh. A skinny old pub with fascinating characters. Plan on an hour, if you're there in the evening.

★ *Jack's Place,* on the Burtonport road just before you come to the village of Annagary. Tiny little old pub with a newly added restaurant offering good basic food at reasonable prices.

★ *Leo's Singing Pub,* near Crolly. Dingy, smoky, awful if you want to talk. But often you'll hear good spontaneous traditional music. For that reason, it attracts people from many countries.

★ *Hudie Begs,* Main Road, Bunbeg. This place is the Fort Lauderdale of Ireland. On spring and summer weekends, especially holiday weekends, youthful singles from all over the country (and from other countries as well) spill from its doors and into the streets. It's an old-fashioned pub, but who's noticing the decor? What are they all there for? The same thing they're after in Fort Lauderdale.

★ *Ostan Gweedore Bar* in the Gweedore Hotel (Ostan Gweedore), down the hill to the sea from the main Bunbeg-Derrybeg road. Sit in this lovely bar/lounge—but don't face the bar. Turn away to the wall of windows that faces a magnificent seascape. If you're lucky enough to be there at high tide, you no doubt will feel you're on a ship in the midst of the rocky, turbid Atlantic. If you've the time, save an hour or two.

★ *McFadden's Bar* in McFadden's Hotel, Gortahork. For years, a pleasant old stopping place on the road to Letterkenny. Quiet, genial, and worth a visit.

★ *Gallagher's Bar* in Gallagher's Hotel, Main Street, Letterkenny. This is really a lounge, not a bar. And it's quiet—in one of Donegal's most bustling communities. If you want to take a break in Letterkenny, this subdued, tasteful, yet practical hotel is the place to do it.

★ *Jackson's Bar* in Jackson's Hotel, just off Main Street in Ballybofey. Pleasant little inland bar with excellent pub foods and adjacent to one of the finest restaurants in the county (see Restaurants).

★ *The Carrigart Bar* in the Carrigart Hotel, the Main Street, Carrigart. Sophisticated for the area, but certainly not outstanding by Irish standards. It's a pleasant place to stop on the brink of an absolutely beautiful landscape—The Atlantic Drive. (See Itinerary.)

SHOPPING

★ C. Bonner & Son, Glenties Road, Ardara. Handknit sweaters, tweed fashions, crystal, china, pottery, rugs, souveniers.

★ Campbell's Tweed Shop, Main Street, Ardara. Tweeds and Irish crafts.

★ Kennedy of Ardara, Main Street. Aran knits, handloomed knitwear (and demonstrations of same), Irish linens, Tyrone crystal, Irish pottery and rugs. Shop insures and mails abroad.

★ J. F. Heron, Main Street, Ardara. Quality handknit sweaters, Irish caps and scarves.

★ Wm. McNelis & Sons, Main Street, Ardara. Tweedwear, knitwear, Irish crystal and china. Tweed is woven on the premises.

★ John Molloy, Main Street, Ardara. Tweeds.

★ Castle Craft Centre, Main Street, Ballyshannon. A variety of Irish crafts.

★ Rogan's, Bridge End, Ballyshannon. Handmade fishing flies.

* The Gift Shop, Main Street, Ballyshannon. A variety of Irish crafts and gifts.
* Cormac Breslin, Main Street, Bunbeg. Irish clothing and crafts, including baskets.
* Nothing but McNutt, Main Street, Carrigart. Handwoven tweeds and other Irish crafts. Restaurant attached. (See Restaurants.)
* The Pharmacy, Main Street, Carrigart. Irish crystal.
* Anthony Gallagher, Middletown, Derrybeg. Cottage craft knitwear.
* Cladyknit Ltd., Main Road, Derrybeg. Handknits and other Irish apparel.
* Magee of Donegal, the Diamond, Donegal town. A wide variety of Donegal tweed items and other clothing crafts.
* Kelly's The Tweed Shop, Main Street, Donegal town. Donegal tweeds and Donegal handknit sweaters.
* The Gift Shop, the Diamond, Donegal town. Water colors and oils of the area, tweed-woven pictures, Belleek, porcelain, other crafts, souvenirs.
* The Antique Shop, the Diamond, Donegal town. Glass, paintings, china, jewelry, brass, silver, oil lamps.
* The Gallery, on the hill above Dunfanaghy. One of Ireland's best antique/craft/painting shops. This place should be at the top of your list if you're visiting Ireland for quality shopping. There are few places with the taste level and the excitement of this shop a la Georgian country home. You should save an hour for it, even if you have to stay overnight in one of the local seaside haunts. This place is truly a gem.
* Tweed and Fashion Shop, Dunfanaghy. Expensive apparel shop with some lovely items.
* Glencolumbkille Craft Shop, Glencolumbkille. Fine local crafts.
* The Inishowen Craft Shop, Malin. Cottage crafts, including superb knitwear from the locals.

Roots: O'Donnell (Donegal Castle and the Franciscan Friary, Donegal town); McSweeney or Sweeney (Doe Castle). Some other prominent Donegal families are: Boyles, Gallaghers, Duffys, Campbells, McFaddens, Wards, Kellys, Dohertys.

SPORTS

This is a wonderful county for swimming (sometimes a mite chilly, mind you) with its virtually empty beaches. WARNING: Be sure to check with the locals before plunging in, even if the waters look calm. There are areas of Donegal where the deep undertows are so severe that they've taken even strong swimmers to their deaths.

Surfing, wind surfing, canoeing, water-skiing are all very popular here. Then there's deep-sea diving, skin diving, snorkeling. And of course, fishing.

Golfing, tennis, running are readily available.

Donegal Literature: Many of the country's Gaelic writers, who are unknown to all but Irish scholars in America, hail from County Donegal. Their writings are so earthy, so humorous, so ribald and ultimately so beautiful (because they sing of life) that it's a tragedy there aren't the funds or the interest to have them translated so we can all share this wonderful heritage. Maybe someday.

Brian Friel, the prominent Irish playwright who rose overnight to fame with his magnificent play *Philadelphia, Here I Come,* which was rushed from

Ireland to New York by producer David Merrick, hails from County Derry and has a house in Donegal. The setting of *Philadelphia* is Donegal.

Ulster Literature: Benedict Kiely (short-story writer) and John Montague (poet) both have their roots in the rich farmlands of County Tyrone. Brian Moore, the well-known novelist (*The Lonely Passion of Judith Hearne* and *The Doctor's Wife*) often writes of his Belfast. Patrick Kavanagh (poet) grew up in County Monaghan.

Irish Eventide

—The fire from the sky keeps the earth and its waters ablaze through eternity.

—from the Celtic, 8th century

CREDITS

Many thanks to the *Irish Tourist Board,* especially Patricia Tunison Preston, Paddy Derivan, Simon O'Hanlon and Joan Ennis.

★ Photography—the *Irish Tourist Board, Joe Kardwell Associates,* and *Marie Fullington.*

★ Editorial—*Robin Sommer Editorial Services* of Greenwich, Ct.

ABOUT THE AUTHOR

Don Fullington is a free-lance newspaper and magazine writer. Born in upstate New York, he lived six years in County Donegal, Ireland, where he was a travel writer for many overseas publications. He and his family currently live in New York City.

National Routes Network

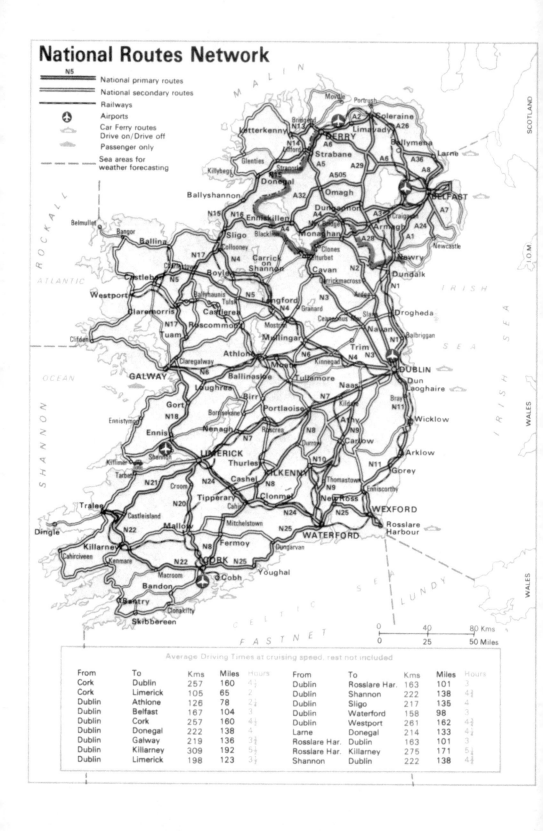

—N5—		National primary routes
		National secondary routes
		Railways
✈		Airports
		Car Ferry routes
		Drive on/Drive off
		Passenger only
		Sea areas for weather forecasting

Average Driving Times at cruising speed, rest not included

From	To	Kms	Miles	Hours	From	To	Kms	Miles	Hours
Cork	Dublin	257	160	4½	Dublin	Rosslare Har.	163	101	3
Cork	Limerick	105	65	2	Dublin	Shannon	222	138	4½
Dublin	Athlone	126	78	2½	Dublin	Sligo	217	135	4
Dublin	Belfast	167	104	3	Dublin	Waterford	158	98	3
Dublin	Cork	257	160	4½	Dublin	Westport	261	162	4½
Dublin	Donegal	222	138	4	Larne	Donegal	214	133	4½
Dublin	Galway	219	136	3½	Rosslare Har.	Dublin	163	101	3
Dublin	Killarney	309	192	5½	Rosslare Har.	Killarney	275	171	5½
Dublin	Limerick	198	123	3½	Shannon	Dublin	222	138	4½

INDEX

Page numbers in italics refer to illustrations

Abbeyglen Hotel (Clifden), 205–06
Abbeyside Castle (Waterford), 102
Abbey Tavern (Howth), 25, 35, 47–8
Abbey Theatre (Dublin), 25, 53–4, 184
à Becket, Thomas, 84
Achill Island (County Mayo), 218–19
Acton's Hotel (Kinsale), 126, 129
Act of Union, 29, 118
adapters, electrical appliance, 14
Adare (County Limerick), 161–2
Aer Arann (Aran Airline), 194
Aer Lingus (Irish Airlines), 4–5, 6
Aghadoe Heights Hotel (Aghadoe Hill), 148, 149
Aghadoe Hill (Aghadoe), 146
Aherne's Pub (Waterford), 107
American Bar (Aran Islands), 197–8
American Embassy (Dublin), 16
American Express Company (Dublin), 16
American International Rent-A-Car, 6
An Cafe Liteartha (Dingle town), 163
Anchor, the (Donegal), 230
An Cuan Restaurant (Aran Islands), 197
Andrews, Mark Edwin, 168
Andy Kinsella's (Wexford), 87
Anglo-Norman invasions, 28, 67, 77, 83–4, 85, 116, 138, 187–8, 213
Annabel's (Dublin), 53
Annagary (County Donegal), 235
Annals of the Four Masters, 230
Annals of Innisfallen, 147
Anno Santo Hotel (Salthill), 188
antiques, displayed, 37, 38, 63, 118, 119, 132, 169, 171, 207, 214, 217, 240
antiques, sold, 57, 58, 63, 97, 106, 123, 151–2, 181, 190, 217, 225, 236, 245
An Tsean Cleibh Restaurant (Aran Islands), 197
Aran Airline. *See* Aer Arann
Aran Bar (Burtonport), 234, 243
Aran Islanders, The (Synge), 198
Aran Islands, *192*, 193–99
Aran knitwear, 106, 174, 181, 198, 244. *See also* craft shops; department stores
Arbutus Hotel (Killarney), 143, 148
Arbutus Lodge (Cork), 113, 117, 119–20, *120*
archaeological sites, 68, 118, 136, 138, 158. *See also* beehive huts; crannog; dolmen; gallan; ogham; prehistoric remains

architecture, Georgian, 24, *29*, 30, 84, 101, 112, 126, 161
Ardagh chalice, 35
Ardara (County Donegal), 231–2
Ardilaun House Hotel (Galway), 185, 188
Ardree Hotel (Waterford), 105–06
Ards Forest Park (County Donegal), 236–7
Ariel House (Dublin), 23, 38–9, 45
Armada Restaurant (Dingle town), 163
Arnott & Co. (Dublin), 46, 52
Arranmore Island (County Donegal), 234
Ashford Castle (Cong), 203, *212*, 213–16
Atlantic Coast Hotel (Clifden), 208, 209
Atlantic Drive, the (County Donegal), 237
Atlantis, legend of, 198
Augustinian Abbey (Adare), 161
Augustinian Abbey (River Cong), 216
Augustinian Abbey of St. Mary d'Urso (Drogheda), 64
Augustinian Red Abbey (Cork), 113
Auto Ireland, 6
Avis Rent-A-Car, 6
Avondale (near Rathdrum), 73, 76
Avondale Restaurant/Craft Shop (Rathdrum), 73

Bailey Pub, the (Dublin), 28, 40
Balfe, William, 86
Ballincar House (Sligo town), 222, 224
Ballinakill House (Waterford), 106
Ballinskelligs (County Kerry), 137
Ballintubber Abbey (Ballintubber), 216
Ballymaloe House (Shanagarry), 104, 117, 120
Ballynahinch Castle Hotel (Ballynahinch), 205
Ballyseede Castle Banquet (Tralee), 164–5
Balor of the Mighty Blows, 235, 236
Bank of Ireland, the, 24, 31
Bantry House (Bantry), 127
Barnacle, Nora, 191
Barnesmore Gap (County Donegal), 238–9
Baroque, Restaurant (Dalkey), 49
Barry, John, 82
Barry Memorial (Wexford), 80, 82
Barry, Robert de, 84
Bay View Hotel (Clare Island), 218
Bay View Hotel (Waterville), 137
Bay View lodging (Aran Islands), 196
Beach View House (Aran Islands), 197

Beara, Princess, 128
Beara Peninsula, 127–8
Beatty, Chester, Library (Dublin), 35
beehive huts, 156, 157
Beer and Bite (Waterford), 106
Beezie's Dining Saloon (Sligo town), 223, 224
Behan, Brendan, 54, 61
Belfast (Northern Ireland), 63
Belleek china shops, 57, 88, 151–2, 174, 190, 209.
    See also craft shops; department stores
'Bells of Shandon, The,' (Mahony), 114–15
Belltable Arts Centre (Limerick), 180
Benbulben (County Sligo), 221, 222
Berkeley Court Hotel (Dublin), 25, 37, 40, 44, 51
Bewley's (Dublin), 23, 45
Bianconi Grill (Cork), 120
bicycling, 135, 171, 181, 218, 226
Biddy O'Barnes Pub (Barnesmore Gap), 243
Billy's Vintage Car Bar (Clifden), 208
Bistro, the (Guardwell), 129
Black Lough (Gap of Dunloe), 145, 146
Blarney Castle (County Cork), 110, 111, 117
Blarney knitwear, 110, 190. See also craft shops; department stores
Blarney Stone, 110, 116–17
Blasket Islands, 156–7
Blathnad, 160
Blind Poet of Ireland, the. See Raftery, Anthony
Bloody Foreland (County Donegal), 235
Bloom's Hotel (Dublin), 25, 37–8, 40–41, 44, 50, 51
Blue Haven Hotel (Kinsale), 126, 129–30
Bluestack Mountains (Donegal), 238–9
boating, 137, 138, 181, 214, 218, 229, 240
Bohemian Girl Pub (Wexford), 86
Bonne Chere Restaurant (Sligo town), 224
Book of Hy-Many, 62
Book of Kells, 24, 31, 35, 231
bookstores, Irish interest, 58, 88, 97, 106, 181, 190, 191, 198, 209, 226
Bord Failte. See Irish Tourist Board
Boru, Brian, 28, 179
Bourne-Vincent Memorial Park (Killarney), 145, 148
Boyle, Elizabeth, 112
Boyle Monument (Dublin), 34
Boyle, Richard, 1st Earl of Cork, 103, 107
Boyne, Battle of the, 33, 34, 63, 105
Boyne Valley Tour, 63–70
Braemor Rooms (Dublin), 52
Bran, son of Febal, 159
Brandon, Mount (Dingle Peninsula), 159
Brazen Head Pub (Dublin), 28, 54–5, 61
Breaffy House Hotel (Castlebar), 219, 220
Brendan, Saint, 159

Brendan Self Drive, 6
Brontë, Charlotte, 191
Brown Thomas Department Store, 46, 52
Browne Doorway (Galway), 185
Brugha, Cathal, 37
Buckley, Timothy [pseud. The Tailor], 110–11
Budget Rent-A-Car, 6
Buithe, Saint, 65
Bull Ring, the (Wexford), 80, 81
Bunratty Castle Banquet (Bunratty), 168, 169, 172
Bunratty Folk Park (Bunratty), 168, 169
Burges, William, 113
Burgh, Thomas, 31
Burlington Hotel (Dublin), 38, 43, 44, 53
Burren, the (County Clare), 169–70
Burtonport (County Donegal), 234
Busaras (bus terminal, Dublin), 20, 22, 23
Bush Courtyard Pub (Waterford), 108
Buswell's Hotel (Dublin), 38
Butler, James (earl of Ormonde), 94
Butler Arms Hotel (Waterville), 137

cabaret, Irish, 25, 38, 52–3, 88
Cafe de Paris (Cork), 120–21
Caherdaniel (County Kerry), 136
Cahirciveen (County Kerry), 138
cairns, 66, 67
Canice, Saint, 93
Cap Con Macken Pub (Wexford), 87
Cappanacuss Castle (County Kerry), 135
Cara, Lough (County Mayo), 216
Cara Restaurant (Killarney), 149
Carmel, Hotel (Kilkenny), 95
Carmelite Friary (Kinsale), 126
car rentals, 6–8
Carrigart Hotel (Carrigart), 241, 242, 244
Cashel (County Connemara), 201
Cashel House Hotel (Cashel), 205
Casper & Guimbini's (Dublin), 25, 44, 50
Castle Golf Club (Rathfarnham), 59
Castlegregory (Dingle Peninsula), 160
Castle Inn (Dublin), 50
Castlerosse Hotel (Kenmare Estate), 148
Cathedral of St. Nicholas and Our Lady (Galway), 185–6
Catholic-Protestant conflict, 63, 64, 92, 94, 105, 158, 160, 161, 164, 179, 238
ceili, 124, 168, 173, 199
Cellar Bar (Galway), 189
Cellar Grill (Galway), 189
Celtic Hotel Pub (Clifden), 208
Celtic Mews (Dublin), 41
Central Hotel (Donegal town), 241–2
Chalet Swiss (Westport), 220
Chambers, William, 30
Charles I (king of England), 92, 116

Chez La Hiff (Dalkey), 49
children, traveling with, 9
Christ Church Cathedral (Dublin), 24, 28
Christ Church Cathedral (Waterford), 101
Church of the Assumption (Wexford), 83
Church of the Immaculate Conception (Wexford), 81, 83
Church of Ireland (Donegal), 229–30
Church of Ireland (Letterkenny), 237
Church Island (Lough Currane), 139
Church Island (Lough Gill), 223
Church of the Most Holy Trinity (Dublin), 33
Church of St. Multrose (Kinsale), 126
Church of St. Peter (Drogheda), 64–5
Church of Sts. Peter and Paul (Cork), 111
C.I.E. (Irish Transport Co.), 20, 194
City Hall (Dublin), 24, 32
Claddagh, the (Galway), 186
Claddagh Festival (Galway), 191
Clare Island (County Mayo), 218
Clifden (County Connemara), 201
Cliffs of Moher (Lahinch), 169, 170, *170*
Clifton House (Limerick), 179
climate/clothing, 13
Clogher Head (Dingle Peninsula), 157
Clontarf, Battle of, 28
Clontarf Castle Show (Dublin), 53
Clontarf Golf Club (Clontarf), 59
Club House Hotel (Kilkenny), 95, 97
Cody, William 'Buffalo Bill,' 83
Coffee Bean, the (Sligo town), 224–5
Coghlan, Eamonn, 59
Collins, Michael, 30
Cois Farraige Restaurant (Dingle town), 163
Colman, Saint, 202
Colmcille, Saint, 196
Columcille, Saint, 230–31, 236, 237
Coman, Saint, 223
Confederation of Kilkenny, 92, 94
Congreve, William, 98
Connacht Restaurant (Dublin), 46
Connemara Gateway Inn (Oughterard), 208
Connemara marble shops, 191, 203, 209. *See also* craft shops; department stores
Connemara National Park, 206
Conor Pass (Dingle Peninsula), 155, 159
Coole Park (Gort), 184
Cooley, Thomas, 32
Coote, Sir Charles, 188
Corballis Public Golf Course (Donabate), 59
Cordon Bleu (Tralee), 165
Cork, Richard Boyle, 1st Earl
Cork (County Cork), *109*, 110–114, *114*, 115–24
Cork Choral Festival, 123
Cork Jazz Festival, 123
Cormac (king of Ireland), 68
Cornmarket (Wexford), 81, 83

Corrib Great Southern Hotel (Galway), 188
Corrigan's Hotel (Cork), 118
cost ranges, comparative, 11
cottage industries, 230, 231
Cottage Island (Lough Gill), 223
County Hotel (Wexford), 85
Court Hotel (Killiney), 49
craft exhibits, 145, 169, 208, 231
craft shops, 57, 58, 63, 88, 96–7, 106, 122, 130, 140, 146, 151, 157, 162, 181, 190, 191, 198, 202, 203, 204, 209, 225, 226, 231, 236, 244–5
Craggaunowen Castle (Quin), 168–9
crannog, 168, 170
Crawford School and Gallery (Cork), 111
credit cards, 11
Croagh Marhin (Dingle Peninsula), 156
Croagh Patrick (County Mayo), 218
Crock of Gold Pub (Killarney), 151
Cromwell, Oliver, 34, 64, 67, 78, 81, 83, 84, 92, 94, 103, 105, 107, 154, 158
Cromwell's Fort (Kenmare), 135
Cromwell's Headquarters (Wexford), 80, 82
Cross of Cong, 35, 216
Crowley, O'Neill, 112
Crown Pub (Wexford), 80, 87
Cruit Island (County Donegal), 234–5
Cuchulainn, 160
Culvy, Rice de, 186
Curragh Racecourse, the (County Kildare), 60
Curran, John Philpot, 34
Currane, Lough (County Kerry), 137
Curran's White Star Pub (Sligo town), 225
Currarevagh House (Oughterard), 207–08
currency, 10
Custom House (Dublin), 23, 31
customs duties/declarations, 14

Dail, the, 24, 30
Dalkey (County Dublin), 73–4
Danes, 105, 179. *See also* Norsemen; Vikings
Dan Ryan Rent-A-Car, 6
D'Arcy Inn (Clifden), 208–09
Davies, Donald, 74
Davis, Thomas, 112
Davy Byrnes Pub (Dublin), 28, 55–6
Deane, Kearns, 114
Deenach Grill (Killarney), 149
Deer Park Hotel Public Golf Course (Howth), 59
department stores, 46, 52, 58, 97, 106, 122, 174, 190
Derryquin Castle (County Kerry), 135
Derrynane Abbey (Caherdaniel), 136
Derrynane House (Caherdaniel), 136
Desmond, Thomas, 8th Earl, 103
Desmond Castle (Adare), 161–2
Desmond Castle Museum (Kinsale), 126

Desmond War, 154, 160–61
de Valera, Eamon (president of Ireland), 36
Devorgilla, 65
Diarmaid, 68–70
Digby's Restaurant (Dun Laoghaire), 48
Dingle Peninsula (County Kerry), 148, 153–65
Dingle town (Dingle Peninsula), *153*, 154–5
Dobbins Wine Bistro (Dublin), 44
Doctor on Call (Dublin), 21
Doctor's Wife, The (Moore), 246
Doe Castle (Creeslough), 237, 245
Dog Bay's Strand (Roundstone), 201
Doheny & Nesbitt Pub (Dublin), 28, 55
dolmen, 35, 135
Dominican Abbey (Youghal), 103
Dominican Church (Cork), 114
Dominican Church (Tralee), 161
Dominican Friary (Drogheda), 64
Dominican Friary (Waterford), 100
Donegal Castle (Donegal), 229
Donegal, County, *227*, 228–46, *246*
Donegal Thatched Cottages (Cruit Island), 235, 240–41
Donegal town (County Donegal), 229–30
Doolan's Pub (Waterford), 106
Dooley's Inn (Waterford), 106
Doon, Daire, 156
Dowth (County Meath), 66
Doyle's Seafood Bar (Dingle town), 163
driver's license requirements, 7
Drogheda (County Dublin), 64–5
Dromineen Castle (County Cork), 118, 119
Dromoland Castle (Newmarket-on-Fergus), 147, 168, 171, *171*, 172
Dromore Castle (County Kerry), 140
Druid Lane Theater (Galway), 191
druids, 74, 135
Dublin (County Dublin), *19*, 20–22, *22*, 23–6, *27*, 28–62
Dublin Airport, 5, 6, 22, 232
Dublin Castle, 24, 28, 32–3
Dublin Horse Show, 15, 20
Dublin Marathon, 59
Dublin Theater Festival, 21, 54
Dublin Tourist Trail, 23
Dun Aengus (Aran Islands), 195
Dun an Oir, fort (Smerwick Harbour), 158, 160
Dun an Oir Hotel (Smerwick Harbour), 158
Dun Aonghasa Restaurant (Aran Islands), 197
Dunbeg, fort (Dingle Peninsula), 156
Dunboy Castle (Castletownbere), 128
Dungloe (County Donegal), 234
Dunguaire Castle (Kinvara), 184
Dunkerron Castle (County Kerry), 135
Dun Laoghaire (County Dublin), 72, 73
Dun Laoghaire Golf Club, 59
Dunloe Castle (County Kerry), 144

Dunloe Castle Hotel (Beaufort), 148
Dun Oghil (Aran Islands), 195
Dunquin (Dingle Peninsula), 157
Durty Nelly's Pub (Bunratty), 168, 173
Dwyer, Michael, 74, 112

Eagan's Lounge Bar (Waterford), 106
Eagle, Mount (Dingle Peninsula), 156
Eamon's Restaurant (Bray), 49–50
Easter Rising (1916), 29, 37, 78, 185, 223
Egan's House (Glasnevin), 39
Egan's Pub (Waterford), 106
1848 Uprising, 100
18th Precinct Restaurant (Dublin), 46
Eirinagreinne Restaurant (Dingle town), 163
E. J. King's Pub (Clifden), 209
Elgin Guesthouse (Dublin), 39
Elizabeth I (queen of England), 30, 32, 100, 107, 117, 154, 160–61
Elizabeth Fort (Cork), 113
Ellen's Pub (Maugherow), 225
Embassy Townhouse (Dublin), 39
emergency telephone, nation-wide, 16, 21
emigration to America, 113–14, 115, 231
Emmet, Robert, 29, 54
Enda, Saint, 196
Enniscorthy (County Wexford), 73, 77–8
Enniscorthy Castle County Museum, 73, 77–8
Enniskerry (County Wicklow), 74
Eogan (prince of Ireland), 128
Entertainment Centre (Cork), 124
Errigal Mountain (County Donegal), 238
eternal youth, legend of, 76–7, 156, 196, 198. See also *Tir ná nog*
Europe Hotel (Fossa), 143, 149
Everyman Playhouse (Cork), 123
Eyre Square (Galway), 185

Faerie Queene, The (Spenser), 107
Fail, Island of, 68
Failte Hotel (Killarney), 149
Fairyhouse Racecourse (County Meath), 60
Falcon Inn Hotel (Glenbeigh), 140
Farquhar, George, 98
Father Matthew Memorial Church (Cork), 112–13
Fechin, Saint, 216
Fee, Lough (Killary), 204
Fenian movement, 116
Fergoman, 232–3
Ferriter, Pierce, 143, 158, 161
Ferriter's Castle (Ballyferriter), 157
Ferrycarrig Hotel (Wexford), 85
Fianna, the, 68–9, 116, 156
Fighting 69th, 101
Finbarre, Saint, 113, 116
Finian, Saint, 137, 147

Finn, 68–70
Fir Bolg, 195, 198, 215, 216
fishing, fresh water, 59, 118, 135, 137, 139, 181, 205, 208, 209, 214, 234
fishing permits, 15, 59, 181
fishing, salt water, 35, 59, 73, 88, 135, 137, 138, 171, 198, 209, 229
fishing supplies, 13, 59, 88, 138, 151, 189, 191, 244
Fitzgerald, Lord Edward, 30
Fitzgerald, John, Earl of Desmond, 155
Fitzgerald, Maurice, 107, 222, 224
Fitzpatrick Castle Hotel (Killiney), 49
Fitzpatrick's Pub (Kilkenny), 95
Fitzpatrick's Shannon Shamrock Hotel (Bunratty), 172, 173
Fitzstephen, James Lynch, 186
Fitzstephen, Robert, 84
Fitzwilliam Square (Dublin), 30
Fitzwilliam Tennis Club (Rathgar), 60
fly/drive packages, 6, 8
Flynn Brothers Self-Drive, 6
Focus Theater (Dublin), 51
Foley, John Henry, 111
Foley's Seafood/Steak (Killarney), 149–50, 151
Folk House Hotel (Guardwell), 129, 130
Folk Village (Glencolumbkille), 231
football, Gaelic, 60, 123, 181
Ford, John, 215
Forge Restaurant (Dingle town), 163
Formorians, the, 235
Four Courts, the (Dublin), 26, 31–2, *32*
Fourteen Tribes of Galway, 187–8
Franciscan Abbey (Galway), 187
Franciscan Friary (Adare), 161
Franciscan Friary (Donegal), 230
Franciscan Friary (Wexford), 83
Freeney's Publ (Galway), 189
French Church (Waterford), 101
Friel, Brian, 245–6
Fruits of the Sea Festival (Kenmare), 133

Gaby's Restaurant (Killarney), 144, 150
Gaelic language centers. *See Gaeltacht*
Gaeltacht, 111, 137, 157, 187, 235
Gallagher's Hotel (Letterkenny), 241, 243, 244
gallan, 155–6, 158
Gallarus Oratory (Dingle Peninsula), 158–9, *162*
Galley Cruising Restaurants (Waterford), 106
gallowglasses, 237
Galway (County Galway), *183,* 184–7, *187,* 188–91
Galway Bay (steamer), 194
Galway Bay International Sea Angling Festival, 191
Galway Horse Show, 191
Galway Museum, 186

Galway Oyster Festival, 191
Galway Races, 191
Gandon, James, 31, 32
Gap of Dunloe (County Kerry), 144, 147
Gas (petrol) stations, 8, 72, 238
Gate Theater (Dublin), 54
Gateway Pub (Cork), 122
Gateway Restaurant (Drogheda), 65
General Post Office (Dublin), 25, 37
George Chapman Restaurant (Waterford), 106
Gilbert House (Aran Islands), 197
Gill, Lough (County Sligo), 223
Gilmartin Pub (Sligo town), 225
Ginkel, General Godart von, 179, 188
Glenbay Hotel (Malinmore), 240, 242
Glenbeigh (County Kerry), 138
Glenbeigh Hotel (Glenbeigh), 140
Glencolumbkille (County Donegal), 230–31
Glendalough (County Wicklow), *71,* 72, 75, *75,* 76
Glengarriff (County Cork), 127
Glen Head (County Donegal), 231, *239*
Glenstal Abbey (Muroe), 170
Glenveagh Castle (County Donegal), 238
Gogarty, Oliver St. John, 73, 184, 206, 207
golf courses, 35, 59, 88, 118, 123, 135, 136, 137, 164, 171, 181, 191, 209, 214, 219, 224, 226, 240, 245
Gore-Booth, Eva, 223, 226
Gorey Arts Festival (County Wicklow), 77
Gougane Barra (County Cork), 110
Governor's Rock (Killarney), 146
Grainne, 68–70
Granary Bar & Buffet (Dublin), 46, 50
Granville Hotel (Waterford), 100–01, 106
Great Liberator, the. *See* O'Connell, Daniel
Great Southern Hotel, Corrib (Galway), 188
Great Southern Hotel, Eyre Square (Galway), 185, 188, 189
Great Southern Hotel (Killarney), 143, 149, 150
Great Southern Hotel (Mulrany), 219
Great Southern Hotel (Parknasilla), 136
Gregory, Lady Augusta (Persse), 184
Gresham Hotel (Dublin), 37, 44, 51
Grey, Lord Henry, Duke of Suffolk, 158, 160, 164
Grey Door, the (Dublin), 43
greyhound racing, 60, 164, 181
Griffen, Gerald, 152
Griffin's Bar & Lounge (Clifden), 208
Griffith, Arthur, 30
Gros, Raymond le, 77, 84
Guinea Pig Restaurant (Dalkey), 49
Guinness, Sir Arthur (later Lord Ardilaun), 213
Guinness, Sir Benjamin, 213
Guinness Brewery (Dublin), 26, 36
Gulliver's Travels (Swift), 61
Gur, Lough (County Limerick), 170

Half Door Restaurant (Dingle town), 163
Harold Cross Stadium (Dublin), 60
Hawk's Well Theater (Sligo town), 226
Healy, Timothy 'Tim,' 127
Hellfire Club, 62, 95
Henry II (king of England), 28, 65–6, 84, 85, 94, 105, 116
Henry VII (king of England), 33, 105
Henry VIII (king of England), 33, 34, 83, 216
Hertz Rent-A-Car, 6
High Kings, the, 68, 76, 216, 222
History of the World, A (Raleigh), 107
Hoare, Gregory, 160
Holy Trinity Church (Cork), 112
home rentals, holiday, 158, 218, 234–5, 240–41
Home Rule, 76, 81
Horn Head (County Donegal), 236
horse racing, 60, 164, 181, 191. *See also* individual racetrack listings
House of Wines (Sligo town), 225
Howth (County Dublin), 35
Hudie Begs Pub (Bunbeg), 244
Huguenot exiles, 101
hunting, 59–60, 97, *97,* 181
hunting licenses, 15
Huntsman, the (Waterville), 140
hurling, 60, *60,* 123, 181
Hyland Central Hotel (Donegal town), 240, 243

Ibar, Saint, 82
Ice Age, 139, 144–5, 148
ILAC Shopping Centre (Dublin), 57
Imperial Hotel (Cork), 118, 121, 124
Inchagoill Island (Lough Corrib), 215–16
Inch Strand (Dingle Peninsula), 154
Inishbofin Island (Connemara), 202
Inishbofin Island (County Donegal), 236
Inishere (Aran Islands), 194
Inishman (Aran Islands), 195
Inishmore (Aran Islands), 194, *199*
Inishtookert (Blasket Islands), 157
Inisfree Island (Lough Gill), 223
Innisfree, Hotel (Sligo town), 224
Innocent X (pope), 94
International Hotel (Killarney), 143, 149, 150
Iona House (Dublin), 39
Iona monastery (Hebrides), 230
Ireland's Eye (Dublin Bay), 35
Ireton, Henry, 179
Irish Airlines. *See* Aer Lingus
Irish china/porcelain shops, 58, 88, 174, 181, 190, 203. *See also* craft shops; department stores
Irish Confederation, 100
Irish Free State, 29, 31, 32, 110–11, 127
Irish glass shops, 58, 88, 106, 151–2, 181, 203, 244. *See also* craft shops; department stores
'Irish Heritage Vacations,' 6

Irish lace sold, 151–2, 190, 233. *See also* craft shops; department stores
Irish Life Centre (Dublin), 57
Irish linens sold, 57, 151, 174, 244. *See also* craft shops; department stores
Irish music, traditional, 25, 28, 47, 48, *48,* 51, 58, 77, 87–8, 96, 106, 187, 189, 191, 208, 209, 225, 226, 234, 235. *See also* cabaret, Irish; *ceili; rinceoil chorcai; seisiún*
Irish Parliament, 29, 31, 64
Irish Republican Brotherhood, 116, 206
Irish Revolution, 36, 37
Irish Times, the, 54
Irish Tourist Board (Bord Failte), 4, 6, 8–9, 15, 21, 23, 54, 59, 60, 82, 88, 97, 100, 107, 124, 169, 181
Irish Transport Company. *See* C.I.E.
Irish tweed shops, 57, 58, 174, 190, 209, 225, 230, 232, 244–5. *See also* craft shops; department stores
Irish Volunteers, 35
Irish Yachting Association, 59
Island Restaurant (Killiney), 49
Islander, The (O'Crioffan), 164

Jack's Place (Annagary), 235, 244
Jackson's Hotel (Ballybofey), 233, 240, 242, 244
James II (king of England), 33, 63, 64, 66, 105, 126
Jane Eyre (Charlotte Brontë), 185
jewelry stores, 58, 97, 181, 191, 225. *See also* craft shops; department stores
Joe Malone's Pub (Limerick), 180
John (king of England), 29, 105, 179
Johnson & Perrott (car rentals), 6
Johnston Castle (County Wexford), 88–9
Johnston-Hernon's Kilmurvey House (Aran Islands), 195, 196
Jorse, Thomas de, 203
Joyce, James, 19, 40, 45, 54, 61, 191
Joyce's Country, 203
Joyce's Tower (Sandycove), 61, 72, 73
Jury's Hotel (Cork), 118, 121
Jury's Hotel (Dublin), 22, 25, 38, 43–4, 46, 50, 51, 53
Jury's Hotel (Limerick), 172, 179

Kate Kearney's Cottage (Gap of Dunloe), 144, 145
Kavanagh, Patrick, 246
Keane's Pub (Maam Cross), 203
Keene, Henry, 30
Kells (County Kerry), 138
Kelly's Pub (Wexford), 83
Kenmare Bay Hotel (Kenmare), 132
Kenmare Town Fair, 133

Kennedy, John F., ancestral home (County Wexford), 89
Kennedy, John F., Memorial Garden (Galway), 185
Kennedy, John F., Memorial Park (Wexford), 89
Kenning Car Hire, 6
Kerry, County, *131*, 132–3, *133*, 135–40, *142*
Kerry Poets Memorial (Killarney), 143
Kevin, Saint, 72, 75–6, 196
Keysers Lane (Wexford), 80, 82
Kiely, Benedict, 246
Kieran, Saint, 76
Kilkenny (County Kilkenny), *91*, 92–8
Kilkenny Arts Week, 98
Kilkenny Castle, 92
Kilkenny Design Centre (Dublin), 46, 52, 58
Kilkenny Design Centre (Kilkenny), 92, 96–7
Killarney (County Kerry), 143–7, 148–52
Killarney Bach Festival, 151
Killarney Lakes (County Kerry), *141*, 146, 147–8
Killary Shop (Leenane), 204
Killeany (Aran Islands), 196
Killiney (County Dublin), 73–4
Killiney cliff walk, 72
Killorglin (County Kerry), 139
Killybegs (County Donegal), 230
Kilmainham Jail (Dublin), 26, 36
Kilmalkedar Church (Dingle Peninsula), 159
Kilmartin's Wine Bistro (Dublin), 44
Kilmurvey Strand (Aran Islands), 195
Kilronan House (Dublin), 23, 39
Kincone Lodge (Wexford), 85
King John's Castle (Limerick), 178, 180
Kings Burial Place (Glendalough), 76
King's Head Pub (Galway), 189
King Sitric Restaurant (Howth), 35, 48
King Williams Glen (County Meath), 66
Kinsale (County Cork), *125*, 126–130
Kinsale Gourmet Food Festival, 130
Kirby's Brogue Inn (Tralee), 165
Kish Restaurant (Jury's, Dublin), 41
Knappogue Castle Banquet (Quin), *167*, 168, 173
Knights of Kerry, 154
knitwear shops, 58, 88, 190, 203, 225, 244–5. *See also* craft shops; department stores
Knockmuldowney Restaurant (Ballisodare), 225
Knowth (County Meath), 66
Kylemore Abbey (Kylemore Pass), 203–4, *204*
Kyteler, Dame Alice, 91, 93, 94–5
Kyteler's Inn (Kilkenny), 93, 95–6

Lacy, Hugh de, 67
'Lake Isle of Innisfree, The' (Yeats), 221, 223
Lansdowne Arms Hotel (Kenmare), 133
Laoghaire (king of Ireland), 73
La Petite France (Castlebar), 220

Laurels, the (Killarney), 150, 151
Lavin, Mary, 70
Leacanabuaile, Fort (County Kerry), 138
Lean, David, 148, 154
Le Chateau Pub (Cork), 122
Le Coq Hardi (Dublin), 23, 39, 41–2
Leinster, James Fitzgerald, 1st Duke, 30
Leinster House (Dublin), 24, 30
Leinster, kingdom of, 64
Leopardstown Racecourse (County Dublin), 60, 73
Leo's Singing Pub (near Crolly), 235, 244
Le Provence (Dublin), 42
Letterkenny (County Donegal), 237–8
Limerick City (County Limerick), *177*, 178–81
Limerick Inn (Limerick), 172, 173, 180
Limerick Marathon, 181
Limerick Ryan Hotel, 179, 180
Limerick Walls, 178
Lion's Tower Pub (Galway), 189
liquor (full) licensing, 12
Lissadel House (Lissadel), 223
Liss Ard House Hotel (Skibbereen), 127
Listowel Writers' Week, 165
Lobster Pot (Dublin), 42
lodgings vouchers, 6, 8
Logue's Pub (Kincasslagh), 235, 244
Long Hall Pub (Dublin), 24, 55, *55*
Longueville House (Mallow), 103, 118–19, 121
Lord Brandon's Cottage (Gap of Dunloe), 145, 147
Lord Edward Restaurant (Dublin), 24, *40*, 42, 50
Lover, Samuel, 34
Lovett's Restaurant (Douglas), 121
Lower Lake (Killarney), 146, 148
Lughnasa, Festival of, 139
Lucky Lamp Pub (Limerick), 180
Lug-or Lugh, Festival of, 159
Lydonhouse Restaurant (Galway), 189
Lydon's Galleon Room (Limerick), 180
Lynch, Sybil, 158

Maamturk Mountains (Connemara), 201, 203
Maas Village (County Donegal), 232, 234
MacArthur's Coffee Pot (Sligo town), 225
MacCarthy, Cormac MacDermot, Lord of Muskerry, 117
MacCarthy, Donal, 145
McCarthy, J. J., 155
McClure, Sir Robert, 81
MacCool, Finn, 156, 226
MacCumhaill, Finn. *See* MacCool, Finn
McDaid's Pub (Dublin), 56
MacDaire, Curaoi (king of Munster), 160
McDyer, Father James, 231
McFadden's Hotel (Gortahork), 241, 244

MacGillicuddy Reeks (Killarney), 139, 144
McGrath's or Abbeyside Castle (Waterford), 102
McIvor, Reginald, 102
MacKinley's Stone (Ballyconnell), 235
MacMurrough, Dermot (king of Leinster), 84, 85, 102
Maghera sea caves (Ardara), 232
Mahony, Francis Sylvester [pseud. Father Prout], 115
mailing restrictions, 14
Malahide Castle (Malahide), 62, 63
Malinmore (County Donegal), 231
Man of Aran, The (Mullen), 198
Manchan, Saint, 158
Man Friday Restaurant (Scilly), 130
manuscript art, 231. *See also* Book of Kells
maps, Geographia Dublin, 20
Marathon Tours, 59
Marble City Bar (Kilkenny), 96
Marconi Tavern & Grill (Clifden), 208
Mareschal, William le, 93
Marie Antoinette (queen of France), 155
Maritime Museum (Wexford), 82
Markievicz, Countess Constance (Gore-Booth), 223
Marlfield House (Gorey), 73, 77
marriage stones, 189
Marsh's Library (Dublin), 60–61
Martin, Richard 'Humanity Dick,' 205
Martyn, Richard, 184
Mary From Dungloe Festival (Dungloe), 234
Mary Rose's Restaurant (Cork), 122
Matthew, Father Theobald, 111
Max's Wine Bar (Kinsale), 130
Meagher, Thomas Francis, 100–101
medieval art, Hunt collection, 168
medieval period, 93, 100, 103, 112, 139, 178, 224
Meeting of the Waters (County Wicklow), 73, 77
Mellifont Abbey (Mellifont), 65–6
Mellowes, Liam, 185
Merrion Square (Dublin), 24, 30
Metropole Hotel (Cork), 119
Mews Restaurant, The (Letterkenny), 243
Michael's Restaurant (Wexford), 86
Middle Lake, also called Muckross Lake (Killarney), 148
Military Road, the (County Wicklow), 72, 74–5
Miller's Bistro (Limerick), 180
Minard Castle (Dingle Peninsula), 154
Mirabeau, Restaurant (Sandycove), 48–9
Mister Bojangles (Cork), 124
Mitchell's Cellars Restaurant (Dublin), 45
Moby Dick Lounge (Waterford), 107
Monaghan town (County Monaghan), 233
Monasterboice (County Meath), 65
Monasterboice Inn (Monasterboice), 65
Montague, John, 246

Mooney's Pub (Wexford), 87
Moore, Sir Edward (Earl of Drogheda), 66
Moore, Brian, 246
Moore, Garret, 66
Moore, George, 211, 216
Moore, Thomas, 73, 77, 88
Moore's Hotel (Cork), 119
Moore Street (Dublin), 26, 36
Moorings, the (Rosses Point), 223, 225
Moran's of the Weir (Kilcolgan), 184
More, O'Sullivan, 144
Mount Brandon Hotel (Tralee), 165
Mount Herbert Hotel (Dublin), 23, 39
mountain climbing, 137, 139, 160, 201, 209, 226, 235, 238
Muckish Mountain (Falcarragh), 235
Muckross Abbey (Killarney), 145
Muckross House (Killarney), 145–6
Muckross Lake, also called Middle Lake (Killarney), 148
Mulhall's Restaurant (Kilkenny), 96
Mullen, Patrick 'Pat,' 198
Mulligan's Pub (Dublin), 28, 55
Municipal Gallery of Modern Art (Dublin), 35
Murphs (Cork), 122
Murphs (Dublin), 46–7
Murphy, Father John, 78
Murphy, Seamus, 143
Murphy Doodle's (Dublin), 47
Murray's Europcar, 6
Murrisk Abbey (Murrisk), 218
Muskerry Castle. *See* Blarney Castle
Myers, Graham, 31

Nagle's Coffee Dock (Wexford), 86
Nairn (County Donegal), 232
Naomh Eanna (steamer), 194–5
Na Mara, Restaurant (Dun Laoghaire), 49
Napoleon Bonaparte (emperor of the French), 230
National Car Rentals, 6
National Concert Hall (Dublin), 51, 54
National Folk Theater (Tralee), 165
National Gallery (Dublin), 24, 35
National Gallery Restaurant (Dublin), 44
National Hotel (Donegal town), 240, 242, 243
National Monument (Cork), 112
National Museum (Dublin), 35
Navigator, the, 216
Neary's Pub (Dublin), 28, 50, 56
Nesbitt Arms Hotel (Ardara), 240, 242
Newgrange (County Meath), 63, 66–7, 67
Newpark Hotel (Kilkenny), 92, 95, 96, 97
Newport House (Newport), 219
Nieves Restaurant (Dalkey), 49
night clubs, 38, 53, 124
'1919' (Yeats), 98

Nore Valley Tour, 90
Norsemen, 28, 102, 116, 224. *See also* Danes, Vikings
Northern Ireland, 228, 232, 233
Northwest Orient Airlines, 5

O'Brien, Cornelius, 169
O'Brien, Donal Mor (king of Ireland), 178
O'Brien, Katherine 'Kate,' 181
O'Brien, Turlough, 162
O'Carolan, Turlough, 34
O'Carroll, Donough (prince of Oriel), 65
O'Casey, Sean, 61, 184
O'Casey's Bistro (Dublin), 45
O'Conaire, Padraic, 185, 191
O'Connell, Daniel (the Great Liberator), 54, 136
O'Connor, Andrew, 35
O'Connor, Cathal (king of Connacht), 216
O'Connor, Frank (Francis), 110, 124
O'Connor, Roderick (king of Ireland), 216
O'Connor, Turlough (king of Ireland), 216
O'Crioffan, Thomas, 164
O'Dalaigh, Gofraidh Fionn, 200
O'Donnell, 'Red' Hugh (Earl of Tyrone), 66, 129, 229, 234
O'Donoghue, Geoffrey, 143
O'Donoghue's Pub (Dublin), 28, 56, *56*
O'Faolain, Sean, 110, 124
O'Flaherty, Liam, 198
O'Flaherty, Thomas, 198
O'Flaherty's Pub (Dingle town), 164
ogham, 136, 144, 158, 159, 161
O'Grady's Restaurant (Clifden), 208
O'Higgins, Kevin, 30
O'Kelly, William Boy, 62
Old Bridge Tavern (Cork), 122
Old Dutch Bistro (Kenmare), 133
Olde Tom Pub (Limerick), 180
Old Granary Restaurant (Wexford), 86
Old Ground Hotel (Ennis), 172, 173
Old Wexford Coaching Inn (Wexford), 80, 81, 85, 86, 87
Olympia Theatre (Dublin), 54
Omagh (County Tyrone), 233
O'Malley, Grace, 202, 203, 218
O'Morgair, Saint Malachy, 65
O'Neill, Hugh (Earl of Tyrconnell), 129
O'Neill, Sir Phelim, 64, 66, 233
Opera House (Cork), 123
O'Rahilly, Aodhgan, 143
Ormonde, James Butler, 2nd Duke, 29
O'Rourke, Tighernan or Tiernan (king of Breifne), 84, 85, 222
O'Shea Brothers, 31
Ossory, kingdom of, 138

Ostann Gweedore or Gweedore Hotel (Bunbeg), 241, 244
Ostann na Rosann or Rosses Hotel (Dungloe), 240, 242, 243, 244
O'Sullivan, Eoghan Ruadh, 143
O'Sullivan, Maurice, 164
O'Sullivan's Beaufort Bar (Beaufort), 151
O'Toole, Laurence (king of Ireland), 76-7
Oughter, MacWilliam, 218
Oyster Tavern (Cork), 122
Oyster Tavern (Spa), 165
Ozzie's Coffee Shop (Castlebar), 220

Paddock Bar (Dublin), 24, 50-51
Paddy Burke's Pub (Clarinbridge), 185
Paddy's Seafood Restaurant (Sneem), 140
pagan era, 68, 128, 139, 146, 158, 159, 160, 170, 198, 231. *See also* druids; High Kings, the
Pain, James, 178
paintings, exhibited, 63, 92, 111, 171, 208
paintings, sold, 88, 97, 151, 190, 236, 245. *See also* craft shops
Palace Bar (Dublin), 57
Pantry, the (Kenmare), 133
Park Hotel (Kenmare), 132, 133
Parknasilla (County Kerry), 135-6
Parliament House (Dublin), 29
Parnell, Charles Stewart, 73, 76
Parsons, Richard (Earl of Rosse), 62
Passage West (County Cork), 115
passports, 13-14
Patrick Guilbaud, Restaurant (Dublin), 42
Patrick, Saint, 28, 33-4, 64, 67, 145, 146, 215-16, 218
Patrick's Bed (County Mayo), 218
Pavilion Restaurant (Cork), 122
Peacocke's Restaurant (Maam Cross), 202-03
Peacock Theater (Dublin), 51, 54
Pearce, Sir Edward Lovett, 31
Peig (Sayers), 164
Pembroke, Richard de Clare (Strongbow), 2nd Earl, 28, 84, 93, 102, 105
Penn, William, 104, 110, 118, 169
Periwinkle Restaurant (Dublin), 26, 47
Perryville House (Kinsale), 129, 130
Petrel's Restaurant (Aran Islands), 197
Philadelphia, Here I Come (Friel), 245-6
Phoenix Park, the (Dublin), 26, 28, 36, 59, 60
Pierce, Richard, 83
Pigeon Hole Cave (County Mayo), 215
Pikeman Monument (Wexford), 81
Pink Bicycle Restaurant (Dublin), 47
Plunket, Saint Oliver, 64
Poison Glen (County Donegal), 238
polo, 36, 60
pony trekking, 136, 229, 240
Popish Plot Affair, 64

Portmarnock Golf Club (Portmarnock), 35, 59
Port Na Blagh Hotel (Port Na Blagh), 241, 242
Portnoo (County Donegal), 232
Portrait of the Artist As a Young Man, A (Joyce), 19, 61
poteen, 78, 144, 145, 232
pottery shops, 108, 140, 204, 209, 226, 244. *See also* craft shops
Powers, Albert, 185
Powerscourt Gardens (County Wicklow), 72, 74
Powerscourt Shopping Centre (Dublin), 24, 26, 57
Poyning's Law, 64
prehistoric remains, 63, 76, 84, 154, 156, 169–70, 195, 216, 223. *See also* archaeological sites; beehive huts; crannog; dolmen; druids; gallan; ogham
Prendergast, Maurice de, 84
Project Arts Centre (Dublin), 54
Prout, Father. *See* Mahony, Francis Sylvester
Puck Fair (Killorglin), 139
Pugin, Alexander (Augustus), 143, 161
Punchestown Racecourse (County Kildare), 60

Quare Fellow, The (Behan), 61
Quiet Man, The (film), 215

Raffles (Dublin), 38, 53
Raftery, Anthony (the Blind Poet of Ireland), 211
Raleigh, Sir Walter, 102–03, 107, 158, 160
Rathass Church (Tralee), 161
Rathmullan House (Rathmullan), 241, 243
Rearden's Cellar Bar (Cork), 122
Reask (Ballyferriter), 158
Rebellion of 1798. *See* Rising of 1798
Redmond Monument (Wexford), 81
Reginald Grill (Waterford), 106
Reginald Lounge (Waterford), 106
Reginald's Tower (Waterford), 102
Renvyle House (Renvyle), 206–07
restrooms, public, 8
Rice, Count James, 155
Richard II (king of England), 33, 64, 188
riding facilities, 88, 123, 137, 171, 181, 191, 205, 209, 218
rinceoil chorcaí, 124
Riordan's Seafood Restaurant (Dingle town), 163–4
Rising of 1798, 29, 74, 77, 78, 81, 85
River Rooms Restaurant (Westport), 220
Riversdale House (Kenmare), 132
road sign and auto terms, 8
Rose Hill Hotel (Kilkenny), 92–3, 95, 96
Rose of Tralee Festival (Tralee), 160, 165
Rosleague Manor (Letterfrack), 206
Ross Castle (Killarney), 146
Rothe House Museum (Kilkenny), 93

Rothe Inn (Kilkenny), 96
Royal Dublin Golf Club (Dollymount), 59
Royal Dublin Society, 30, 51
Royal George Hotel (Limerick), 180
Royal Hotel (Glendalough), 72
Royal Munster Fusiliers, memorial (Cork), 112
Royal Tara china stores, 57, 190. *See also* craft shops; department stores
running, locations for, 15, 59, 123, 135, 137, 164, 171, 181, 198, 202, 209, 214, 226, 245
Ryan's Daughter (film), 148, 154, 157
Ryan's Pub (Dublin), 26, 55

Sachs Hotel (Dublin), 38, 42, 51
sailing, 107, 123, *123,* 137
Sail Inn Restaurant (Killybegs), 242, 243
Saint Aidan's Mews (Wexford), 86
Saint Anne's Church of Shandon (Cork), 114–15
Saint Brendan's Oratory (Inishtookert), 157
Saint Buithe's Abbey (Monasterboice), 65
Saint Canice's Cathedral (Kilkenny), 93, 94
Saint Crohane's Hermitage (Caherdaniel), 136
Saint Eunan's Cathedral (Letterkenny), 237
Saint Finbarre's Cathedral (Cork), 113
Saint Francis Abbey (Kilkenny), 98
Saint James Church (Dingle town), 155
Saint John's Cathedral (Limerick), 178
Saint John's Church (Sligo town), 222
Saint John's House and Abbey (Youghal), 103
Saint Lawrence's Gate (Drogheda), 64
St. Leger, Sir Anthony, 100
St. Leger, Colonel John 'Jack,' 62
Saint Mary's Cathedral (Killarney), 143
Saint Mary's Cathedral (Limerick), 178
Saint Mary's Church (Dingle town), 155
Saint Mary's Collegiate Church (Youghal), 103
Saint Mary's Pro-Cathedral (Cork), 114
Saint Patrick's Cathedral (Dublin), 24, 33–4, *34*
Saint Patrick's Church (Wexford), 81, 83
Saint's Road, the (Dingle Peninsula), 159
Saint Stephen's Green (Dublin), *19,* 36
Sally Gap (County Wicklow), 72, 74–5
Sand Castle Restaurant (Dalkey), 89
Sand House Hotel (Rossnowlagh), 229, 239–40, 241, 243
Sandycove (County Dublin), 73
sauna facilities, 37, 38, 39, 85, 95, 118, 136, 137, 148, 149, 188, 224
Sayers, Peig, 164
Scheilig Hotel (Dingle town), 155, 162–3, 164
Schomberg, Frederick Herman von, 1st Duke, 34
Seagan Ua Neachtain Pub (Galway), 187, 190
Seanachie Pub (Cork Road), 102
Seanad, the, 24, 30
Sean O'Craig's (Aran Islands), 198
Seaview Hotel (Bunbeg), 242

seisiún, 88, 97, 107, 124, 180
Selskar Abbey (Wexford), 81, 83, 84
Shanakee Pub (Guardwell), 130
Shandon Tavern (Cork), 122
Shanganah Vale (County Dublin), 74
Shannon Airport, 174, 228
Shannon Duty-Free Shop, 174
Shannon Shamrock Hotel, also called Fitzpatrick's (Bunratty), 172, 173
Shaw, George Bernard, 61, 140, 184
sheepskin goods sold, 151, 190, 203, 226. *See also* craft shops
Shelbourne Hotel (Dublin), 22–3, 25, 37, 43, 44, 47, 50–51, 57
Shelbourne Park (Ringsend), 60
Sheppard, Oliver, 78, 81
Shop at Jury's (Dublin), 35, 38, 58–9
Shrimps Wine Bar (Dublin), 45
Silver Swan Hotel (Sligo town), 224, 225
Silver Teal Restaurant (Moycullen), 203
Simnel, Lambert (the Yorkist Pretender), 33, 105
Singh, Ranjit, 205
Sitric the Dane, 105
Sitric Restaurant (Waterford), 100
Skeffington Arms Hotel (Galway), 188, 189
Skelligs Rocks (County Kerry), 138
Skipper's Restaurant (Kinsale), 130
Sky Road (Connemara), 201–02
Skywoman of Kerry, the (Killarney), 143
Sligo Abbey (Sligo town), 222
Sligo County Museum (Sligo town), 222–3
Small Home Restaurant (Dublin), 43
Smugglers Restaurant (Waterville), 140
Snaffles (Dublin), 43
Solomon Grundy's (Dublin), 47
South Pole Inn (Annascaul), 154
Spain, trade with, 154, 157, 188
Spaniard Pub (Scilly), 130
Spanish Armada, 157
Spanish influence, 185, 186, 188, 189
Spenser, Edmund, 78, 107, 109, 112, 158, 160, 164
Springhill Hotel (Kilkenny), 95
Stag's Head Pub (Dublin), 51, 57
Staigue Fort (County Kerry), *134,* 136
State Library, the (Dublin), 35
Statutes of Kilkenny, 93–4
Stonecourt Gourmet Restaurant (Waterford), 102, 106
Stone of Cu, 223
Stowaway Bar (Kinsale), 130
Strabane (County Tyrone), 233
Strawberry Fair (Enniscorthy), 77
Strongbow. *See* Pembroke, Richard de Clare
Sweeney's Hotel (Dungloe), 240, 242, 243
Sweeney's Oughterard House (Oughterard), 207
Swift, Jonathan, 34, 60–61, 98

swimming, locations for, 35, 59, 88, 135, 137, 139, 164, 181, 198, 219, 229
swimming pools, 37, 38, 85, 86, 95, 118, 136, 137, 148, 162, 164, 188
Switzers Department Store (Dublin), 58
Synge, John Millington, 76, 153, 154, 164, 184, 198

Tailor, The. *See* Buckley, Timothy
Tailors Hall Theater (Dublin), 51
Talbot Hotel (Wexford), 80, 82, 85, 86, 87
Tandoori Rooms (Dublin), 43
Tara Brooch, the, 35
Tara, Hill of (County Meath), 68
taxi fares, 12
Teach Culainn Bar/Restaurant (Cahirciveen), 140
Teampall MacDuach (Aran Islands), 195
Teampall na Skellig (Glendalough), 76
Ted's Brazen Head Grill (Limerick), 180
temperance movement, 111, 112
tennis facilities, 60, 73, 95, 107, 118, 136, 137, 162, 164, 171, 181, 214, 219, 224, 229, 240
Thackeray, William Makepeace, 124, 152, 205
Thatch Bar, the (Burtonport), 234, 244
theatre group, Gaelic (Galway), 191
Theatre Group, New (Kilkenny), 97
Theatre Royal (Waterford), 107
Theatre Royal (Wexford), 88
theater vouchers, 54
theater workshop/*Teach Siamsa* (Tralee), 165
Thomas Moore Tavern (Wexford), 83, 87
Thomond, kings of, 169
Thoor Ballylee (County Galway), 184
Three Lakes Hotel (Killarney), 143, 149, 150
time changes, 13
Timmerman's Wine Cellar (Dublin), 47
Tim's Tavern (Wexford), 87
tipping, 12
Tir ná nog, 157
Tom Malony Tours (TM Nationwide), 6
Tommie Regan's Pub (Sligo town), 225
Tone, Wolfe, 54, 112
Toner's Pub (Dublin), 57
Torca Cottage (Dalkey), 74
Tory Island (County Donegal), 235, 236
Tower Hotel (Waterford), 106
Towers Hotel (Glenbeigh), 140
Transamerica Airlines, 5
Trident Hotel (Kinsale), 129
Trim Castle (County Meath), 67–8
Trinitarian Abbey (Adare), 161
Trinity College & Library (Dublin), 24, 30, *30,* 31, 35, 51, 61
Tullig House (Beaufort), 143
Twelve Bens, the (Connemara), 195, 201

Tynan's Bridge House Bar (Kilkenny), 93, 96
Tyntes Castle (Youghal), 103

Ulster, province of, 64, 92, 228
Ulysses (Joyce), 35, 40, 55–6, 61, 73, 207
University College (Galway), 186–7
Upper Lake (Killarney), 147, 148
Upstairs Downstairs (Cork), 122

Ventry Strand, Battle of, 156
Viking House Restaurant (Kincass...
Vikings, 35, 82, 84, 229. See also Danes; ...
    men
Vinegar Hill massacre, 78
Vintage Restaurant (Kinsale), 130

Wadding, Father Luke, 102
Wander Inn, the (Kenmare), 133
Warbeck, Perkin, 105, 116
Waterford (County Waterford), 100–107
Waterford crystal sold, 88, 106, 174, 181. See also
    craft shops; department stores
Waterford Glass Factory, 100, 101–02
Waterford International Festival of Light Opera,
    107
water sports, 137, 191, 198, 205, 209, 219, 226,
    229, 240, 245. See also boating; swimming, lo-
    cations for; swimming pools; yachting
Waterville Lake Hotel (Waterville), 137
Wavecrest Bar (Wexford), 87
Wednesdays Restaurant (Dublin), 43

Will...
    33, 63, ...
wine licensing, ...
Woodfield House (Lime...

yachting, 35, 59, 73
Yeats, John Butler (father), 35
Yeats, John 'Jack' (brother), 223
Yeats, William Butler, 98, 184, 207, 221, 222,
    223, 226
Yeats Country Ryan Hotel (Rosses Point), 224
Yeats Memorial Museum (Sligo town), 222
Yeats Society, 226
Yeats Summer School, 226
Yeats Tavern (Drumcliffe), 225
Youghal (County Cork), 102–03, 107–08
Young Ireland Party, 100